THE DEVIL BEHIND THE MIRROR

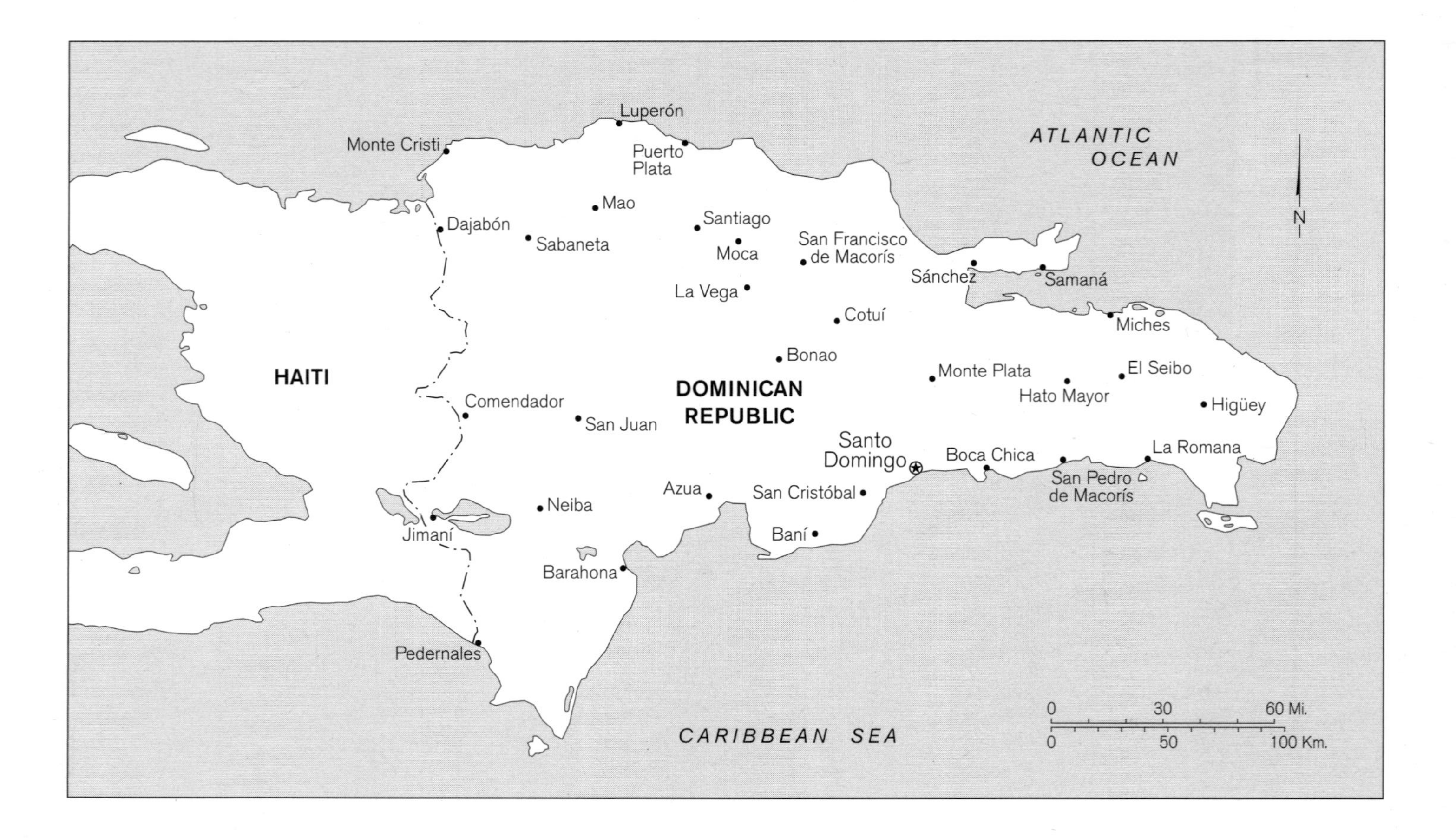
ATLANTIC
OCEAN
N
Luperón
Monte Cristi
Puerto
Plata
Mao
Dajabón
Sabaneta
Santiago
Moca
San Francisco
de Macorís
Sánchez
Samaná
La Vega
Cotuí
Miches
Bonao
HAITI
DOMINICAN
REPUBLIC
Monte Plata
El Seibo
Hato Mayor
Higüey
Comendador
San Juan
Santo
Domingo
Boca Chica
La Romana
San Pedro
de Macorís
Azua
San Cristóbal
Neiba
Jimaní
Baní
Barahona
Pedernales
CARIBBEAN SEA
0
30
60 Mi.
0
50
100 Km.

The Devil behind the Mirror

Globalization and Politics in the Dominican Republic

STEVEN GREGORY

UNIVERSITY OF CALIFORNIA PRESS Berkeley Los Angeles London

University of California Press, one of the most distinguished university presses in the United States, enriches lives around the world by advancing scholarship in the humanities, social sciences, and natural sciences. Its activities are supported by the UC Press Foundation and by philanthropic contributions from individuals and institutions. For more information, visit www.ucpress.edu.

University of California Press
Berkeley and Los Angeles, California

University of California Press, Ltd.
London, England

Library of Congress Cataloging-in-Publication Data

Gregory, Steven, 1954–.
The devil behind the mirror : globalization and politics in the Dominican Republic / Steven Gregory.
p. cm.
Includes bibliographical references (p.) and index.
ISBN-13: 978–0–520–24727–7 (cloth : alk. paper)
ISBN-10: 0–520–24727–2 (cloth : alk. paper)
ISBN-13: 978–0–520–24929–5 (pbk. : alk. paper)
ISBN-10: 0–520–24929–1 (pbk. : alk. paper)
1. Dominican Republic—Foreign economic relations. 2. Globalization—Dominican Republic. 3. Globalization—Political aspects—Dominican Republic. 4. Dominican Republic—Economic conditions—1961– 5. Dominican Republic—Social conditions—1961– 6. Tourism—Dominican Republic. I. Title.

HF1502.G74 2007
330.97293—dc22 2006005032

Manufactured in the United States of America

15 14 13 12 11 10 09 08 07 06
10 9 8 7 6 5 4 3 2 1

The paper used in this publication meets the minimum requirements of ANSI/NISO Z39.48–1992 (R 1997) (*Permanence of Paper*).

For Susan

The publisher gratefully acknowledges the generous contribution to this book provided by Columbia University.

Contents

List of Illustrations

Acknowledgments

I have relied on many friends, colleagues, and acquaintances to complete this project. In the Dominican Republic, I am especially grateful to Milquella Reyes, my research assistant for much of 2001. Ms. Reyes offered me sound advice, support, and friendship, and her research contributed immensely to this project. Ronald Graham, Minaya Sánchez, and Gabriel Zapata offered me their support, hospitality, and friendship through the course of my research, and I owe them a great deal. Many others in Boca Chica and Andrés generously shared their time, knowledge, and kindness with me. I thank Yahira Ruíz Acosta, Gérard Avin, Josefina Carmona, Noella Castro, Jean Paul Déliard, Eddie Dorsainville, Danny Guzmán, Sonia Martínez, Héctor Matos, Mabel Núñez, "Tapa" Ortega, Elwin Polanco, Fomerio Rodrigues and the staff of Turivisión, Solange Saint Paul, Fanfan Salnave, Rosa Sánchez, José Torres, and the officers and members of Junta La Unión. Without their kindness, hospitality, and generous assistance, this project would not have been possible.

In the United States, the collegiality and encouragement of the faculty, staff, and students at the Institute for Research in African American Studies (IRAAS) at Columbia University sustained me during the course of this project. Among them, I am especially grateful to Farah Griffin, Sharon Harris, Kecia Hayes, Manning Marable, and Shawn Mendoza.

Over the years, friends and colleagues have generously offered comments and conversation at different stages of this project. I especially thank Thomas Beidelman, Marianella Belliard-Acosta, Arlene Dávila, Manthia Diawara, Rachelle Charlier Doucet, Sherry Ortner, Cecilia Salvatierra, and the students in my spring 2005 undergraduate seminar, "Globalization in Anthropological Perspective." Lisa Maya Knauer served as my research assistant during the early stages of this project and, as my colleague in 2005, closely read the manuscript. Her valuable comments and suggestions greatly improved this book. I am grateful to Milagros Ricourt for copyediting the Spanish text and for her valuable suggestions. Jake Kosek, Donald Moore, and Anand Pandian, editors of *Race, Nature and the Politics of Difference* (Duke, 2003), in which an earlier version of chapter 4 appeared, provided very helpful comments on that chapter. Finally, I am grateful to Naomi Schneider and the University of California Press readers for their insightful and invaluable comments and suggestions for revising the manuscript.

Introduction

Paco's Café sat at the bustling intersection of Calle El Conde and Palo Hicado, a broad avenue that formed part of the traffic-choked ring road surrounding Parque Independencia at the edge of Santo Domingo's Colonial Zone. A favorite meeting place for foreign expatriates and Dominicans, Paco's was jammed with patrons who would pass the hours talking and watching the throngs of people that circulated through El Conde, a pedestrian promenade lined with fast-food restaurants, clothing stores, and street vendors.

From my table I could see the military honor guard posted at the Puerta del Conde (Gate of the Count), an imposing redbrick arch and belfry that is the main entrance to the tree-shaded park. It was there, in 1844, that Dominican patriots had proclaimed the birth of the Republic, marking the beginning of the war for independence from Haitian rule. Two young soldiers dressed in nineteenth-century-style white tunics and baggy blue trousers stood at rigid attention, rifles shouldered, indifferent to the traffic melee before them. It was late in the afternoon, and the pedestrian traffic along El Conde was emptying into Palo Hicado and the park beyond. Shoppers, students, and working people, free for the day, fearlessly dodged the traffic as they made their connections to public minivans and *guaguas* (buses) for the journey home.

I was killing time. I had an appointment later in the evening, and it was too hot to do anything productive. A tall, lean man approached my table and greeted me in Spanish. He was a licensed tour guide and was wearing a New York Yankees baseball cap and a plastic ID card clipped to the pocket of his neatly pressed white shirt.

"*Ahí,*" I replied, trying to sound Dominican and indifferent. He paused. I could see that he was trying to figure out what I was.

"You're from Puerto Rico?" he continued in Spanish. "*Boricua!*"[1] He shook my hand with enthusiasm. (A San Juan–based cruise ship had docked in the port earlier, and many of the tourists now exploring El Conde were Puerto Rican.) I told him that I was from the United States and that I was working in the Dominican Republic. He frowned.

"But you look Hispanic," he continued in English. I explained that my father was African American and my mother white. After puzzling over that for a few moments, he sat down at my table and introduced himself as Alberto.

Alberto, it turned out, had lived in Washington, D.C., for five years and spoke English with an African American southern accent. "Ain't that some shit," he remarked, twisting his mouth in irony after he described to me how he had been deported by the U.S. Immigration and Naturalization Service (INS) while looking for work in Tacoma. Once he was back in the Dominican Republic, a motorcycle accident had left his right leg mangled. No longer fit for manual labor but fluent in English, Alberto had found work as a tour guide.

Two shoeshine boys approached our table, wooden boxes tucked under their tiny arms. "*Limpia!*" (Shoe shine!), cried the older boy, beaming and placing his shoeshine box at my feet. "*Boricua!*" shouted the other, gleefully mistaking me for a Puerto Rican.

Alberto made eye contact with the older boy and shook his head in disapproval. The boy hesitated, frowned, and then began to unpack an odd assortment of plastic bottles filled with white and caramel-colored liquids.

"Child, he doesn't want one," Alberto said firmly. His face relaxed into a smile. The children pouted but stood their ground. Alberto looked to me with an expression of pride and amusement and then gave each boy a worn bronze peso.

"You see, I'm not hard on them," he said, watching the children race down El Conde. "Their parents need the money. But they must have respect."

Alberto was still trying to place me, to figure out how I fit into the social landscape of the global economy. He asked me if I worked in Las Américas Free Trade Zone (FTZ) at one of the export processing factories. I told him that I was a college professor and that I was doing a study on the impact of globalization and tourism in the Dominican Republic.

Alberto thought for a moment and lit a cigarette. Tourism was not helping the country, he said, because the government's policies prevented poor people from benefiting from it. "The rich people in this country want to keep it all for themselves," he continued, clasping his hands and squeezing. "They don't care about the poor." Alberto pointed with his cigarette at the throng of people waiting for buses.

"Today I have no work. You see me, I am here all day hanging out, not doin' shit." The thought angered him, and his gestures and facial expressions seemed to me more African American than Dominican. Alberto explained that he charged 750 pesos (US $45)[2] to take a group of tourists on an all-day tour of the colonial city. But with the rise of the all-inclusive resort hotels, these excursions were now arranged by the hotels with on-site tour operators who charged as much as US $50 per head. "It's crazy, man! They want it all for themselves and the people have nothing to live."

A bald, sunburned man, looking somewhat disoriented, sat at a nearby table and ordered a beer. Alberto caught his eye and smiled. *"Deutschlander?"* (German?).

"No," the man replied in English. "I am from Norway." The Norwegian pulled a guidebook from his backpack and set to work.

Alberto lost interest and returned to our conversation. "The government we have now, they make many projects and spend money, but it's not for the people. It's for the rich. *Only* for the rich." He gazed at the large banner ads for Burger King and Nokia suspended between the kiosks on El Conde. "You see all this shit? It's just paper." Alberto eyed the four-foot-wide Whopper with Cheese. "It does nothing for the country. It's only a mirror. And the devil is on the other side."

Alberto's metaphor stunned me. There was no better way to put to language the seductive lure of the commodity than as a Narcissus-like engagement with a mirror. And there was no better way to represent the ravenous will-to-profit of transnational capital than as a devil, poised behind the mirror as if to ensure that the relation between the subject and the object of consumption would be immediate and mute—a surface not of reflection, as Jean Baudrillard (1990: 67) put it, but of absorption.

This book proceeds from Alberto's deft metaphor and examines the dissonance between what transnational capital promises and what it delivers as this tension is lived, interpreted, and acted upon in the everyday lives of working people. On the one hand, I examine how distinct economic, cultural, and social processes that have been associated with "globalization"[3] and neoliberal economic reforms have restructured the lives and livelihoods of people in the Dominican Republic. On the other hand, I explore the ways in which working people and communities responded to and, in some cases, contested these developments, which ranged from the expansion of tourism and the privatization of state-owned industries to the dissemination of new technologies, media, and cultural forms.

A key aim of this study is to highlight and tease out the contextually distinct and uneven manner in which transnational flows of capital, culture, and people were realized in a specific sociocultural and political context—namely, the adjacent towns of Boca Chica and Andrés on the southern coast of the Dominican Republic. Much of the discussion and debate surrounding globalization has been abstract and lacking in empirical research.[4] Efforts to conceptualize globalization and assess its myriad effects on the world system have often drawn evidence from developments within and among affluent nation-states (e.g., those represented by the G8, the OECD,[5] and the European Union) and, as a consequence, have formulated generalizations that shed more light on the development histories of the industrial and postindustrial world than on the less developed nations that have borne the brunt of the dislocation and depredation resulting from economic restructuring. This tendency has led to narratives of globalization that disregard key asymmetries in the sovereignty, economic influence, and, indeed, military power among contemporary nation-states—disparities that are effects, in the main, of the enduring legacies of imperialism and colonialism (Mishra 2001; Mutman 2001; Petras and Weltmeyer 2001).[6]

The muting of these historically forged differences is particularly evident among researchers who have stressed—and, I argue, exaggerated—the "deterritorialized" status of the contemporary world with respect to the organization of political economies and the reproduction of cultures. In these narratives, technological innovations, coupled with the rise of institutions of global integration and governance, have released the processes of capital accumulation and cultural production from spatial constraints, undermining place-based identities and politics, as well as the sovereign powers of nation-states. Although strong globalization arguments are frequently peppered with qualifications recognizing important differences among states, cultures, and transnational processes, rarely do these differences rise to the level of analysis. This suppression of difference—of sociospatial contingency—exaggerates the autonomy and determinacy of capital-*cum*-technology vis-à-vis states and leads to perspectives that locate *anti*capitalist agency in cosmopolitan subjects, who have the power, wherewithal, and sophistication to negotiate national borders (Ong 1999; Kiely 2000; Brennan 2004). As a consequence, struggles against sex or gender inequalities, racial discrimination, contemporary imperialism, and economic restructuring itself are often neglected, pressed below the horizon of the "Global Now" (Appadurai 1996: 2; see also Mishra 2001).[7]

Strong deterritorialization accounts also share a propensity for treating space as a container in which things happen and into which people, things, and media move—what Edward Soja (1980) has termed "contextual space"—rather than as a social product that is, in its own right, deeply political and ideological in character (see also Lefebvre 1991). Indeed, the well-worn appeal to the language of "border crossings" begs an accounting of what is taking place within those borders—what Doreen Massey (1993: 61) has termed the "power geometry of space-time compression." As Soja (1980: 211) has pointed out, "social and spatial relationships are dialectically inter-reactive" and the "social relations of production are both space forming and space contingent."[8]

It is precisely this lack of attention to the space-*forming* and space-*contingent* character of the relations of production (and of cultural reproduction) that has led some to regard late capitalist accumulation aspatially (as "footloose") and, more generally, to construct "the economic" as external to the political field of the state—as "global" capital-*cum*-technology that washes over states and, in the process, over important political questions.[9] By stressing the deterritorialized character of contemporary capitalism, some have neglected not only the critical role played by states in constituting and disciplining labor power—the question of "governmentality" for Michel Foucault (1991)—but also the multitiered spatial politics that enable *and* disable the transnational movement of capital. As Aiwa Ong (1999: 15) cogently put it, "the nation-state—along with its juridical-legislative systems, bureaucratic apparatuses, economic entities, modes of governmentality, and war-making capacities—continues to define, discipline, control, and regulate all kinds of populations, whether in movement or in residence." Capital and its production processes may be more portable and increasingly governed by putatively international institutions such as the International Monetary Fund (IMF), the World Trade Organization (WTO), and the

World Bank, but its social division of labor remains firmly anchored in space and, importantly, in politics.

Discourses of globalization are very much about movement, typically at the expense of an analysis of stasis and the spatial politics that fix much of the world's population in space. As Silvio Torres-Saillant (1992: 42) has pointed out, though Dominicans have been portrayed as archetypal transnational subjects in the scholarly literature and media, few Dominicans—or, for that matter, few inhabitants of the planet—have the wherewithal to reap the benefits of the "hallucinatory movements . . . of capital, people, consumer products and telecommunications" (see also Pérez 2004).

As I completed this book, I was haunted by the images of a hurricane's aftermath: scenes of affliction, death, and devastation; of tens of thousands of black people and low-income others imprisoned in space, marooned as much by their race and poverty as by the rank floodwaters of New Orleans, Louisiana. The images on CNN and in other media were eerily familiar and reminded me of another disaster, Hurricane George, which devastated the Dominican Republic in 1998, leaving hundreds dead and tens of thousands homeless and without food or water. As in New Orleans, it was the poor and the racially marked who had been unable to escape the storm's fury—people immobilized in place by a global system of political and economic inequality.

A few days after Hurricane Katrina struck New Orleans in August 2005, my research assistant, Milquella Reyes, emailed me from the Dominican Republic. Milquella had suffered through the fury of Hurricane George: her home had been destroyed and her neighbors killed, and she had weathered the storm with her son in a cinder-block latrine. Milquella had also been watching CNN. She wrote to me that she could not believe that the images were coming from a city in the United States because they so closely resembled the aftermath of Hurricane George in the squatter community where she lived: the anguish, the devastation, and the feelings of anger and abandonment. For this reason, she wrote, she was once again plagued by *pesadillas* (nightmares).

This book turns attention to the nightmare face of globalization seldom addressed in the scholarly literature: to the lives, livelihoods, and struggles of people unable to move and "fixed" in space by economic hardship and by spatial practices restricting movement, citizenship rights, and access to a living wage. It should come as no surprise, then, that the people with whom I worked in the Dominican Republic spoke about their problems in spatial terms: as an inability to move, whether into the policed enclave of the tourism economy or across national borders or, more generally, through the social division of labor (see Guarnizo and Smith 1998).

I begin chapter 1 by introducing the area where I conducted ethnographic fieldwork: the adjacent towns of Andrés and Boca Chica, located about thirty kilometers southeast of the capital city, Santo Domingo. Andrés was settled as a sugar *batey,* or company town, associated with the Boca Chica *ingenio* (sugar mill); Boca Chica, developed as a seaside resort popular among both Dominican and foreign visitors. I present an overview of the area's development since about the turn of the nineteenth century and then examine the impact of neoliberal economic reforms on the lives and livelihoods of residents. Taken together, Andrés and Boca Chica characterize in microcosm wider transformations that have occurred in the Dominican economy since the late 1970s: a transition from the production of primary agricultural exports to international tourism and export-oriented manufacturing and services.

Structural adjustment policies led to a dramatic increase in informal economic activities throughout the Caribbean and Latin America, that is, to economic activities outside formal wage-labor relations and unregulated by the state (Itzigsohn 2000). In Andrés and Boca Chica much of this informal economic activity centered on tourism. The informal economy provided alternative and often illicit sources of income for under- and unemployed people (in this sense, a "coping strategy"), but its workers also challenged power-laden definitions of *what* constituted productive labor and the race- and sex/gender-inflected meanings and values assigned to laboring bodies.

In this context I focus attention on citizenship as a disciplinary technology, consisting of discourses and practices governing national belonging, exercised by state authorities to channel access to social rights and regulate, among other things, the social division of labor (Ong 1996). Attending to these everyday struggles over labor, identity, and national belonging highlights critical antagonisms within, and resistances to, the organization of productive relations in late capitalism and the specific practices of governmentality exercised by nation-states to produce and reproduce their sociospatial orders of accumulation.

Chapter 2 considers this sociospatial order within the frame of international tourism by investigating the spatial discourses and practices through which that order was imagined, produced, and contested in Boca Chica. Elite discourses concerning the nature of tourism and its *ambiente* (atmosphere) fabricated the *zona turística* (tourism zone) as a racialized, gendered, and class-stratified landscape where access to the tourism economy was strictly regulated. I investigate the production of these spatial meanings and relations and demonstrate some of the ways in which working people and communities transgressed this imagined geography and produced alternative spatial meanings. A critical fault line in this spatial politics was the distinction that residents and authorities drew between *la comunidad* (the community) and the *zona turística*. I explore the ambivalence that many residents expressed to the *zona turística* and its economy: perceived, on the one hand, as a magical sector of modernizing prosperity; on the other, as a venue for the penetration of corrupting foreign influences held by some to undermine a deeply gendered sense of Dominican cultural values, economic prerogatives, and sovereign powers.

This elite fabrication of the *zona turística* as an enclave of accumulation distinct from, and threatened by, the "social disorder" of surrounding communities was contested and reimagined by residents at different spatial scales. In chapter 3 I explore how residents critically engaged and drew upon transnational fields of experience and signification to produce and reassert local knowledge, identities, and interests in ways that complicated and stretched beyond Boca Chica's overdetermined image as an international tourism center. Here, as elsewhere, I emphasize the bidirectional, interreactive relationships between transnational flows of media and place-based networks of power and meaning. An analysis of the role of the imagination in contemporary social life must consider this interreaction of transnational mass media with the space- and meaning-producing projects of social agents—projects that imagine "possible lives" in ways that are sometimes distinct from, and even opposed to, those proffered in the mass media (see Appadurai 1996). For this reason, gender, racial, and class relations figured prominently in this situated politics of representation, highlighting their contested status within Dominican society and the degree to which the division of labor is constructed along these axes of difference (Ong 1991; Safa 1995).

Chapter 4 addresses these gendered networks of space, power, and labor through an examination of sex tourism in Boca Chica. I situate sex work within the everyday construction of heteronormative male identities among male "sex tourists" and within other preserves of male power in the wider political economy. From this vantage point sex work appears as one among many domains of labor where the exploitation of women was enabled and exacerbated by heteronormative discourses and practices of sexual regulation stretching from the household to the factory. I argue that for women in Boca Chica, the economically driven decision to engage in sex work was reasoned in relation to forms of paid and unpaid labor that similarly restricted their autonomy in relation to male power. The critical political question, then, is not whether sex work was, or was not, a form of wage labor; more profoundly, it is whether wage labor for many Dominican women was but a variant of sex work within capitalism's sex/gendered structures of exploitation. I then demonstrate the ways in which women disrupted these structures and discourses of male power, claiming forms of agency and autonomy that challenged the male heteronormative imperative and its race- and class-shaped discursive supports.

Race-*cum*-culture was also a critical fault line in Boca Chica's social division of labor and in the disciplinary reckoning of citizenship. Chapter 5 examines the complex and ambiguous relationship of Haitian migrants and Dominicans of Haitian descent to the Dominican body politic. Elite discourses constructed people of Haitian descent as radically external to the nation and as embodying pathological alterity. These racialized constructions of Haitian identity, shaped by Dominican history, U.S.-Dominican relations, and enduring patterns of Haitian labor exploitation, informed evaluations of Haitian subjectivity and, to be sure, Haitian bodies, conditioning their insertion into the tourism industry and wider political economy. I demonstrate how persons of Haitian descent disrupted these stigmatizing constructions of their identity, in part by stressing and politicizing their embeddedness in black diasporic cultures and politics.

I take issue with Paul Gilroy's (2000: 13) assertion that the mass-mediated, "planetary commerce in blackness" has led to a decline in the dissident cultures of the African Diaspora—to mere "repetition" rather than resistance—and show how both Haitians and self-identified black Dominicans appropriated African diasporic cultural practices (e.g., hip hop aesthetics, Rastafarian poetics, and Dominican "meren-rap" and "Reggaetón" music),[10] not only crafting and reasserting themselves as hybrid cultural subjects but also bringing that hybridity to bear against reductive and pathological constructions of black bodies.

Chapter 6 presents an analysis of the contested approval process of a multinational corporation's plan to construct a deepwater "Megaport" and Zona Franca (Free Trade Zone) at Punta Caucedo, just to the west of Andrés–Boca Chica. In the globalization literature "global capital" often has been represented as aspatial *and* disembodied, obscuring the processes through which capitalists act as a political force harnessing support for their projects, inveigling skeptics, and engaging in negotiations with states and other political actors. Capitalists must speak and make sense of their strategies and actions, not only to economic and political elites, but also to an assortment of other constituencies and interest groups.[11] As Henri Lefebvre (1991: 347) has pointed out, a global flow—of capital, technology, or media—is "only effective to the extent that it enters into relationship with others. . . . The coordination of such flows occurs within a space."

Chapter 6 examines this process of spatial coordination, teasing out the disparate discourses and practices that were employed by CSX World Terminals (a U.S.-based multinational) and its Dominican partners to muster support for the Megaport project among state officials, the business community, labor, and other constituencies. The most organized and severest critic of the Megaport was Boca Chica's luxury tourism industry, and I examine the competing, often contradictory claims made by both faces of capital as they fabricated and appealed to the nation's identity and economic interests. The dispute over the Megaport highlights the complex composition of multinational capital and the degree to which its flows are channeled, deflected, and resisted by the specific histories, political economies, and cultures of nation-states.

1

The Politics of Livelihood

La República Dominicana es un país creado por Dios para el Turismo, me he atrevido a decir algunas veces, estimulado por la belleza de su potencial.

[The Dominican Republic is a country created by God for Tourism, I have dared to say sometimes, excited by the beauty of its potential.]

Don Angel Miolán, director of Dominican tourism, 1967–1974

I had been in Boca Chica for two weeks and still had not seen Minaya. I made it a daily practice to walk from one end of the beach to the other to cultivate relationships with people who, like Minaya, made their living selling goods and services to foreign tourists. I would begin at the fortresslike Coral Hamaca Beach Hotel and Casino at the eastern end of town and walk west, pausing along the way to speak with vendors, guides, and touts who worked at the bars and restaurants along the beach. Midway along the trek I would stop at an Italian-owned restaurant to visit my research assistant, Milquella Reyes, who worked there as a waitress. I would then continue to Hostal Zapata, a midsized hotel owned by Gabriel Zapata, a Dominican who had lived in Washington, D.C., for many years. I had stayed at Zapata's hotel often, and, sharing an interest in politics, we had become friends.

Next to Zapata's hotel was the Boca Chica Resort, the second of the town's all-inclusive resort hotels. Rumor had it that the site had once been occupied by the beach house of the mother of Dominican dictator Rafael Leónides Trujillo Molina (1930–1961). West of the Boca Chica Resort was a large parking lot used by Dominicans who visited the beach from the capital and elsewhere. Scattered throughout the lot were food stalls selling fried fish, *yaniqueques* (johnnycakes), and beverages.[1]

Beyond the parking lot the beach continued for another two kilometers until it reached the neighboring town of Andrés, signaled by the towering red-and-white-striped smokestack of Ingenio Boca Chica. With few exceptions, the western end of the beach was used by Dominican visitors, especially on weekends and holidays when busloads of people arrived from the capital.

My daily tour of the beach was also an effort to persuade people that I was not a tourist in an economy in which wealth differences between foreigners and most residents were enormous, indisputable, and endlessly reiterated by the symbolic and spatial order of things. To that end, I would often carry a clipboard with me and wear long pants and a dress shirt with two pens prominently displayed in the pocket. It was the only time in my career that I have tried to look like an anthropologist.

I had met Minaya two summers earlier and made it a point at the end of each trip to buy two or three shirts from the huge bundle of garments that he lugged back and forth along the beach in the afternoon heat. We had spoken often about his work and my own, and he had introduced me to many of his coworkers. Like the other vendors, Minaya was a good listener. To sell things to tourists, one had to be alert to subtle inflections in the voice that suggested some direction in their fickle desire to consume or a shift in the precarious balance between interest and irritation.

It was March 2001, and tourism was slow in the wake of the global recession. Many of the vendors, hair braiders, and others who worked the beach had gathered under the palm trees in front of the Boca Chica Resort. Within the walled compound one hundred or so tourists were stretched out on chaise longues. Every so often vendors would approach the low concrete wall, display their wares, and then retreat once more to the shade of the palms.

I found Minaya resting against a palm tree with his cousin, a cigar vendor. Minaya explained to me that he had just returned from San Juan de la Maguana, his birthplace, where he had attended a funeral. His brother-in-law had been electrocuted while trying to jerry-rig an electrical connection to his home from the power line that passed above it—a tragic, yet not uncommon, accident. Since business was slow, Minaya told me, he could leave work early, and he invited me to his home in Andrés for dinner. It was his daughter's fifth birthday, and his wife was making *sancocho,* a hearty soup often served on special occasions.

Minaya slung the motley bundle of garments over his shoulder, and we headed for the narrow alleyway next to the Hotel Don Juan, where the vendors gathered at the end of the day and stored their goods. It

1. Vendors displaying their wares in front of the Boca Chica Resort. The boy holding the sack is collecting bottles for their deposits. Photo by the author.

was also the meeting place of Boca Chica's Sindicato de Vendedores (Vendors' Union). Here the vendors gathered daily to discuss their trade, resolve disputes, and organize their activities so as to ensure that on any given day there would not be too many selling the same commodities in the same places. When business was slow, the *síndico* (union president) staggered the work schedules of members to ensure that everyone sold enough to make ends meet.

Vendors lined the shaded alley, some wearing the pale blue smocks issued to those who were licensed by the Policía Turística, or POLITUR, the specialized tourism police. Two Haitian women sold fried fish and sausages from a rough-hewn wooden stall. Neatly arranged stacks of clothing, cigar boxes, and wood carvings imported from Haiti were set up along the alley's walls. Manolo, the union president, was involved in a heated discussion with a jewelry vendor about the power plant that was being built across the Bay of Andrés by the AES Corporation, a U.S.-based global power company. From the alley we could see the plant's bulbous liquid gas tank and the delicate silhouette of the jetty where tankers would one day dock. The jewelry vendor was arguing that the new power plant would solve the problem of the *apagones* (blackouts) that were a daily occurrence in Boca Chica and across the nation.

"*Ven acá*" (Look here), Manolo snapped, glaring at the man. "The blackouts are not the result of a lack of power," he insisted. "That's a lie. There is plenty of electricity in the country. What is happening is that the power companies, the foreigners, want to make more money. They make the blackouts to force the people to pay more. It's an abuse."

"Yesterday," a cigar vendor chimed in, "they killed two in Capotillo," referring to two men who had been shot dead by the National Police in a poor barrio of the capital during protests against the blackouts.

In fact, the recently privatized power distribution companies had been shutting down service to neighborhoods in the capital and elsewhere where bill collection rates were low. Intended to discipline a recalcitrant population and the Dominican government into paying newly inflated electric bills, the power outages had incited widespread, unrelenting protests throughout the country.

In Boca Chica the power issue had become a lightning rod for public debate about privatization, economic justice, and the behavior of foreign corporations within the nation. The daily blackouts were often greeted with cries of *"Sé fue la luz!"* (The lights have gone!), a refrain sampled from a popular merengue, and caustic commentaries on the nation's economy and political leadership. In everyday speech, Dominicans punned the noun *poder* (power) to form such phrases as *"Aquí, no hay poder"* (Here, there is no electricity/political power).

For beyond the inconvenience, the blackouts injected a rhythm of crisis into everyday life, disordering the taken-for-grantedness of neoliberal assertions of economic development and giving rise to a "heretical discourse," as Bourdieu (1977: 170) put it, of social justice and defiance. Graffiti spray painted onto the wall of the AES Corporation's office in Boca Chica read, *"El pueblo demanda poder!"* (The people demand power!).

Minaya enjoyed controversy and turned to me. "Tell me, Gregory, they say that we pay more for the lights in this country than they do in New York. Is it true?"

I replied that I didn't know but that I thought that an average electric bill might be about $30 a month. There was a pause as we made the calculation.

"Five hundred pesos," Minaya remarked. "The same, maybe less."

We left the beach and headed for Calle Duarte to hire *motoconchos* (motorcycle taxis) for the three-kilometer trip to Minaya's home in Andrés.

Calle Duarte was Boca Chica's main street and ran parallel to the beach from the western end of town to the Coral Hamaca Beach Hotel and Casino, about two kilometers to the east. Midway along Calle

Duarte were the town's Catholic church and plaza. Facing the tree-shaded plaza were the police station and the offices of the *ayuntamiento,* or municipal government. Clustered around the plaza were an assortment of bars, restaurants, money exchanges, gift shops, and other businesses that catered largely to foreign tourists.

Crosscutting Calle Duarte was Calle Juan Bautista Vicini, which extended north from the plaza to Carretera de Las Américas, the highway linking Boca Chica to the capital in the west and to San Pedro de Macorís in the east. North of the town center were a patchwork of residential neighborhoods interspersed with budget hotels, grocery stores, and other small businesses. Calle Vicini and the grid of paved streets continued on the other side of the highway, where I lived, but soon dissolved into unauthorized settlements *(arrabales)* of cinder-block and wood-frame houses, connected by a tangle of dirt roads.[2]

We reached the town plaza and hired two *motoconchos* for the trip to Andrés. Because I wanted to photograph the sugar factory, we took the road that skirted the coast, past Ingenio Boca Chica and the Port of Andrés, and farther on to Punta Caucedo. Along the way trucks loaded with equipment and building materials roared past us, kicking up dust and gravel as they made their way to the unfinished power plant. Ingenio Boca Chica appeared to be abandoned. The corrugated steel panels that covered the factory's milling and boiling areas were missing in places, and chunks of machinery were strewn about the yard. A security guard dozed at the entrance, a shotgun cradled in his lap.

I asked Minaya about the factory. He drew his index finger across his throat, *muerto* (dead). Ingenio Boca Chica and other government-owned sugar mills had been recently "capitalized," that is, leased to private corporations, which were expected to invest in them and enhance their profitability. As yet, the factory's new operator—a Mexican multinational corporation—had not begun the renovations needed to return it to operation. As a result some three thousand workers had lost their jobs. Once a bustling, albeit poor sugar settlement, or *batey,* Andrés was now a community without an economy.

We continued on foot along the coastal road, and Minaya told me about his life. He had been born in San Juan de la Maguana and had come to Andrés in 1988 to work at the *ingenio* (sugar mill), where his uncle was a foreman. With no formal schooling, he told me, his employment prospects had been bleak. At the factory he labored as a *vagacero,* whose job it was to remove the spent cane after milling. It was back-breaking and poorly paid work, and after a few months on the job he

2. Ingenio Boca Chica as seen from the coastal road in 2001. Photo by the author.

quit. With money borrowed from his uncle, Minaya purchased his first stock of goods to sell on the beach. "It's better to have your own little business," he told me, "and have more freedom."

After years of scraping and saving, Minaya bought two adjacent wood-frame casitas on the outskirts of Andrés and sent for his mother, brother, and three sisters from San Juan. Other family members soon followed. Eventually, Minaya bought a cinder-block house next to the others and married a woman from his hometown. His brother and cousins worked with him on the beach as vendors, and two of his sisters managed a *colmado* (grocery store), which the family rented from a neighbor. Minaya enrolled his youngest sister in elementary school at the age of nineteen.

We turned off the coastal road and followed a narrow dirt path that led into Andrés, past crumbling wooden houses and newer cinder-block buildings that were stalled at various stages of construction. Minaya pointed to the house that his eldest sister was building—a roofless, concrete rectangle with cavities yet to be filled with windows and doors. The poor, he explained, built their houses "little by little" as they saved money to buy fixtures and allotments of cinder blocks.

We arrived at his home, located at the end of an unpaved cul-de-sac at the edge of town. Children were gleefully sifting through the remains of a birthday piñata while their mothers stood by, cake in hand, impatient to leave. Minaya noticed me peering at the tangle of illicit wire connections to the power lines overhead and grinned. "In my house," he quipped, "there is power."

We entered the enclosed porch, and Minaya brought out chairs from inside. He told me how he had gathered his entire family on the cement porch when Hurricane George flattened his mother's house and blew away the roof of his own in 1998. "There were twenty of us gathered here on the patio—who knows, maybe thirty." He gazed at the cement ceiling. "But this ceiling is strong. It stayed."

Minaya's wife, Jocelyn, and his three sisters came out to greet us with coffee, followed by a procession of nephews, nieces, and cousins. With her second, newborn child in her arms, Jocelyn told me about her business selling hair care products to neighbors. Poor economic conditions had prompted many women to create microenterprises to contribute to household budgets. An assortment of plastic bottles and glass jars were neatly arranged in a homemade display case on the porch. When we finished our coffee, Jocelyn invited us inside to eat.

The main room of the two-room house was divided by a wall unit that separated the living room from the cooking area in the rear. The family of four slept in a small side room subdivided by curtains. A sofa, a coffee table, and two chairs were squeezed into the front room. A television set and portable CD player occupied the wall unit, along with family photographs, a porcelain serving dish, and empty bottles of imported liquors, which I had often seen displayed in the homes of poor families. Less a display of conspicuous consumption than a keepsake of special occasions, the bottles were symbols of the just, though infrequent, desserts of hard work.

After dinner Minaya invited me to the family's *colmado*. Minaya's eldest sister was busy serving an elderly woman, who was complaining about the size and price of each item as it arrived—an onion, two carrots, a bullion cube, and a clump of tomato paste sealed in a plastic bag. Minaya chuckled as he reached into the freezer for a beer. "*No es fácil, Doña Julia,*" he said. Not looking up, the woman agreed, "No, life's not easy."

We sat out front on plastic chairs. Minaya's cousin Feo was playing dominoes with friends. It was now dark, and we could see the warm glow of the massive Coral Hamaca Beach Hotel across the bay and the headlight trail of cars driving east on the highway toward San Pedro de Macorís.

3. Minaya and Jocelyn Sánchez on Diana's fifth birthday. Photo by the author.

"Tell me, Gregory, how is the book going?" Minaya asked.

"Little by little," I replied. I took the opportunity to remind him about my work. I told him that I was writing about the changing economy—tourism, privatization, and so on—and about the impact of these changes on people's lives.

Minaya thought for a moment. "Here we are all poor," he said, grinning as he did when preparing a joke in his mind. "So you will have to write a very big book!"

We stayed at the *colmado* for another hour, bringing each other up to date on our lives. Just as I was about to leave, Minaya asked about my trip to Cuba the year before. I replied that although there were shortages and other problems, people seemed to have enough to eat and access to health care and other essential services.

"But, Gregory," he countered, leaning toward me, "they say that in Cuba there is no freedom—there is no democracy." His face became stern, wrinkles forming across his brow.

"Yes, that's what they say." I did not want to argue politics with a friend.

"Here, in the Dominican Republic, we have plenty of freedom," Minaya continued, "plenty of freedom. And democracy too." His tone was solemn, but I could see the telltale grin beginning to form. Feo and the others looked up, dominoes cradled in their palms. "Here we have the freedom to work. And to struggle. *And we have the freedom to be poor!*" Minaya burst into laughter and insisted that I stay for one last beer.

The ironic notion of having the freedom to be poor recalls Karl Marx's (1964) account of the unfreedom of "free labor" under capitalism and the multifaceted relationships between the structures of coercion that govern the lives of working people and the modes of agency, maneuver, and resistance available to them. At the crux of these everyday struggles was the capitalist labor process: the power relations and practices through which labor was, as Marx put it, subsumed by capital. Indeed, for Minaya and for others with whom I worked, this struggle for livelihood was not merely one of earning a living. Equally important, it was a struggle over power-laden definitions of *what* constituted productive labor and of the bodies in which it was to be found—that is to say, a struggle over the political, symbolic, and spatial ordering of the social division of labor.

This chapter begins an examination of the production and policing of this division of labor and the myriad inequalities that it both expresses and secures. My interest in the division of labor—a category that has received relatively scant attention in the social science literature—is driven by both interpretive and theoretical concerns (Garnsey 1981).[3] The most pressing problems facing the people with whom I worked were at once economic (in the narrow sense of earning a living) and positional, having to do with their social location vis-à-vis commingling and multiscaled power arrangements, stretching from the proximate community to the global order. The value and qualities of their labor were politically constructed through the iteration of social distinctions (among them, race, gender, sexuality, and citizenship) and by means of a variety of practices in which state authorities played critical, although not exclusive, roles. In short, the politics of identity was inexorably fused with the everyday politics of making a living. Though this social positioning was, in large part, a function of class (taken as one's location within capitalist relations of production), it was irreducible to class identity, or, for that matter, to any category that, to sustain its identity, must be abstracted from its muddled spatial and temporal contexts. Rather, class identities were embodied in and lived through a matrix of social differences that located one in the social and spatial order of the capitalist labor process (Ong 1991).[4] By examining the everyday structuring of the social division of labor, its power differentials and social distinctions, I focus attention on a field of antagonism and conflict that was axial in the lives of the subjects of this ethnography.

An analysis of the social division of labor and the sociospatial practices of division that constitute it also provides an approach to theorizing class, not in relation to other differences, but through the sociospatial fields within which racial, gender, ethnic, and other differences are crafted and lived.[5] This spatial understanding of class, as it is embodied in marked subjects, emphasizes and renders problematic the subject's dynamic and practically structured relationships, not merely to the "point of production," but also to the wider social field of the extended reproduction of capital. This strategy resists the logic of "intersectionality" that has often accompanied attempts to conceptualize class in relation to race, gender, and other social distinctions. Instead, I approach class formation and its politics of livelihood as a process that is realized through the sociospatial ordering of differences, that is, as the social division of labor.[6]

DOMINICAN COUNTERPOINT: SUGAR AND TOURISTS

Andrés and Boca Chica are located on the southeastern coast of the Dominican Republic, about thirty kilometers from Santo Domingo. Until recently the two towns were part of the National District of Santo Domingo and were represented by the *síndico,* or mayor of the capital. Surrounding the city of Boca Chica proper were a number of settlement areas (e.g., Monte Adentro, Los Tanquecitos, and Caucedo), some of which were developed as squatter communities by migrants. This larger area, 149 square kilometers, was referred to by residents and the authorities as greater Boca Chica (Sección de Boca Chica) and was considered a single political community. In 2002 (after I conducted fieldwork) Andrés and Boca Chica and neighboring settlements were reorganized as a *municipio* (municipality)—one of four constituting the newly created province of Santo Domingo. In 2000 the population of greater Boca Chica was estimated to be 73,149 (CIECA 2001).[7]

Once a settlement of fishermen, Andrés developed as a sugar *batey* with the construction of Ingenio Boca Chica at the end of the nineteenth century by Juan Bautista Vicini, an Italian-born merchant capitalist who migrated to the Dominican Republic in 1882 (Cabrera 2001). The Dominican sugar industry blossomed in the late nineteenth century, spurred by the disruption of sugar production in Cuba during its wars of independence (1868–1878) and by the decline in sugar beet production in Europe during the Franco-Prussian War of 1870.[8] The development of large-scale sugar plantations was driven by foreign capital and technical expertise provided by Cuban, Italian, North American, and Puerto Rican immigrants, some of whom, like Bautista Vicini, married into elite Dominican families, forming what Emilio Betances (1995: 26) described as "a local sugar bourgeoisie based on foreign resident planters." These planters entered into an alliance with the administration of President Ulises Heureaux (1881–1899), from which they received loans and profitable concessions to build and operate an infrastructure of ports and railroads.

However, in the face of declining sugar prices (especially during the crisis period 1881–1889), many of these factories foundered, forcing their owners to sell to foreign corporations that, like the U.S.-controlled Porto Rico Sugar Company and the Cuban-Dominican Sugar Company, were rapidly consolidating their control over Dominican sugar production (Knight 1939; Betances 1995). U.S. involvement in the Dominican political economy increased when the New York–based San Domingo Improvement Council (SDIC), backed by the U.S. government, purchased the Republic's debt in 1893 from the Dutch firm of Westendorp and took control of Dominican finances (Veeser 2002). In 1904 Theodore Roosevelt appointed U.S. officials to collect Dominican customs revenues on behalf of the SDIC. The Dominican-American Convention, signed by President Ramón Cáceres in 1907, legalized the customs receivership and extended U.S. control over accounting and budget procedures, reducing the Dominican state to a "semi-protectorate of the United States" (Betances 1995: 72).

The consolidation of foreign, primarily U.S. control of the sugar industry was strengthened during the U.S. military occupation of the Dominican Republic (1916–1924). In 1920 the U.S. military government issued Executive Order No. 511, a land reform measure authorizing a cadastral survey and a new system of land registration that further undermined the system of *terrenos comuneros* (common lands), making it possible for the sugar corporations to legally expropriate peasant holdings and dramatically extend the acreage under their control (Betances 1995). Only the year before, the military government had imposed a tariff system that exempted U.S.-made industrial products from import duties, thereby undermining both the local manufacture of goods and the export of raw agricultural commodities (Moya Pons 1990).

By 1916 Ingenio Boca Chica, along with other mills, had been absorbed into the U.S.-controlled Cuban-Dominican Sugar Company (Betances 1995). In the same year twenty-five-year-old and soon to become dictator Rafael Trujillo was employed at Ingenio Boca Chica as a *guardacampestre* (security guard), initiating an enduring connection between the Trujillo family and the coastal area. Trujillo's employers at Ingenio Boca Chica would later provide him with a letter of reference when he applied to the Guardia Nacional, the National Guard established by the U.S. military occupation in 1918.

Over the course of the twentieth century, Ingenio Boca Chica and its associated cane fields drew upon a diverse labor force, which included *cocolos* (migrant workers from the British West Indies) and Haitian braceros. Although the sugar industry had employed seasonal Dominican workers in its early years of development, low wages on the estates and price inflation in the late nineteenth century discouraged rural Dominicans from abandoning subsistence cultivation for wage labor. Orlando Inoa (1999) reported that the first group of West Indian migrant workers arrived in 1872. By the early decades of the twentieth century, thousands of workers were arriving each year from the Leeward Islands (Antigua, Nevis, and St. Kitts) and elsewhere in the Caribbean and, after 1915, increasingly from neighboring Haiti (Martínez 1995).

During the 1950s, Rafael Trujillo began buying out the holdings of the U.S.-controlled sugar companies, expanding the Trujillo elite's monopoly of the Dominican economy. In 1956 Trujillo bought Ingenio Boca Chica and four other mills from the West Indies Sugar Company. After Trujillo's assassination in 1961 the Trujillo-owned mills were nationalized and placed under the management of the government's Consejo Estatal del Azúcar (CEA; State Sugar Council), created in 1966 (Chardon 1984).

Although the early 1970s witnessed a sugar boom as a result of a spike in prices on the U.S. preferential market (from 6.9 cents a pound in 1970 to more than 60 cents by the mid-1970s), sugar prices fell precipitously after 1976, leading to a decline in production (Betances and Spalding 1995). By 1986 revenues from traditional exports (e.g., sugar, cacao, coffee, and tobacco) had dropped from 51.9 percent of hard currency in 1977 to just 22.8 percent. Sugar accounted for only 8 percent of export revenues in 1991, compared to 40 percent provided by the rapidly growing tourism industry (Itzigsohn 2000). By the 1990s the fulcrum of the region's economy had shifted from Andrés and its declining sugar industry to Boca Chica and international tourism.

Boca Chica, located roughly three kilometers down the coast from Andrés, developed gradually in the early decades of the twentieth century as a seaside resort, frequented by affluent *capitaleños* (residents of the capital), who built vacation cabañas along the shore. Much of the land in Boca Chica was owned by Juan Bautista Vicini, who built the town's Catholic church and initial infrastructure. Boca Chica's beach, facing what is reputed to be the largest coral-ringed lagoon in the Caribbean, remains one of the most popular seaside resorts for Dominicans and hosts a variety of public festivals, such as Semana Santa (Holy Week), that draw huge crowds from Santo Domingo and elsewhere.

In 1952 the Trujillo regime constructed the Hotel Hamaca, the first of Boca Chica's resort hotels, as part of a largely unsuccessful campaign to stimulate domestic and international tourism during the prosperous post–World War II period (Meyer-Arendt, Sambrook, and Kermath 1992). Although occupancy rates remained low at most of the seaside and mountain resorts built by Trujillo, the Hotel Hamaca attracted wealthy, predominantly North American tourists and celebrities throughout the 1960s, in part because of its proximity to the capital and the international airport.

Beginning in the late 1960s and spurred by the aggressive promotion of tourism as an economic panacea by the World Bank, the Inter-American Development Bank (IDB), and other international agencies, the administration of President Joaquín Balaguer began an aggressive campaign to promote tourism. Tourism was presented by its international boosters as a means to advance from a primary sector–based economy to one based on services, without passing through a phase of industrialization, as had been attempted through earlier import substitution policies.[9] As Malcolm Crick (1989: 315) observed for the Caribbean as a whole, "Tourism was represented as an easy option for development because it relied largely on natural resources already in place—e.g. sand, sun, friendly people—and therefore required no vast capital outlays for infrastructure."

In 1971 legislation was passed granting a 100 percent income tax exemption, duty-free imports, and other generous concessions to tourism industry investors. The Department of Tourism Investment and Infrastructure (INFRATUR) was created within the Central Bank to provide low-interest financing and other incentives to domestic and foreign investors and to stimulate infrastructural development. In the same year

Edes Mendar, a Spanish consulting firm, conducted a study for the IDB that examined the southern coast's potential for tourism (Báez 2000). The final report identified measures to promote the development of infrastructure and recommended the relocation of residents from the *zona playera* (beach zone).

In 1973 the Balaguer government issued Presidential Decree No. 3134 authorizing the state to purchase and, if necessary, expropriate privately held coastal lands in Andrés and Boca Chica that were earmarked for tourism development. The resulting speculation in land led to a massive displacement of people from the *zona playera.* Clara Báez (2000) noted that this displacement led, in effect, to the transfer of coastal properties from residents to foreigners. "The tourism development plan," Báez concluded, "viewed the resident population more as a nuisance to be relocated far away than as a human and cultural resource to be integrated into the development of tourism in their community" (66).

Designated in 1973 a Polo Turístico (Tourism Pole) by presidential decree, Boca Chica, along with the tourism industry as a whole, grew rapidly during the 1980s and 1990s (especially in the aftermath of the 1983 currency devaluation), witnessed by the renovation and expansion of the twenty-eight-room Coral Hamaca Beach Hotel (formerly the Hotel Hamaca), the construction of two additional all-inclusive resort hotels, and the establishment of dozens of small and midsized hotels, restaurants, gift shops, and other businesses catering to the growing number of foreign tourists.

Boca Chica's rapid transformation into an international tourism destination was mirrored at other seaside resorts, such as Puerta Plata, La Romana, and Playa Bávaro. Whereas in 1970 only 89,700 foreign tourists visited the Dominican Republic, by 1992 their number had grown to 1.6 million. Although tourism contributed only US $368.2 million in hard currency to the Dominican economy in 1985, that figure skyrocketed to US $1,046.4 million by 1992 (Betances 1995). Between 1991 and 1996 the number of tourist rooms in Boca Chica and neighboring Juan Dolio (forming Pole I) increased from 2,614 to 4,040 (Abt Associates 2002).

The expansion of tourism in Boca Chica drew migrants from other areas of the country who settled in Andrés and Boca Chica and in expanding squatter settlements to the north. A resident interviewed by Báez (2000: 67) described Boca Chica's residents as a "floating population of migrants." Many of these new arrivals came from rural areas that had been impoverished by the decline in agricultural exports. Many came with the expectation of earning a living in tourism-related services.

4. Musicians playing for tourists in front of the Hotel Don Juan. Photo by the author.

A thirty-eight-year-old man who moved with his family to Boca Chica from San Cristóbal in 1995 told Milquella Reyes, "When I was in my town, everyone was saying, 'Over there, in Boca Chica, there are many tourists. You can make money and improve yourself and have a better life.' But now I am here, and there is no work. Nothing."

In fact, the growing tourism economy provided few jobs for local people. In 1996 the Asociación para el Desarrollo de Boca Chica (Boca Chica Development Association) calculated that hotels and restaurants in Boca Chica employed only 1,662 of the 42,869 residents. A more recent survey estimated that the hotel industry employed only 1,800 persons directly (Mouchel Consulting, Ltd. 2001). With the exception of unskilled, low-paying work in hotel services (e.g., security, housekeeping, and commercial laundries), few residents of Andrés and Boca Chica possessed the skills and other credentials required to work in the formal tourism sector.

The failure of tourism to promote job growth in Boca Chica was consistent with the situation elsewhere in the Caribbean. As Crick (1989) has argued, luxury tourism typically employs expatriate management and staff brought in from elsewhere and, consequently, seldom stimulates local job growth. Moreover, luxury tourism tends to form enclaves of economic activity—exemplified by the all-inclusive resort model—that remain insulated from local economies, reproducing, as Crick put it, "the dualistic structure, the plantation system, of the colonial economy" (317; see also Pattullo 1996). Equally important, hiring patterns in Boca Chica's tourism industry were shaped by subtle and not so subtle forms of race-*cum*-color discrimination. Many residents reported to me that tourism-related firms did not hire persons who were perceived as *morenos* (relatively dark skinned) for positions that brought them into contact with foreign tourists, for example, positions as clerks, waiters, bartenders, or dealers in hotel casinos. Frequently, these "front desk" employees were recruited from the capital.

The majority of the residents of Andrés–Boca Chica thus fell between the cracks of a rapidly changing economy: between a moribund sugar industry and declining traditional export economy and an expanding tourism sector that offered few job prospects for low-skilled and racially marked people. Although some residents found work in the export manufacturing factories located in Las Américas FTZ, these factory jobs were difficult for most to secure, and the low wages and forced unpaid overtime (ranging between fifty-six and eighty total hours per week) made them untenable livelihoods for many.

For example, twenty-three-year-old Yahaira Brito, married and the mother of two toddlers, took a job at a garment factory in Las Américas FTZ when her husband, a construction worker, could no longer find enough work to support the household. Yahaira's starting salary of $3,500 pesos (US $215) per month barely covered the family's expenses after deducting her monthly rent of RD $1,200 and transportation costs to and from the factory, which averaged RD $600 monthly. When her diabetic mother became ill and could no longer baby-sit her children, Yahaira was forced to quit the factory job. When I met the couple in 2001, both were unemployed and increasingly in debt to relatives and local merchants. Yahaira and other women with whom I spoke agreed that few export processing jobs paid a living wage and, from the standpoint of women, the jobs presupposed households with male wage earners (see Safa 1995).

STRUCTURAL ADJUSTMENT AND THE NEW ECONOMIC POLICY

In 2000–2001 neoliberal economic reforms legislated by the administration of former President Leonel Fernández were implemented in Andrés–Boca Chica and elsewhere in the nation, further eroding the livelihoods of residents. Responding to pressure from the IMF, the World Bank, and the IDB, the Dominican Republic put into action a program to "capitalize" state-owned industries, notably the sugar and power industries. The privatization of state-owned industries was one component of a sweeping package of economic and political reforms, anticipated in earlier IMF agreements, that consolidated a restructuring of the Dominican economy.

In 1990, shortly after having been reelected president, Balaguer embarked on a comprehensive program of economic reforms, which came to be known as the New Economic Program (NEP). Faced with worsening economic conditions—rising inflation, growing trade deficits, and increasing debt arrears to the IMF and other international lenders—the Balaguer administration was obliged to negotiate an agreement with the IMF, conditional on the implementation of fiscal reforms (e.g., price liberalization, exchange rate devaluation, and decontrol of interest rates), tax and banking reforms, and the elimination of food subsidies (IMF 1999).

These "structural adjustment" policies, informed by neoliberal economic theory—a resurrected version of classical liberal economic thought dominant in the United States and Great Britain before the Great Depression—were based on the view that only an unregulated capitalist system—a "free market" economy—can achieve optimum performance with respect to economic growth, efficiency, technological progress, and distributional justice (Kotz 2002). In the neoliberal view state involvement in the economy should be minimal and the regulatory policies associated with the welfare state dismantled by sharply cutting back social welfare spending, privatizing public assets and functions, and reducing taxes on businesses and investors. At the international level the neoliberal program advocates the free movement of capital, goods, and services across national borders.

In the Dominican Republic 1990 tax reforms opened national markets to foreign competition by reducing tariffs and eliminating most import quotas and licensing requirements. The Foreign Investment Law, passed in 1995, opened key sectors of the Dominican economy to foreign investment, extended to foreign investors the guarantees granted domestic investors, and eliminated all restrictions on profit remittances and capital repatriation. The devaluation of the peso, by depreciating the value of Dominican labor, attracted foreign investment in tourism, export processing, and other growth areas of the economy (Betances 1995).

A 1999 IMF report presented a glossy evaluation of the NEP's results at the end of the millennium:

> The response to the stabilization program was positive. Economic growth resumed, driven especially by those sectors that were more open to competition, such as tourism and tourism related activities, construction, non-sugar manufacturing, and telecommunications. In 1991–95, the average rate of GDP growth accelerated to over 4 percent, while inflation slowed sharply. (IMF 1999: 13)

Although the NEP lowered inflation, accelerated the nation's growth rate and stimulated a massive influx of direct foreign investment, NEP structural adjustment policies led to increases in underemployment and poverty and to a sharpening of social inequalities. As José Itzigsohn (2000: 50) has noted, the reforms of the 1980s and 1990s resulted in a dramatic reduction in the state's role in providing social services and employment-related benefits (indirect salary), notably in health care and education. For example, by 1990 real capital expenditures in education were equal to only 45 percent of what they had been in 1980. In health care 1990 expenditures amounted to 81 percent of what they had been ten years earlier. And in 1992 the real minimum salary was only 77 percent of its 1980 level and 58 percent of its 1970 level.

This deterioration of wages and public services was aggravated by reductions in social security. By the early 1990s the Instituto Dominicano de Seguro Social (Dominican Institute of Social Security) was near bankruptcy and was reducing the subsidies it paid to insured workers: $7.2 million in constant 1988 pesos in 1979, compared to only $2.8 million in 1989 (Itzigsohn 2000). As a result, although unemployment decreased and participation in the labor force increased as a consequence of restructuring, wages, benefits, and social security deteriorated both in the downsized public sector and in "growth sectors" of the economy. In fact, Itzigsohn (2000) has suggested that it was this deterioration in real wages, coupled with sharp cutbacks in social security, that forced Dominican households to send more workers into the labor force, yielding higher employment rates.[10]

The Fernández administration, which came to power in 1996, gave renewed impetus to this process of neoliberal economic restructuring, advancing policies of trade liberalization, privatization, and fiscal and monetary discipline. In 1997 the Public Enterprise Reform General Law was passed that authorized increased private sector participation in economic sectors dominated by state-owned enterprises such as the sugar, power generation and distribution, and mining industries.[11]

In September 1999 management of the ten publicly owned sugar mills operated by the CEA was auctioned off to private corporations, which were granted thirty-year leases on the mills and a package of financial incentives. Management of Ingenio Boca Chica and four other mills was transferred to Conazucar, a Dominican subsidiary of the Mexican Zucarmex Group. In accordance with the agreement, all mill employees—thirty thousand nationwide—were dismissed to ensure that the transfer to private management would occur free of labor obligations. For the 1999–2000 harvest, only two mills—Boca Chica and Consuelo—were run at near-capacity, and equipment from the other mills was cannibalized to sustain the former. Only five hundred of Ingenio Boca Chica's three thousand employees were rehired.

In March 2001 Conazucar, embroiled in disputes with the government, labor unions, and independent sugar growers, sold its leases on the five mills to Consorcio Pringamosa, a consortium of Dominican and foreign investors. During the 2000–2001 harvest cycle, as Pringamosa negotiated with the government over the disposition of its new holdings, Ingenio Boca Chica remained idle and in disrepair. One laid-off mill worker complained to me that he was owed nine months' back wages but, in the ownership shuffle, did not know which "foreigners" were in charge.

If the capitalization of the sugar industry further weakened labor markets in the area, the privatization of the power industry escalated the cost of living. In April and May 1999 the Dominican government completed the sale of its power-generating and distributing assets, formerly managed by the state-owned Corporación Dominicana de Electricidad (CDE). In the capitalization plan, the state invited private corporations to submit bids for part ownership of the state's power assets. The winning bidders would receive half ownership and full management control (IMF 1999). The distribution of electricity was taken over by Unión Fenosa (a Spanish company) and the U.S.-based AES Corporation, and the state began buying power from private generators, such as Cayman Power, AES, and Smith Enron, the owner of a controversial power plant in Puerto Plata.

Beginning in late 2000, electric meters were installed in Andrés and Boca Chica, and many households that had never been billed for electricity found themselves paying as much as RD $500 per month—roughly 15 percent of the minimum private sector wage. In some poor barrios deemed unprofitable by the power distribution companies, meters were not installed and residents were charged flat fees irrespective of their actual consumption. In general, prices to consumers more than doubled as the power distributors were allowed to index rates to inflation and the price of oil. The Dominican government agreed to subsidize much of this increase at an expense of US $5 million a month. Moreover, in an effort to enforce bill collection, the power distributors began deliberately blacking out sections of the capital and elsewhere that were not paying their bills in a timely manner. These punitive blackouts were a daily occurrence throughout the nation in 2000–2001 (and beyond), provoking mass protests that were often brutally repressed by the armed forces.

IMPROVISING A LIVELIHOOD: THE INFORMAL ECONOMY

Neoliberal structural adjustment policies pushed many residents of Andrés and Boca Chica into the informal economy, into economic activities that were outside of formal wage-labor relations and avoided state regulation.[12] The informal economy had been expanding in the Dominican Republic before the adoption of the neoliberal, export-oriented model of development in the 1980s. However, labor deregulation, reductions in public sector employment, and other adjustment policies contributed to a substantial increase in underemployment and informal employment in the Dominican Republic and throughout the Caribbean and Latin America (de Oliveira and Roberts 1993; Mullings 1999; Itzigsohn 2000).

The privatization and de facto abandonment of Ingenio Boca Chica had left some three thousand workers unemployed and their households bereft of a source of income. Both formal and informal enterprises that were dependent on the sugar economy and the income of its workers suffered as well. Many households were forced to improvise livelihoods, wholly or partially, through informal economic activities. For example, when the father of sixteen-year-old Yamily Rodriguez was laid off from Ingenio Boca Chica in 2000, she and her sister quit school and began working as unlicensed masseuses and manicurists on the beach and her mother began taking in laundry.

As in Yamily's household, women often responded to worsening economic conditions by intensifying both their unpaid household labor and their paid informal work (Espinal and Grasmuck 1997; Wilson 1998a). In some cases this involved what Susan Vincent (1998: 121) has described as the "commodification of domestic labor." For example, Milagros Peralta converted her living room and porch into dining areas and opened a six-table *comedor* (restaurant). While Milagros and her mother prepared food, her younger sisters waited tables. Most of her regular customers were coworkers of her husband, a policeman. Other women established similar microenterprises in their homes, such as hair salons, laundries, or shops that offered clothing and other goods.

When Paredes García found that his salary as a schoolteacher no longer provided a living wage for his family, he quit his job and began working as a welder at a curbside car and motorcycle repair shop. Elwin Polanco lost his job at a bakery in Andrés when its business declined. Like many young men, Elwin turned to the tourism economy, improvising a living as an unlicensed tourist guide, marijuana dealer, and occasional pimp.

Many of these informal economic activities were clustered around Boca Chica's tourism economy. Men mostly sold a variety of products, ranging from clothing, crafts, and cigars to shellfish, fruits, and other foods. Women mostly worked on the beaches as masseuses, manicurists and pedicurists, and hair braiders, catering largely to foreign tourists. Young men worked as *motoconchos,* providing inexpensive transportation to residents and tourists alike. *Motoconchos,* who numbered in the hundreds in Boca Chica and its environs in 2001, typically rented their motorcycles at a per diem rate of about RD $200 (US $12). Men with whom I spoke viewed working as a *motoconcho* as an alternative—albeit a very dangerous one—to strenuous, sporadic, and low-paying work as day laborers in construction, one of the few jobs available to the unskilled.

The one exception to the gender-segregated nature of the informal economy that I encountered during the period of my fieldwork was a jewelry vendor of Haitian descent, who was described to me by her male coworkers as a "lesbian." Vendors with whom I spoke offered two explanations for the gendered division of labor, neither of which conceded willful discrimination. One common view was that men were better suited to conduct business in the *zona turística* because they are more aggressive; another was that men are more savvy at negotiating with foreign tourists. Both male views implied that women were more suited to economic activities that made use of their "natural" female abilities and support research that has shown that "women's work comes to be seen as related to the domestic sphere no matter what they do" (Vincent 1998: 122).[13] As I show, these constructions of women's roles and capacities also informed the discourses and practices of the police and other authorities.

Although state authorities issued a limited number *carnetes* (licenses) for some of these economic activities—vending and massage, for example—few workers could afford the licensing fees charged to work legally in the *zona turística.* As a result most of those who earned their liveli-

5. Informal day laborers working at a seaside restaurant. Photo by the author.

hoods on the margins of the tourism economy did so illicitly and were subject to harassment, arbitrary arrest, and stiff fines by the National Police and POLITUR. Although there had been at least one attempt to regulate the *motoconchos* by issuing them identification cards and distinctive, police-issued vests, the effort was resisted by the *motoconchos* (who feared licensing fees and restrictions on their areas of operation), and enforcement was lax. Consequently, *motoconchos* were routinely stopped by the police, sometimes in townwide operations, and fined for lacking proper documents. As Beverly Mullings (1999: 70) has pointed out for Jamaica, the efforts of the tourism industry and public authorities to "formalize or eliminate" informal activities have not only further reduced tourism's benefits to the population at large but have also turned areas serving tourists into "virtual war zones."

Another significant area of informal economic activity in Boca Chica was sex work, targeting the largely European and North American tourists who visited the area. During the 1990s, Boca Chica became a notorious destination for male sex tourists due, in part, to the proliferation of U.S.-based Internet web sites dedicated to "single male travel" (see chapter 4). Much of the town's tourism infrastructure—small and midsized hotels, restaurants, bars, and discotheques—owed their livelihood to this predominantly male, sex-oriented tourism. The prospect of making money *trabajando con turistas* (working with tourists) attracted young women and men from the capital and other impoverished areas of the country and from Haiti to work in Boca Chica's discotheques and bars as hostesses, bartenders, and sex workers.

Ivelisse, a twenty-six-year-old mother of three from San Pedro de Macorís, explained to me that she made more money in one weekend working with tourists than she had earned in one month as a machine operator in the San Pedro FTZ. Moreover, the long hours and forced overtime at the factory made it impossible for her to care properly for her children. Like Ivelisse, many women who worked with tourists were single mothers and, often, heads of households and viewed their work, not always involving sex, as the only option available to them to support their families and gain access to health care. Sex work was tolerated by the authorities, but those who pursued it, like others working in the informal economy, were routinely arrested and fined by the police, typically for lacking proper identification. Like Ivelisse, many viewed informal work as a less onerous and, in some cases, more lucrative alternative to wage labor in the formal economy, whether in FTZ factories or in low-paying tourism-related services.

Beyond its importance as a source of livelihood, the informal economy also gave rise to social relations and cultural practices that challenged elite, power-laden definitions of the labor process. As a strategy for avoiding regulation, informality brought its practitioners into routine conflict with state authorities. These social conflicts did not merely involve disputes over licensing requirements; equally significant, they implicated and aggravated deeper antagonisms related to the hierarchical organization of the tourism economy, its sociospatial division of labor, and its underlying ideologies of racial, sexual, gender, and class difference.

This oppositional side of informal economic activities has been muted, if not neglected, in much of the literature on informality. As John Cross (1998: 2) has pointed out, researchers have tended to treat informal workers as "passive economic subjects rather than economic actors—as those who had 'lost out' in the struggle for 'formal' jobs rather than as people attempting to win the struggle for a decent living." Against this tendency, Aili Mari Tripp (1997), writing on Tanzania's urban informal economy, has underscored the significance of noncompliance with regulation as an important "weapon of the weak," a modality of agency and resistance capable of contesting and influencing state policies. Tripp attributes the neglect of these oppositional aspects of informality to a narrow view of politics that stresses formal political structures at the expense of the "texture of the everyday" (9). I push this argument further and argue that these practices of noncompliance stretched beyond labor regulations to implicate power-laden constructions of both labor and identity.

To be sure, the notion of informality embraces disparate activities, which differ considerably with respect to their linkages to formal capitalist enterprises and the degree to which they are tolerated, overlooked, and, in some cases, even promoted by the state (Crichlow 1998). Alejandro Portes (1994a) has pointed out that the informal economy contributes to the process of capital accumulation because it provides cheap goods and services by lowering the costs of the reproduction of labor and by using low-cost, unregulated labor through "off the books" hiring and subcontracting arrangements. In Boca Chica many formal enterprises such as restaurants, gift shops, and construction companies hired informal and, in many cases, undocumented workers in order to avoid labor regulations governing the minimum wage, mandatory bonuses, and other benefits. In such contexts informal workers (and their employers) were generally, although not always, disregarded by state authorities and not prosecuted.

However, the vast majority of informal workers in Andrés–Boca Chica were self-employed and, within the highly regulated and policed economy of tourism, were routine targets of the state. Moreover, given the low wages in the formal tourism-related services sector, there were few incentives to employ or subcontract informal labor.[14] In short, formal and informal labor was distinguished less by wages and benefits than by illicit versus licit activities and, importantly, laboring bodies that were stigmatized versus those that were not.

I examine the everyday production and policing of this boundary between informal and formal economic practices and between bodies deemed productive and of social value and bodies marked and devalued

6. A corn vendor and his son working on the beach. Photo by the author.

and, in elite discourses, stigmatized as *delincuentes* (delinquents). Indeed, it was along the hotly contested edges of the formal economy that the sociospatial relations and discourses of difference that constituted the social division of labor were most legible and vulnerable to dispute. Alternatively, I examine the ways in which the laboring poor circumvented, challenged, and reworked this distinction and, in the process, exercised alternative and, often, oppositional conceptions of productive labor, economic value, and social justice. I approach informality as a field of offstage cultural production—a "hidden transcript," as James Scott (1990) put it—across which the laboring poor improvised and exercised modes of subjectivity and practice that brought them into conflict with the dominant, neoliberal regime of accumulation and its discourses of difference.

Further, I argue that the central contradiction or, better, field of antagonism in late capitalism is less the "structural" relationship of labor to capital than the political cleavages that result from the social *and* spatial structuring of the division of labor—a field of antagonism and conflict that is indissolubly economic, political, *and* symbolic and in which the state remains analytically central. From this vantage point, informality is not merely a strategy of noncompliance that skirts and sometimes resists state regulation; equally significant, it produces social practices, relations, and forms of consciousness that call into question the capitalist labor process and the division of labor in which it is rooted. Through their everyday struggles for livelihood, the laboring poor contested power-laden constructions that defined both the nature of productive labor and the capacities of the bodies in which that labor was to be found—constructions of labor power that were shot through with asymmetrical evaluations of racial, gender, and cultural differences. Attending to these everyday struggles illuminates key antagonisms and resistances to the reorganization of the labor process in late capitalism.

CITIZENSHIP AND THE POLITICS OF EXCLUSION

The ability of residents to secure a livelihood, whether in the formal or informal economy, was conditioned by the strength of their claims to citizenship. The possession of documents certifying Dominican nationality (notably, *actas de nacimiento,* or birth certificates, and *cédulas,* or national identification cards) was required to secure jobs in the formal economy and, more generally, to establish one's legality vis-à-vis state authorities. The "policing of citizenship," through the routine checking of identity papers, was a leading technology of power by which the police and other authorities governed the movement of people within and across the social division of labor and through the spaces of the tourism economy. Being *sin papeles* (without papers) was a widespread and serious problem for the laboring poor, locking many out of jobs in the formal economy, undermining their access to goods, services, and rights associated with citizenship, and subjecting them to arbitrary harassment and arrest by the police.

For a variety of reasons, many people in Andrés and Boca Chica did not have birth certificates, which were needed to obtain other forms of identification. Following the birth of a child, parents are required to present themselves at an office of the Registro or Oficialía Central del Estado Civil (Civil Registry) to officially declare the birth so as to be issued a birth certificate. When a person reaches the age of eighteen, this certificate must be presented at an office of the Junta Central Electoral (Central Electoral Board) to obtain an adult *cédula,* which is required for voting, securing employment in the formal sector, opening a bank account, and obtaining licenses and other documents.

Many people, especially those in rural areas, delayed or neglected registering their children's birth, through oversight, ignorance, or lack of resources to travel to the nearest Oficialía and pay the required taxes.

For example, Josefa Sánchez, a forty-five-year-old mother of four, had been trying to find employment for years. Finally, in 1998, she secured a housekeeping job at the Boca Chica Resort. However, when she was unable to produce a *cédula* at the end of her three-month probationary period, she was fired.

Over the years Josefa had hired investigators, called *buscones,* to find people who could testify to the facts of her birth in accordance with a complex legal procedure necessary to secure a "late" birth certificate. These failed efforts had drained the family's resources, and Josefa had given up trying. Not long before I met her, Josefa had opened an illegal gambling parlor in her home to supplement the income she earned from washing clothes. However, being without papers, Josefa feared arrest by the police and, worse, being mistaken for a Haitian immigrant and deported. As Milquella put it, Josefa was an "invisible woman—a woman without an identity."

This was not an uncommon problem among the poor. José Beato, a community activist based in Andrés, estimated that at least 32 percent of the adult population there (excluding persons of Haitian descent) lacked birth certificates and other identity papers and, "from the state's perspective, [did] not exist" (*Listín Diario,* June 3, 2001). In the case of Dominicans of Haitian descent, the situation was far worse. Because Dominican authorities generally did not issue birth certificates to children born of Haitian parents (Martínez 1995), the vast majority of Dominicans of Haitian descent living in Andrés–Boca Chica were barred from the public school system, the formal economy, and electoral participation.[15]

The citizenship status of some residents was compromised as a result of their encounter with the police and the criminal justice system. Most employers, especially in the tourism industry and FTZs, required job applicants to present a Certificado de Buena Conducta (Certificate of Good Conduct) along with a *cédula* and other supporting documents. Issued for a fee by the National Police, the Certificate of Good Conduct certified that the applicant did not have a criminal record and was otherwise in good standing with the law. This document was also required when applying for licenses (e.g., to work as tour guides or vendors) and when applying for visas at foreign embassies and consulates. People who had been arrested by the police (not infrequently for lacking identity papers and working informally) had difficulty obtaining this critically important document.

Lack of a Certificate of Good Conduct was also a problem for the growing number of Dominicans who had been deported from the United

7. Josefa playing with her granddaughter on her porch in Andrés. Photo by the author.

States under the strict guidelines of the Illegal Immigration Reform and Immigrant Responsibility Act of 1996 (IIRIRA). Under IIRIRA, foreign-born, permanent residents of the United States can be deported for a variety of offenses, including ones that previously had been classified by the INS as misdemeanors, such as shoplifting, illegal gambling, and marijuana possession. The IIRIRA was made retroactive and placed unprecedented restrictions on rights to judicial appeal. Although it was not possible to estimate the number of *deportados* (deportees) living in Boca Chica, I met eleven Dominican Americans who had been deported under the act (see also Hernández 2002; Brotherton 2003).

One of these Dominican Americans, Tomás Ortíz, migrated to New York with his family in 1974 at the age of fourteen. After graduating from high school, he completed one year of study at Hostos Community College. At twenty-five he married a Dominican-born woman who was a U.S. citizen. Although he was a permanent resident (his wife and his three children were U.S. citizens), Tomás was deported from the United States in 2000 after having pled guilty to a charge of marijuana possession and after having been imprisoned at an INS detention facility in Louisiana for eight months. Unable to return to his family in New York, Tomás settled in Boca Chica, reasoning that his fluency in English would help him to find work in tourism. However, despite his language skills and other credentials, his status as a *deportado* made it impossible for him to obtain a Certificate of Good Conduct. When I met Tomás in 2001 he was working as an unlicensed tour guide, arranging excursions, car rentals, and other services for tourists. On the day of our interview, Tomás was scheduled to appear before Boca Chica's prosecutor to answer charges of operating tours without a license.

As the above cases illustrate, citizenship—understood as "a continuing series of transactions between persons and agents of a given state in which each has enforceable rights and obligations" (Tilly 1995: 8)—constituted a critical and contested field of power relations and practices where struggles over access to employment, political participation, and other rights and goods were conducted between state authorities and the diverse population under their control. This ongoing series of transactions implicated in the making, policing, and unraveling of citizenship formed a node of disciplinary practices, enabling and disabling the movement of people through space and labor markets and constituting them as class-, gender-, and racially marked subjects with weakened or nonexistent claims to the nation and its resources.

Indeed, it was through the policing of citizenship—its enabling discourses, practices, and logics of verification—that differences tied to race, class, gender, and national origin were embodied and articulated as a system of exclusions that was the foundation of the social division of labor. In Josefa's case, her unverifiable citizenship status (the result, in part, of her family's class and rural origins) not only excluded her from employment and other social rights and services but also rendered her vulnerable to being (mis)taken by the authorities for an illegal *Haitian* immigrant, that is, to being racialized and criminalized, as have been many Dominicans of unverifiable identity (Human Rights Watch 2002). As Michael J. Mitchell and Charles H. Wood (1998: 1007) observed in their study of race and police brutality in Brazil, "perceived social status is a defining characteristic of citizenship" (see also Da Matta 1987), and, far from a legal identity, citizenship was produced through everyday interactions that transposed socially constructed distinctions into formal systems of exclusions (see also Caldeira 2000). As Ong (1996: 737) has put it, citizenship is a "process of subject-ification."

In Andrés–Boca Chica this politics of citizenship centered on the tourism economy, where identity-based exclusions served to insulate the profits, most notably, of the all-inclusive resort hotels. Because these profits depended in large part on tourists spending their money within the resort complexes, the hotel industry in Boca Chica exerted considerable pressure on state authorities to police competing informal economic activities. Acting largely through the Asociación Pro-Desarrollo Turístico de Boca Chica (Boca Chica Tourism Development Association), a group dominated by representatives of the area's three major resorts, the tourism industry pressured police to crack down on unlicensed vendors, *motoconchos,* sex workers, and others who provided comparatively inexpensive goods and services to tourists. These campaigns to *limpiar la calle* (clean up the street) typically constructed informal activities as criminal ones that threatened tourists and *el ambiente turístico* (atmosphere for tourism). Typically, those with the weakest claims to citizenship tended to be criminalized and marginalized, spatially as much as economically, within the stratified tourism economy.

TOURISM'S OTHER: *LA FIESTA DE TÍGUERES* (THE HUSTLERS' PARTY)

I arrived in Los Coquitos just after 8:00 P.M. and parked my scooter in the narrow alley next to Colmado La Gloria. A compact barrio overlooking the western end of the beach, Los Coquitos had a bawdy but lively reputation among residents and was held by some to be a den of thieves, hustlers, and drug dealers. Colmado La Gloria sat at a bustling intersection, across the street from a popular pool hall and catty-corner to a noisy *motoconcho* stand where a dozen or so drivers would gather to wait for customers, occasionally racing the engines of their Yamahas in anticipation of a fare.

La Gloria was reputed to have the lowest beer prices in Boca Chica, and young men gathered there in the evenings to drink and socialize amid the staccato melodies of bachata music booming from two huge speakers. Inside La Gloria high-tech gambling machines—new to Boca Chica in 2001—lined one wall. Behind the counter was the familiar inventory of commodities: neatly stacked bottles of Brugal and Barceló rum, olive oil, and vinegar; cans of evaporated milk, beans, peeled tomatoes, and Vienna sausages; boxes of Pampers; and round plastic cases filled with locally produced candies. Two teenage boys in Red Sox baseball caps manned the long wooden counter. A middle-aged woman was fastening party balloons to the walls and ceiling.

As the cost of living skyrocketed and the economy worsened, *colmados* had become important entertainment venues for a population that could no longer afford bars, nightclubs, and restaurants. *Colmadones* (the term used to refer to *colmados* with music and seating) such as La Gloria were engaged in cutthroat competition for regular patrons.

I had been invited to a birthday party for Elwin Polanco, a twenty-three-year-old man-about-town who had the reputation of being one of Boca Chica's most infamous *tígueres*. In the Dominican Republic *tíguere* is a versatile term typically used to refer to men whose behavior and disposition place them beyond the pale of respectability and, often, the law. Commonly, it was used to refer to hustlers and criminals or, more generally, to people engaged in behaviors that victimized others. I was sometimes warned to avoid certain neighborhoods—Los Coquitos, for instance—because *allá, hay muchos tígueres* (there, there are many *tígueres*).

Tíguere was also applied to men who were womanizers and seducers or who otherwise exploited women emotionally, sexually, or financially. Though the concept of the *tíguere* indexed qualities typically coded as male—notably, predatory masculinity—it was not reserved for men alone. Women who displayed these characteristics could also be viewed as being *tíguere*. For example, Minaya explained to me that his one-year-old daughter was *más tíguere* (more *tíguere*) than his five-year-old daughter because she only rarely smiled or cried and seemed to possess a forceful personality.

Moreover, the idea of the *tíguere* conveyed a sense of daring, rebelliousness, and, above all, savvy: to be *tíguere* was to surmount obstacles, flaunt conventions, and skillfully, if not always ethically, manipulate the world to one's advantage. Among the laboring poor, not surprisingly, the figure of the *tíguere* evoked considerable ambivalence. For example, I was once present among workmen at an informal auto repair shop when one of them related an incident involving a cousin in the capital. One day the cousin was approached by an officer of the National Police, who insisted that he repair the brakes of a relative's truck at no charge. Surmising that he had no choice, the cousin complied and spent most of a

8. Patrons dancing to bachata at a *colmadón* in Andrés. Photo by the author.

day working on the truck. However, determined to recoup his losses, the injured mechanic also loosened the bolts securing the truck's rear axle. One week later the policeman's relative returned with a broken axle and, in the end, paid for work three times the value of the unpaid job. At the story's end and amid the laughter of his coworkers, a man exclaimed, "*Que tiguerazo. Él sabe mucho!*" (What a big *tíguere*. He knows a lot!).[16] For some, *tígueres* are as much admired as they are feared for their ability to manipulate, if not subvert, a social system stacked against the poor and the powerless.

Elwin arrived on his scooter with a passenger in tow. He told me that the birthday party was running late because his friend's motorcycle had been confiscated by the police in a security sweep. He and his distraught passenger had just returned from the police station where Elwin had pleaded the latter's case to no avail.

"*Perfecto,*" Elwin said, surveying the party decorations and the dozen or so plastic chairs that had been arranged on the sidewalk in front of La Gloria. "Tonight, brother," he said to me, "there will be nothing missing—beer, whiskey, food. Everything perfect." Elwin told me that he had spent $1,000 pesos (US $60) on the birthday party.

Elwin was slender, dark, and handsome and wore his hair in short dreadlocks that he often covered with one of his trademark assortment of hats. This evening he wore a brown felt, bowler-shaped hat that was down so far that it made his ears stick out at right angles. Elwin once confided to me that he displayed his dreadlocks on the beach to attract tourist women but kept them covered at other times to avoid problems with the police, who associated the "Rasta" look with drug dealing.

I had met Elwin one year earlier and interviewed him soon after. He had told me to meet him at a German-owned restaurant on the beach where he sometimes worked as a *fisgón* (tout). The job paid little, but it provided him with a venue to meet foreign tourists. Elwin arrived for the interview with a teenager, whom he introduced as his assistant. The boy was from the capital, a distant cousin, and Elwin was showing him the ropes of *la vida playera* (life on the beach). Elwin had dressed for the occasion: neatly pressed jeans, a black vinyl hat, and a white shirt, buttoned to the neck. It was clear that he wanted to convey to me both his success and the appropriateness of his presence in the heavily policed *zona turística*.

Born in a small pueblo in the Cibao valley, Elwin moved to Boca Chica with his family in 1990, where his father found a job as a security guard at the Boca Chica Resort. The family had been farmers but could no longer make ends meet in the countryside. For four years Elwin worked at a bakery in Los Coquitos but, to the dismay of his parents, was attracted to life in the streets. When he lost his job at the bakery, he began hanging out on the beach and in the bars and discotheques on Calle Duarte. For a time, Elwin earned money as a *chulo,* a pimp of sorts, procuring Dominican women and sometimes men for tourists. He also set himself to meeting foreign women by working as a male escort, or "Sanky Panky," taking them around town and to the capital and providing amusement and other services.

Not long after my interview with Elwin, I was accosted by his "assistant," Junior, in the capital. Only moments before Elwin and his protégé had been escorting two women from Germany on a shopping trip in the Colonial Zone when Elwin was nabbed by a police lieutenant for not having a *cédula*. Junior wanted me to speak to the officer and vouch for Elwin's identity. We raced down El Conde and caught up with Elwin, handcuffed and pleading his innocence, and the officer near Parque Independencia. I approached the officer and explained that I knew Elwin from Boca Chica and could vouch for his identity. I presented him with my New York University business card. "It doesn't matter," the officer replied curtly before depositing Elwin into a police car. After a night in jail and a fine of 500 pesos, Elwin reappeared in Boca Chica the next day.

By the age of twenty, following the retirement of his father, Elwin was supporting his household through his informal economic projects, creating what Tripp (1997) has termed a relationship of "reverse dependency" with his parents. In the 1990s and early 2000s many young people and women working in the informal economy earned more income than did the adult male wage laborers in their households, leading to a reversal of economic obligations and prerogatives from men to women, on the one hand, and from parents to children, on the other. Tripp, addressing an analogous situation in Tanzania, noted, "In creating these reverse dependencies, the new direction of resource flows gave women and even children a greater amount of freedom and autonomy within the household than in the past as a consequence of their economic leverage" (4).

During the interview, Elwin explained to me his attitude toward wage labor and, by contrast, how he made his living:

> I don't work, Esteven. I don't ever work. I don't want to work anymore. Because you know what happens with the jobs here. You work so much for very little money. So when I don't have money, I look for a little snack *(una picadera)*. I speak to people, bring out the chaise longues for the tourists so that I can make some money. And if I want to nibble *(picar)*, I go down to the beach and find whichever white woman I can and talk to her quietly. This is working in a way that one can have fun. Because there are many women, tourists, who come here for the black man. You understand? To pay them. Whichever little brown guy *(morenito)* they like, they take him to the hotel and pay. It's almost like prostitution. I've done it a lot of times—many, many times. But now I'm more tranquil because, like I told you, I have a girlfriend. But two years ago, you would not have seen me here relaxing, because I was searching. I was stronger then. I nibbled. I was more *tíguere*.

This contrast between working *(trabajando)* as a wage laborer in the tourist economy and "snacking" *(picando)* on the source of its profits (the tourist dollar) was often drawn by workers in the informal economy. It illuminates culturally constituted ways of thinking about the labor process and economic justice and highlights a critical axis of class antagonism and conflict that pitted the laboring poor against capitalist enterprises and the state. This was not a struggle between capital and labor but a more foundational antagonism resulting from the structuring of the division of labor itself—a process that implicated not only the organizing and disciplining of labor power but also the social construction of power-laden definitions concerning the nature of productive labor and the bodies in which it was to be found. For in rejecting wage labor and subverting the wage-labor relationship, many workers like Elwin also challenged race-, gender-, and class-based stereotypes that relegated them to performing devalued and highly exploitative work in the capitalist economy.

For example, Elwin's activities as a Sanky Panky (or, as he would prefer to be called, "guide") violated the organization of the labor process in the tourism industry not only by avoiding wage labor (instead, short-circuiting, or snacking, on the source of its profits) but also by transgressing the symbolic order on which it was based—one that constructed the tourism experience, economy, and spatial order in race-, gender-, and class-inflected ways. As a black Dominican with little formal education, Elwin told me, his only opportunity for steady work was in the construction industry. "But to work like that," he said, "in construction, or cutting cane, is to work like a black slave *(esclavo prieto)*." By contrast, to work in tourism-related activities, formally or informally, was to avail oneself of knowledge, skills, and relationships that would enable one to overcome *(superarse)*, to move ahead *(moverse)*, and to turn things around *(resolverse)*—verbs that stressed movement and change, as opposed to the coerced stasis of a slavelike slot in the social division of labor.

One by one Elwin's guests began to arrive, most of whom I knew or had seen in and around Boca Chica. Like Elwin, most earned their living snacking in various ways on the tourism economy. Ramón, for example, worked as a tout and helper for a scuba diving shop but made his money selling marijuana to its clients. Flaco and Leonel (the former, a *deportado* from the United States) worked occasionally as *motoconchos* and organized unlicensed tours for tourists to nightclubs in the capital, taking advantage of their English-speaking abilities.

One of the last to arrive was Bunny, a tall man with shoulder-length dreadlocks who had taken his nickname from the Jamaican reggae great Bunny Wailer. Bunny spoke Spanish in a slow, cadenced manner that mimicked the linguistic style of Jamaican Rastafarians. He peppered his speech with such expressions as "Jah love" and "Hail Rastafari" and, like his role models, referred disparagingly to the police and authorities as "Babylon." This simulation of Rastafarian style was as much an identification with rebel cultures as it was a lure to attract tourists, some of whom found the image of the dreadlocked man on the beach (the so-called rent-a-dread) familiar, if not appealing (see also Ebron 1996). Moreover, for Rasta-style *tígueres* such as Bunny and Elwin, the counter-cultural, antiauthoritarian, and pro-African reputation of the Rastafarians indexed historical, cultural, and political referents that were external to, and subversive of, the symbolic economy of the tourism industry.

Bunny arrived at the party with three German women whom he had met the night before at the Coral Hamaca Beach Hotel's discotheque. Elwin and the others brought out chairs and offered the women drinks, fried chicken, and Moro rice. The women were from Frankfurt and had arrived in Boca Chica the day before on a ten-day charter. Elwin introduced everyone in English and told the women that it was his birthday, that they were his guests, and that they should enjoy themselves without worries. "Everything is perfect here," he said, using a favorite phrase. "Here we are all friends."

"One love," Bunny added, throwing his dreadlocks back with a shake of his head. Bunny whispered into the ear of one woman, and she reached into her backpack and took out a 500 peso note, which he used to buy a half gallon of McAlbert whiskey.

Elwin and the others explained to the women that this was "the real" Dominican Republic and that the Coral Hamaca was "a trap" *(una trampa)*—an elaborate scam to get tourists to pay exorbitant prices for food, drink, and amusement. "Here," Elwin added, "you can see how the people really live. Everything tranquil, everyone having fun." Bunny translated his words into German. The women smiled, nodded their heads, and then gaped in wonder at the mayhem around them.

Tranquilo (tranquil or at peace), often heard as a response to a greeting, was a word that peppered the everyday speech of the poor. Beyond the sense of tranquillity, the word connoted a more specific sense of being relatively free from pressing economic needs and unmet familial obligations.

I asked Bunny where he had learned to speak German. He explained that he had lived in Zurich for three years, and then he pulled an expired Swiss driver's license from his wallet to show me. While working as a waiter at the Hotel Don Juan, Bunny had met a Swiss woman, and the couple had fallen in love. During the woman's third visit to Boca Chica, they were married. Bunny went to live with his new wife in Zurich, but the marriage ended after a year, and Bunny found a job as a bouncer at a bar and brothel in Zurich's red-light district. At the brothel Bunny fell in love with a Brazilian sex worker and persuaded her to return with him to the Dominican Republic. When the manager of the bar refused to return the woman's passport until she had settled her debts, a fight ensued, and Bunny stabbed the man, though not fatally. Bunny was arrested, imprisoned for one year, then deported to the Dominican Republic.

Midway through the story, a pickup carrying three policemen, armed with shotguns and dressed in gray camouflage uniforms, passed the *colmado*. We watched the brake lights flash as the truck stopped twenty meters away, before slowly backing up to where we were sitting.

"*Ven acá!*" (Come here!), the officer in the driver's seat commanded. Elwin jumped from his chair and approached the open window with his *cédula*. As he spoke, he turned toward us, gesturing with his arm as if to explain the tableau before them. The door swung open, and the police sergeant stepped out, tugging at his belt.

"What hotel are you staying at?" the sergeant asked the women.

"The Hamaca," Bunny answered. One of the women held up her arm to display the red plastic wristband provided by the hotel.

The sergeant nodded and then, to no one in particular, announced, "These tourists do not belong in this area. This is not a tourist zone. This area is dangerous for tourists."

"Everything is peaceful here," Elwin protested. "Everyone is having a good time, without problems, without conflict."

The sergeant ignored him and addressed the women directly in English: "You must leave this place. It is not safe for you here. We will take you back to the Hamaca for your security."

There was a flurry of conversation among the women before they grabbed their belongings and climbed into the back of the pickup.

Elwin was livid. As the truck took off down the hill, he stood, arms flailing in the air. "*Coño!*" (an expletive), he yelled at the vanishing truck. "They don't have the right to do this. We are Dominicans. It's an abuse."

A crowd gathered as Bunny tried to calm Elwin, and a discussion ensued about Sergeant Guerrero. A woman, cradling a baby in her arms, proffered that she knew the sergeant's sister and that the family was originally from Bani. A *motoconcho* related that Guerrero had once shaken him down for five hundred pesos for a missing license plate. "That one," he said, "is a scoundrel!"

Elwin sat fuming, eyes bloodshot, still peering down the hill. "You know, Esteven," he said to me. "In this country there is a lack of respect. That one thinks that because I am black, I am not worth anything." He tugged at the skin of his forearm to show me. "It's racism. They don't want us to work with the tourists because they are greedy. They don't want us to progress, to be at peace."

"Who?" I asked.

"The police, the rich, all those who have the power . . ."

"Babylon!" Bunny proffered.

Elwin filled everyone's glass with whiskey and rekindled his good cheer. "But to me that doesn't matter, because I know that I'm going to overcome all of this. Do you know why? Because I have the knowledge to beat them at their own game." Elwin lit a cigarette and relaxed his body into the plastic chair.

"Tell me, Esteven," he continued, tilting his head back and smiling, "what do you think about all of this? About what we are doing here tonight—everybody friends, having a good time. Everything peaceful."

"It's perfect," I replied, not knowing what he was looking for. "It's like a party of *tígueres.*"

"Exactly!" Elwin exclaimed, grinning. *"Una fiesta de tígueres."*

If Elwin's birthday party was a spectacle of transgression, a violation of the symbolic and spatial order of the tourism industry, then the police action was an attempt to reassert that order. Elwin was right to interpret the evacuation of the German tourists, not as a "security" matter, but as an act that reiterated and realigned the system of social distinctions and evaluations that structured, and were structured by, the social division of labor—that is, the allocation of laboring bodies within the political economy of neoliberal capitalism. As such, both its transgression and reiteration exposed, if only fleetingly, the chain of equivalences that fastened the value of laboring bodies to an array of social distinctions within the spatial order of late capitalism.

The *fiesta de tígueres* was very much a spectacle, a theater of the marginalized and poor, which invited its guests to celebrate and indulge in an alternative political and moral economy beyond the pale of the tourism industry—one in which the relationships between "hosts" and "guests," and the nature of the tourism experience itself, could be contested and renegotiated. Blackness could be interesting, desirable, and, indeed, hospitable, and *tígueres* too could share their good cheer and fortune with foreign guests. At stake for Elwin and the others in their encounter with the police was not merely an opportunity to share in the profits of tourism, an economic "rational choice," but also an attempt to recalibrate the relationship between who they were and what they could become within the symbolic economy of late capitalism.

This encounter between police and *tígueres* exemplifies many of the everyday "cultural struggles" over the capitalist labor process that pit the state and capital against those who subsisted outside its normalizing practices (Ong 1991: 281). Clearly, not everyone working in the informal economy brought to those activities the oppositional dispositions exercised by Elwin and his associates. However, what I want to emphasize is that informality constitutes a structural position vis-à-vis the division of labor and its arrangements of power where the discourses and practices underpinning the latter appear in plain view and, therefore, are subject to dispute and contestation. For Elwin and the others, the enforcement of the asymmetrical geography of tourism by the police provoked a recognition of the arbitrariness of the distinctions between formality and informality, legality and illegality, and blackness and its other.

It is to this geography of power and difference, and the spatial practices through which it is constituted, that I now turn. For neoliberal economic restructuring promoted a specific spatial order and spatial politics in Boca Chica. As Jane Jacobs (1996: 1) has noted in a related context, "These expressions and negotiations of imperialism do not just occur *in* space. This is a politics of identity and power that articulates itself *through* space and is, fundamentally, *about* space." In the next chapter I focus on the spatialization of antagonisms and struggles that were associated with the evolving capitalist labor process in Andrés–Boca Chica—struggles that implicated gender, class, and racial differences, as well as questions concerning the nature and status of Dominican sovereignty under conditions of globalization.

2

The Spatial Economy of Difference

Boca Chica is a fantasy, it does not exist. In reality, Boca Chica is suffering, it is hunger, it is poverty. These things cannot be seen with the eyes.

Milquella Reyes

But a new political economy must no longer concern itself with things in space, as did the now obsolete science that preceded it; rather, it will have to be a political economy of space (and of its production).

Henri Lefebvre

Gabriel Zapata's Hostal Zapata, on prime beachfront next to the Boca Chica Resort, was considered one of the best-managed businesses in Boca Chica. In the 1970s Zapata's parents had sent him to the United States to escape political persecution under the regime of Joaquín Balaguer, who became president after the overthrow of Juan Bosch and the U.S. military intervention in 1965. As a leftist student activist and supporter of Bosch's Partido Revolucionario Dominicano (PRD), Zapata had been a likely target of Balaguer's military and paramilitary forces. In the United States Zapata became a successful businessman and eventually owned real estate and clothing stores in Washington, D.C. In the late 1980s, after training in hotel management with the Marriott Corporation, he returned to the Dominican Republic. At the time José Peña Gómez was mayor of Santo Domingo and head of the PRD, and with his assistance Zapata was able to acquire the land for his hotel.

Zapata once told me that he had left the United States to escape the racial prejudice he encountered there, and in the management of his hotel he remained alert to guests' attitudes and behaviors that suggested racism or lack of respect. "I am a black man," he told me one evening as we sat in the dining room, "and some people who stay here think that they don't have to show me respect. They think that they can do whatever they want." Only the night before, Zapata had evicted a group of drunk and disorderly policemen vacationing from New York City. Zapata went on to tell me that the reason he displayed his diplomas in the luggage room was to make sure that tourists understood he was a Dominican *and* a black man with an education.

Zapata managed his hotel with an eye to pedagogy, if not discipline, adopting policies that disrupted what he described as the fantasies animating tourism in the Dominican Republic. Chief among them, he often observed, was the notion that the Dominican Republic was a society without rules, which led some tourists to believe that they could act in ways that would not be tolerated in their own societies. And the fact that Hostal Zapata was one of the few beachfront hotels owned by a Dominican, he believed, contributed to the sense of license felt by many of his guests. My conversations with Zapata's guests had confirmed his observation. For example, during a 1999 visit, a German man explained to me, "Here, there are no rules like there are in Europe or in the United States. People do what they want. You are free to do whatever you want. You can see this when people come here from Europe and stay a long time. They change, they slow down, they become stupid, they take less care of themselves. Here it is completely different. People think only about the present, never about the future."

Zapata had adopted an arsenal of measures to disabuse his guests of this impression. Every day beginning at 6:00 A.M., his staff performed their ritual maintenance program, systematically cleaning and ordering every object and surface in the hotel. As this cleaning regimen typically continued beyond eight o'clock, when breakfast was served, it was not uncommon to find guests watching the spectacle from their tables while they waited for the staff to redirect their energies to serving food.

"When they see this," Zapata said to me one morning as we watched an employee methodically raking sand in the hotel's open courtyard, "then they understand that there is order here and that there are rules just like in the United States, or wherever." In fact, to avoid disturbing the courtyard's raked sand and Zen garden appearance, Zapata's guests would carefully follow the narrow concrete paths that led circuitously and inconveniently from one guest house to another and to the beach.

This vignette underscores the significance of spatial practices in materializing relations of power and difference in Boca Chica's symbolic and political economy. Zapata's spatial work gestured in microcosm to wider struggles over the social meanings and uses of space that implicated gender, racial, and class differences and underscored the contested status of Boca Chica's myriad attachments to the global order. Moreover, these spatial practices suggest that the significance of the nation-state and, more generally, of place in structuring a sense of belonging and political commitment is far from settled in the contemporary global economy.

Struggles over the meaning, organization, and social uses of space typically pitted the tourism industry, supported by an assortment of state agencies, against the laboring poor and the neighborhoods in which they lived. At stake in these disputes were discourses and practices that constructed the *zona turística* as a "fortified enclave," as Teresa P. R. Caldeira (2000) put it, insulating its profits from the surrounding community and projecting the tourism industry's particular, transnationally defined interests as those of the common good. Put differently, these conflicts were disputes over the spatial scale at which the nation's economic interests were to be reckoned. As Anna Tsing (2000: 120) has pointed out, scale is not a neutral dimension of spatial relations "but must be brought into being: proposed, practiced, and evaded, as well as taken for granted." Whereas tourism elites invoked a transnational and undifferentiated model of tourist desire and expectations (crystallized in the "all-inclusive" resort experience), which had to be fabricated and policed, residents appealed to the particularity of locality, stressing its contingency and pliability. These competing assertions of scale, I demonstrate, were not monolithic but were themselves subjected to dispute by diverse representatives of the state, capital, and community in the service of interests and agendas that were far from congruent.

FABRICATING THE ATMOSPHERE OF TOURISM

Residents and the authorities in Boca Chica drew a sharp distinction between the *zona turística* and *la comunidad*. This distinction had spatial referents—the *zona turística* was, to some degree, discrete and concentrated—but it also indexed cultural practices, power relations, modes of consumption, and a sense of cultural citizenship that differentiated *dominicanos* from *turistas* and the sociospatial fields they inhabited. The boundaries between the community and the *zona turística* were, therefore, porous, contested, and reshuffled in everyday practice.

The spine of the tourist zone was a roughly one kilometer section of

9. The elevated causeway of the Boca Chica Resort (right). Photo by the author.

beach that extended from the Coral Hamaca Beach Hotel and Casino to the Boca Chica Resort—an area that residents referred to as the *zona playera.* The separation of the *zona playera* from the surrounding town was secured and reiterated by the design features of the resort hotels and by the policing practices of public and private security guards. For example, the 589-room Coral Hamaca Beach Hotel was surrounded by an eight-foot concrete wall that restricted access to the resort complex and private beach to hotel guests. Only those wearing Hamaca-issued plastic wristbands were permitted onto hotel grounds.

At the opposite end of the *zona playera,* the beach facilities of the 437-room Boca Chica Resort were surrounded by a low concrete wall and policed by private security guards. The hotel's main compound (guest accommodations, swimming pools, dining rooms, etc.) was located about three hundred meters away, in the center of town, and communicated with the beach by means of an elevated causeway, which, according to the resort's brochure, "guarantees the privacy of hotel guests." The causeway enabled guests to travel between the hotel and the enclosed beach facilities without entering public space or encountering the town's inhabitants.

The 224-room Hotel Don Juan, the third of Boca Chica's all-inclusive resorts, sat midway along the *zona playera.* Though the chaise longues, volleyball courts, and other guest facilities occupied the public beach, the aggressive policing of private security guards served, de facto, to privatize the area facing the hotel. In 2000 the management of the Hotel Don Juan attempted to cordon off this area by erecting palm-thatch barriers but met with stiff community resistance. The Vendors' Union, supported by community activists, protested that the barriers were part of a systematic effort by the hotel industry to privatize the public beach. The controversy, publicized by a local, community-based cable television station, brought public pressure to bear on the resort, and the barriers were eventually removed.

This trend toward privatization was also challenged by Dominican visitors to the *zona playera,* who typically disregarded the extralegal exclusions. For example, on a public holiday that drew many *capitaleños* to Boca Chica, I witnessed a dispute erupt between a Dominican family and security guards employed by the Hotel Don Juan. The family of eight had placed their blankets among a phalanx of chaise longues that were occupied by hotel guests. A security guard instructed the family to move because, he contended, they were disturbing hotel guests. "We are Dominicans," a woman shot back, "you can't tell us where to go. This is a public beach." The family held their ground, and the dispute escalated, joined by a second security guard and by a crowd of sympathetic vendors and Dominican beach users. "This," a man argued, pointing to the ground, "is the Dominican Republic—not France, not Germany, not New York. We are Dominicans. Go to hell, *coño!*" The security guards relented, and the tourists and their chaise longues were gently relocated a short distance away.

This spatial insulation of the all-inclusive resorts and the social exclusions that it imposed were intended to safeguard *el ambiente turístico,* as a hotel manager told me, and to ensure that hotel guests would spend their money at the restaurants, gift shops, and other facilities located on hotel grounds (see also Pattullo 1996; Mullings 1999). For example, the Coral Hamaca Beach Hotel staged an outdoor vendors' market on hotel grounds that replicated the commodities sold by Boca Chica's vendors. Merchants and beach vendors often complained to me that employees of the resort hotels discouraged guests from leaving their grounds, warning of street crime and unsanitary conditions in town.

This logic of exclusion, far from improvised, guided the development of the industry as a whole. A 2002 report prepared for the Office of the

10. A public festival sponsored by the Presidente Beer Company. Photo by the author.

Secretary of State for the Environment and Natural Resources by Abt Associates, a U.S.-based consulting firm, explained why the sociocultural environment *(el entorno sociocultural)* surrounding centers of tourism required the policing of cultural differences in order to produce an "attractive" infrastructure for foreign visitors:

> The sociocultural environment is also of great importance in the quality of client offerings, along with the hotel infrastructure that has been created in coastal areas of the country. The culture of the fishing villages, so attractive at the outset of the development of this industry, has been internationalized, [and] one encounters today a mixture of behaviors, styles and ways of life, which neglect and negate the cultural values of the coastal regions, which took hundreds of years to form. (20)

Cultural hybridity (a consequence, in part, of international tourism) is targeted as a threat to the seamless atmosphere of tourism and as a principle of social exclusion. This unruly hybridity risks disrupting the binary oppositions undergirding the industry's symbolic economy—between "guests" and "hosts," between subjects and objects of consumption, and between cosmopolitan modernity and the static charm of a fantasized native culture, in this case, that of the "fishing village." It was precisely this subversive hybridity, a symbolic as much as an economic threat, that the hotel industry and tourism authorities worked to exclude.

The lead agency in this policing of difference was the Policía Turística, or POLITUR, specialized tourism police that operated under the aegis of the secretary of state for tourism. Although the National Police had jurisdiction over Boca Chica and Andrés, they rarely operated in the *zona playera* or on Calle Duarte, where the majority of restaurants and bars serving foreign tourists were located.

The responsibilities and prerogatives of POLITUR stretched well beyond law enforcement to include the policing of the atmosphere of the *zona playera,* for example, by ensuring that tourists were not annoyed by licensed vendors and that unlicensed vendors, beggars, sex workers, and others who were viewed as detrimental to tourism (largely, those working in the informal economy) were excluded from the *zona turística.* POLITUR also engaged in periodic cleanup campaigns to clear rubbish and other signs of disorder from the tourism zone. The phrase *limpiar la calle* was used to refer both to rubbish removal and to the expulsion of undesirable social elements, such as sex workers and, not infrequently, Haitian migrants. During one such street cleaning action sponsored jointly with the Boca Chica Tourism Development Association, POLITUR's director explained to a reporter, "The principal goal of this expedition is to make it possible for tourists and vacationers to enjoy themselves in an atmosphere of cleanliness and order, in keeping with the attractiveness and security that our country offers to foreign visitors" (*Listín Diario,* May 20, 2001, 2A).

Members of POLITUR were reputed to be better educated and more rigorously screened than members of the National Police and included women. POLITUR recruits were required to be high school graduates, which officials maintained better prepared them to interact with foreigners and be sensitive to the aesthetics of the tourism experience. In contrast to the National Police, POLITUR officers were not recruited locally, which was intended to ensure that their police work would not be compromised by familial or other ties to local residents. This lack of attachments to the local population was also said to disincline them to practice graft, reported to be rampant among the poorly paid National Police. Finally, the uniforms worn by POLITUR were less militaristic looking than those worn by the National Police, who frequently patrolled in combat fatigues armed with shotguns. Generally, when patrolling on the beaches, POLITUR officers did not carry sidearms. All this, a POLITUR lieutenant told me, made tourists feel more comfortable about the heavy police presence.

Unlicensed vendors and others pursuing informal economic activities

11. POLITUR officers patrolling the beach. An unlicensed vendor (lower left) is being transported to the police station after arrest. Photo by the author.

bore the brunt of POLITUR's policing practices, and such persons were subject to random arrest and fines of as much as 500 pesos. Since fees for licenses could cost as much as 1,000 pesos per month, few vendors, manicurists, and others selling goods and services in the *zona turística* could afford to operate there legally. Consequently, informal economic activities tended to be projected beyond the frontiers of the tourism zone and the patrol range of POLITUR.

Moreover, people with compromised or nonexistent claims to citizenship were unable to assemble the documents necessary to apply for licenses. Haitian migrants and Dominicans of Haitian descent, for example, were forced to limit their economic activities to the western end of the beach—an area not frequented by foreign tourists or heavily patrolled by POLITUR. In this way, weak claims to citizenship—a status conditioned by racial, gender, and class identity—served to reiterate a spatially inscribed economic marginality vis-à-vis the tourism economy. The division of labor, hierarchically ranked according to social differences, was both constituted through and expressed by spatial practices of exclusion. Informal workers had a clear sense of this socioeconomic geography and adjusted their movements through space accordingly. For example, a Haitian-born vendor of wood carvings explained to me that he avoided the zones of influence of the all-inclusive hotels by detouring through the town in a zigzag pattern, reentering the beach only at points where there were bars and restaurants that catered to local residents.

Vendors and others working in the informal economy played a cat-and-mouse game with POLITUR, testing the frontiers of the *zona playera* and the resolve of the authorities to enforce them. On weekends and on holidays POLITUR sometimes extended its patrol range to the western, predominantly Dominican end of the beach, scattering the informal workers. In late 2001, as POLITUR, equipped with additional manpower and resources, increased its presence, conflicts often erupted between POLITUR and the National Police over jurisdiction and law enforcement practices. A merchant whom Milquella interviewed explained that POLITUR's policing of the *zona turística* had also undermined the elaborate system of graft payments to the National Police by informal workers and others for protection against arrest and harassment. Sex workers and Haitian migrants were especially vulnerable to this system of graft.

However, the antagonism between the two policing authorities ran deeper than the protection racket: POLITUR officers were viewed by many as outsiders who, with higher salaries and social status, held themselves to be superior to the local police. "The government gives them white shirts and four-wheelers [four-wheel motorcycles]," a sergeant in the National Police told me, "and they think that they're better than us. But they don't care about the people of Boca Chica. They are here only to protect the tourists." One day, as I interviewed a hair braider, a fist-fight broke out between two POLITUR officers and an off-duty member of the National Police. The off-duty policeman, who was spending the day at the beach with his family, had seen the two POLITUR officers accost his teenage sister in an ID check and leaped to her defense. The policeman was arrested and handcuffed, provoking outcries from a crowd of vendors and residents. When the POLITUR officers, alarmed by the angry crowd, had confirmed his identity, they released him.

This intensive policing of informal economic activities in the *zona turística* tended to construct those pursuing them as *delincuentes,* the term typically used by POLITUR and other authorities to name the diverse categories of people who were viewed as disturbing *el ambiente turístico*. These "delinquents" included unlicensed workers and panhandling children—often described by officials as runaways, or *palomos* (pigeons)—as well as men and women who were taken to be *tígueres* or sex workers. Young women—in particular, women who were racially marked and poor—were routinely stopped by POLITUR in identity checks on the premise that they were *mujeres de la calle* (streetwalkers) and potential lawbreakers. The hierarchical landscape of the tourism zone, thus, was structured in gendered terms since women were not only more likely than men to be viewed as being out of place there but also more likely to be seen as exploiting their sexuality. As a POLITUR officer said to me, as we watched a group of teenage women cross the beach in front of the Boca Chica Resort, "Those women are not here to bathe, to spend time with their families, their boyfriends. They are here to rob, to prostitute themselves."

Haitians, in particular, were targets of this aggressive policing strategy within the tourism zone. Though there were no official estimates of the number of Haitian migrants and people of Haitian descent living in Andrés and Boca Chica, their presence was significant. This population included Dominican-born Haitians who historically had been associated with Ingenio Boca Chica and its cane fields and new migrants who were drawn to the area by its tourism economy. Among elites, in particular, people of Haitian descent were regarded with disdain as threatening the cultural, economic, and political integrity of the nation (see chapter 5). Haitians were viewed by many as a foreign and decivilizing influence on the nation, and the fact that Haitians, with few exceptions, were confined to the informal economy supported that view.

For example, shoeshine boys *(limpia botas)* and other children who sold goods or panhandled within the *zona turística* were often described to me as runaways from the Haitian sugar *bateyes,* implying that they were the offspring of negligent and opportunistic parents. A commonly used term to refer to Haitian women who worked as hair braiders and food vendors was *mau-mau,* which, aside from its historical reference, conveyed a sense of rapacious, if not illicit, economic activities.[1] Solange, a twenty-three-year-old Haitian hair braider, complained to me that she had been repeatedly harassed by POLITUR because, as she put it, "they think that all Haitian women who come to this country are prostitutes and are here to rob tourists." Moreover, Haitian immigrants were often accused of being carriers of HIV/AIDS and drug traffickers, a topic that I address at some length in chapter 5.

This racialized and gendered construction of the *zona turística* and the policing of its ambience, therefore, not only excluded many residents and migrants from participating licitly in the tourism economy (an exclusion already secured, in part, by the all-inclusive policies of the resort hotels) but also stigmatized those who were excluded as delinquents—a category invested with commingling evaluations of class, gender, racial, and cultural difference. Indeed, it was through these everyday practices of producing and policing the social division of labor that disparate social distinctions were applied to laboring bodies as a sociospatial class hierarchy.

THE VIEW FROM ABOVE

The state's aggressive policing of the *zona turística* was actively promoted by the Boca Chica Tourism Development Association (TDA), a group dominated by the area's three all-inclusive resort hotels. The TDA functioned as an advocacy group, lobbying public officials on behalf of the hotel industry and organizing support for its interests among merchants and other business owners, although with mixed success.

Many residents expressed the opinion that the TDA, rather than Boca Chica's *ayuntamiento* (municipal government), was the real governing body in the area and that its interests were paramount in public policy making. As the owner of a hair salon put it to Milquella, "In reality, the *ayuntamiento* doesn't exist, because the work that has to be done here in Boca Chica is done by the Boca Chica Tourism Development Association. And in my opinion, it's an antidevelopment association."

The TDA also had the lead role in structuring the discourses through which the nature and interests of the tourism industry were represented, and TDA meetings and public forums, more often than not, attracted the attention of the national media. In short, the national and international image of Boca Chica was heavily shaped by the TDA.

In 1999 I was invited by Gabriel Zapata to accompany his twenty-year-old son to a meeting of the TDA. Zapata had been invited to join the group as the representative of Boca Chica's small and midsized hotels. The purpose of the meeting was to provide an opportunity for TDA members to discuss the tourism industry's problems with an assortment of public officials, including the deputy secretary of state for tourism (Region I), the secretary general of the *ayuntamiento,* representatives of POLITUR and the National Police, and officials from the Departments of Youth, Health, and Immigration. The meeting was also attended by representatives of the three major resort hotels, the Boca Chica Merchants Association, and the national print media. Save for one journalist and two secretaries who took notes, all the representatives were male.

The meeting was held in a well-appointed conference room at the Hotel Don Juan. The twenty-five or so attendees took seats around a long mahogany table, on which cell phones, notepads, and military caps were displayed before their owners. Henry Pimentel, deputy secretary of state for tourism, opened the meeting by inviting the attendees to introduce themselves and their respective purviews. Zapata had told me to say that I, along with his son, was there to represent him. I said that, then added that I was an anthropologist from New York City doing research in Andrés and Boca Chica. After highlighting a number of agenda items—crime, wild dogs, uncollected garbage, solid waste, and child prostitution—Pimentel invited the others to identify topics for discussion.

A restaurant owner and member of the merchants association began. "*Haitianos,*" he said, pausing for effect. "Haitians." Others around the table nodded their heads in agreement. A cell phone sounded "Jingle Bells." "Here, in Boca Chica," he continued, "there are many, many Haitians living and working without—without any kind of controls. For example, in construction. Almost all—maybe all of the construction workers here in Boca Chica are Haitians."

Pimentel nodded sympathetically. "Yes, that's a real problem in the entire country," he replied. "But does that affect tourism?"

"Of course!" the merchant blurted. "They are working, not only in construction, but also in tourism. Every tourism institution here in Boca Chica employs Haitians, illegally, and without controls of any kind."

"In that case," Pimentel replied, "that is a problem for POLITUR." The director of the tourism police gravely nodded his head.

"Good," Pimentel said. "Let's move on. Another theme."

An Italian-born hotel owner continued in heavily accented Spanish. "Noise from the discotheques and bars until four and five in the morning. And the *motoconchos,* all night, when people are sleeping. And there is the child prostitution. Horrible! Children, four and five years old, out in the streets until six in the morning. And the tourists ask me, 'What is this? How can this go on?' "

The discussion turned to the problem of prostitution in general and among minors in particular. The representatives of POLITUR and the National Police reported that they did not have the manpower to police the beach and Calle Duarte into the early hours of the morning. Pimentel agreed, adding that the problem was not merely prostitution but also the drugs and crime that went along with it, all of which were affecting the *salud del ambiente* (environmental health). In the case of prostitution by minors, Pimentel called for better coordination between the police and the Department of Youth.

A lieutenant in the National Police spoke up. "Basically, the problems of the minors and the prostitutes are very complex ones because they have social roots." The room fell silent.

> Maybe, it's not anyone's fault, because we are all Dominicans living here, and all of us are responsible for what is happening. Unfortunately, the educational system that has operated in the country has not been the best. And maybe we need legislation to make it the obligation of parents to educate their children. Because these children in Boca Chica and in other tourist zones—for example, in Santo Domingo, in Sosúa, and in Cabarrete—these children are growing up with delinquency and will become delinquents. This is not a problem unique to Boca Chica. It is a national problem. And we don't have the resources to control it. I don't know, *caramba* . . .

"There is no specialized program," Pimentel proffered. "This is why we need better coordination between POLITUR and the Department of Youth."

"Perhaps," the lieutenant replied. "But the question of the prostitutes is a very controversial one because prostitution is the oldest profession there is. But, unfortunately, here in Boca Chica, there are many merchants, many persons, who are complicit in this problem. Because this is all happening under their noses. The prostitutes are having relations with the tourists that come here because, internationally, Boca Chica is promoted on the Internet as a sexual paradise."

There was an outburst of disagreement and comments from some of the merchants and hotel representatives in the room. Pimentel raised his hand for calm.

"Excuse me," the lieutenant continued. "I am not telling lies. It is on the Internet. An investigation was conducted—it was in *El Nacional* [a newspaper] that Boca Chica and other areas are promoted as sex paradises. Then the tourists come here looking for prostitutes, and for minors. How is it possible for the police to do their job, with low salaries and bad conditions, to combat prostitution? What happens is that—All of the merchants on Calle Duarte are involved in this. If there wasn't prostitution, they wouldn't sell this quantity of rum or whatever. Here in this town there is a lack of social conscience, especially among the merchants, and in the society as well."

Ignoring the dissension and the comments, the lieutenant went on. "But we must confront this assault. Because if not, unfortunately, this place will become *worse* than Sosúa.[2] This is what I say. And because of that, the future will be as dismal for tourism as it will be for the police. But you, the majority, are involved in this thing. But for me, as a Dominican, it hurts. Understand?"

The Cuban-born manager of the Hotel Don Juan objected. "I agree with much of what you have been saying, but not *all* of Boca Chica participates in this. This has not been proven."

"I did not say all of Boca Chica," the lieutenant replied. "I said Calle Duarte. Clearly, the Don Juan and Hamaca hotels are not involved . . ."

The Italian hotelier interrupted. "Lieutenant, lieutenant. This, you know, benefits only four or five business on Calle Duarte. There are not many others involved."

Pimentel again called for calm. He suggested that the discussion turn to seeking solutions to prostitution and the other problems that were hurting tourism.

The TDA meeting reiterated the boundaries of the tourism industry's symbolic economy (albeit from the vantage point of its elite interests) and exposed fractures and antagonisms both among local interests and in relation to transnational capital. Before the lieutenant's intervention, the social forces threatening the atmosphere of tourism had been imagined to be external to Boca Chica's political economy—an invasion of Haitians, delinquents, sex workers, and unsupervised children. In the case of Haitians, the claim that they were working in tourism was sufficient to index a multifarious and racialized threat to the industry's and nation's integrity. As was often the case, prostitution was posed as a problem of corrupted minors. Although prostitution among minors existed in Boca Chica, framing the issue in this way erased the agency of adult women who were involved in sex work and enabled the construction of a narrative that presented the origins of prostitution and other social problems in a process of corruption, dissociated from tourism and the wider political economy.[3]

In this evolutionary narrative, prostitution and other "delinquencies" were imagined to be effects of modernity's corrupting influence on categories of persons that were incapable of participating in, and profiting from, its modernizing power. "[Children] come to Boca Chica," one merchant explained to me, "and they see the tourists, with their money and cell phones, enjoying themselves, and they want this too. And they will do anything to get it—steal, prostitute themselves, anything. Because they don't have the education *(la preparación)* to understand how tourism functions." What the categories named in this and similar narratives of threat and corruption shared from the vantage point of male elites was an absence of *logos,* the "civilizing power" of reason.[4] It was this putative absence of reason that made these deeply gendered and racialized categories of persons unworthy of full citizenship.

The lieutenant's remarks disrupted this narrative of corruption not only by pointing to prostitution's socioeconomic origins but also by arguing that everyone—Dominican society as a whole—bore responsibility for the problem. By asserting that merchants and others in the *zona turística* were complicit in, and profiting from, prostitution, he situated the origins of prostitution in the process of capital accumulation rather than in an evolutionary narrative of degeneration. The charge that Boca Chica was promoted on the Internet as a sexual paradise was true; but it also placed responsibility on the tourism industry as a whole, which marketed the Caribbean as a land of "sun, sex, and sand" (Kempadoo 1999; Mullings 1999).

The discussion also exposed a tension that was central in the politics surrounding tourism in Boca Chica—between what was perceived as the encroachment of foreign capital, interests, and influence, on the one hand, and the weakening of Dominican culture, values, and sovereignty, on the other. The lieutenant's statement that, "as a Dominican," prostitution hurt him, recast sex workers as members of the community rather than as criminalized outsiders; moreover, it implied that the international interests represented in the tourism industry were in conflict with the interests of the nation. In fact, most of the bars, discotheques, and hotels that catered to sex tourists were owned by foreign, primarily European expatriates and investors. However, the simple binary of Dominican versus foreign interests did not adequately represent the complex composition of capital in the tourism industry. The Coral Hamaca Beach Hotel, for example, was owned by the Coral Hotels and Resorts Corporation, a subsidiary of the Dominican Grupo BHD. In short, global capital and the interests that it served crossed national frontiers.[5]

Nevertheless, the claim that foreign capital was encroaching on Dominican cultural values and sovereignty was a leitmotiv in everyday spatial politics in Boca Chica and a persistent subtext at TDA meetings (see also chapter 6). In 2001, for example, Dominican members of the TDA charged that expatriate bar owners on Calle Duarte were "colonizing" Boca Chica by putting tables and chairs in the public street. As a Dominican restaurateur put it to me, "Dominican families no longer feel comfortable walking through the town, or on the beach, because foreigners have turned the streets into one big discotheque, with noise, delinquency, and vices." In the national media foreigners were often accused of being ringleaders in the recruitment of sex workers and in the trafficking of Dominican women abroad. A persistent rumor that circulated among Dominicans and expatriates alike was that the Italian devel-

12. A condominium under construction in Boca Chica in 2002. Photo by the author.

opers who were building condominiums in Boca Chica were laundering money for mafia organizations. These accusations, some of which were founded, exposed tensions and conflicts within the tourism industry linked both to the variegated composition of its capital and to anxieties concerning its impact on Dominican political, economic, and cultural sovereignty.

The TDA meeting also exposed discrepancies in the discourses and interests of state agencies. For example, whereas POLITUR officials tended to affirm the dominant ideology of tourism outlined by Deputy Secretary of State Pimentel and the TDA, the National Police lieutenant challenged that view, teasing out complexities that were elided by conflating prostitution with crime and moral otherness. In fact, as the meeting continued, the Department of Youth official came to the lieutenant's defense, pushing this complexity even further. "In some quarters," he began, "prostitution is not considered a profession of disrepute. Today, we don't speak of prostitutes, we speak of sex workers *(trabajadores sexuales),* and this is a new concept recognized universally by international organizations. All prostitution is not equal, and we must recognize a distinction between minors and adults. And from this perspective, a healthier approach would be to develop a plan to control it."

However, the concept of sex workers (a term popularized in the Dominican Republic by sex workers themselves), along with his recommendations, fell on deaf ears. Instead the meeting turned to formulating policies to control the atmosphere of tourism—policies that focused squarely on disciplining space. The first measure, which had been proposed by POLITUR, was a plan to close Calle Duarte to vehicular traffic. The intent of the street closure was to exclude *motoconchos* from the heart of the *zona turística* and, by extension, impede the mobility of sex workers and other "delinquents."

Further, it was agreed that *motoconchos* were to be licensed by POLITUR in order to weed out operators who lacked *cédulas,* ownership papers, and driver's licenses. In 2001 these measures were implemented. Calle Duarte was blocked off to vehicular traffic from dawn to dusk. (It was this street closing measure that enabled the "colonization" of Calle Duarte by foreign merchants.) Although an attempt to regulate the *motoconchos* was made—through document checks and the issuance of fluorescent orange vests to licensed drivers—the plan was soon abandoned because of enforcement difficulties and the noncompliance of the *motoconchos.*

To address Haitians working in the tourism zone and the involvement of minors in sex work, it was agreed that those present should lobby for the establishment of permanent offices for the Departments of Youth and Immigration next to POLITUR's headquarters on Calle Duarte. However, the major responsibility for controlling tourism's atmosphere was to fall to POLITUR. It was agreed that POLITUR's resources needed to be greatly increased in order to extend their patrol range and intensify their enforcement capabilities. The targets for this revitalized strategy of policing were identified as Haitian migrants, sex workers, *motoconchos* (and others working without licenses and *cédulas*), and criminals, including drug traffickers.

Last but not least, the assembly raised the problem of the *fisgones* who worked on the beaches soliciting customers for restaurants and bars. *Fisgones* (sing. *fisgón,* meaning "snoop" or "snooper") were often identified as one of the most potent symbolic and economic threats to the tourism industry. Typically, *fisgones* worked in association with beachfront restaurants and bars, soliciting customers and renting them tables and chairs. In a common arrangement, a bar or restaurant manager would allow a *fisgón* to pocket a rental fee of 50 to 100 pesos for the use of a table with the expectation that the customer would purchase refreshments of much greater value. Though *fisgones* were not paid employees, they had a critical role in attracting customers in the hypercompetitive environment of the *zona playera*. *Fisgones* also procured other goods and services (hence the sense of "snooping") for their customers, for which they received small commissions from the vendor or service provider. For example, like Elwin, *fisgones* used their positions to broker services, ranging from guided tours and currency exchange to massages and sex. In short, *fisgones* made their livings brokering transactions between tourists and their personal networks of merchants, vendors, and service workers.

In this capacity, *fisgones* exercised significant influence. The quality and extent of their social networks, marketing skills, and relations with other *fisgones* affected the profitability and reputation of the beachfront businesses. For example, an eighteen-year-old *fisgón* whom I knew became embroiled in a dispute with a German bar owner when the latter refused to allow him to rent tables on the beach for more than 50 pesos. In retaliation, the *fisgón* began directing customers elsewhere and sabotaging other economic transactions on which the bar depended.[6] After a few days the bar owner conceded. That few of the expatriate business owners were fluent in Spanish made them particularly vulnerable to the maneuverings of the *fisgones*.

Moreover, in their role as brokers, *fisgones* typically developed foreign-language skills and were attuned to mass-mediated popular cultures and styles, ranging from U.S. popular music to Jamaican Rastafarianism. This heterogeneous linguistic and cultural repertoire enhanced their ability to communicate with, and broker services to, foreign tourists. It was this "unstable hybridization of cultures" that branded the *fisgones* as subversives par excellence in a tourism economy that equated profitability with the capacity to control its sociocultural milieu (Turner 2000). As a Dominican gift shop owner who had lived in the United States put it to me, "[The *fisgones*] have never even been [to the States], and yet they want to be gangsters, criminals like in the rap videos. They were born here, but they are no longer Dominicans" (see also Pérez 2004: 117).

As the meeting came to a close, the deputy secretary of state for tourism described the *fisgones* as "a band of delinquents, who have nothing, no restaurant, nothing[,] . . . [and who] make their money stealing from tourists." POLITUR's director referred to them as a "a plague" and observed that they "had their hands in everything—drugs, robberies, prostitution." A merchant argued that beachfront businesses should charge a table minimum rather than allow *fisgones* to rent the tables. This, he said, would solve the problem. The deputy secretary agreed but lamented, "But you know that this will not be easy, these *fisgones* are an institution here in Boca Chica."

The observation that *fisgones* "have nothing" and yet were able to wrestle a livelihood from the tourism economy was frequently cited as an especially disturbing fact. For in contrast to other workers in the tourism economy, *fisgones* sold neither goods nor services but merely brokered their exchange, snooping in the exchange process and raking off surplus value. Like other types of brokers (e.g., stock and real estate brokers), the livelihood of the *fisgones* depended on specialized knowledge (in this case, the mastery and manipulation of cultural codes) and on their ability to analyze markets and interpret the markets' underlying structures of desire.

Indeed, the work of the *fisgones* stretched beyond that of brokers: they served as middlemen in commodity exchanges, manipulating the very meaning of the commodity (the tourism experience) and, in the process, intervening in structuring tourists' desire. For example, their engagement with African American and Caribbean popular cultures and styles, a trademark of the occupation, proffered alternative and, indeed, oppositional iconographies for the tourism experience, ones in which blackness was valued and, in some cases, commodified. A popular cottage industry for some *fisgones* was the burning and marketing of reggae, rap, meren-rap, and bachata music mix CDs. Bachata, a Dominican music genre that historically has been associated with the poor and less than respectable performance venues, was never played in the resort hotels or in mainstream tourist venues (see Pacini Hernandez 1995).

This stretching of the tourism experience challenged the static and seamless package of Dominican culture staged by the resort hotels and tour operators, for example, folkloric dance performances and merengue dance lessons, the sine qua non of the resort hotel entertainment program.[7] The cultural practices of the *fisgones* recapitulated and performed what Frank Moya Pons (2004: 47) referred to as the *diversidad olvidada* (the forgotten diversity) of Dominican culture and identity. Indeed, a form of "nibbling" that was practiced by the *fisgones* and that preoccupied the authorities was the marketing of unlicensed tours to tourists—shopping trips to department stores in the capital, visits to nightclubs in neighboring Andrés. Such tours not only cut into the profits of the resorts and tour operators but also, as the Tourism Development

Association rightly surmised, threatened the atmosphere of tourism as it had been fabricated by industry elites and enforced by the police.

It was this double transgression, cultural as much as economic, that cast the *fisgón* as the tourism industry's archetypal Other. On the one hand, as interlopers in the cultivation and exploitation of tourists' desire, *fisgones* recalibrated the tourism experience in ways that challenged hegemonic industry narratives. On the other hand, as brokers who neither sold their labor nor owned anything (snooping and snacking, instead, on exchange value), their relationship to the capitalist labor process assumed, from the vantage point of elites, a fetishlike form, as Marx put it—that of a "plague" that violated both the logic and the process of capital accumulation.

The dominant discourses of the tourism industry and its technologies of spatial production also found critics beyond the *zona turística*. Although the TDA, backed by state authorities and the media, exercised substantial influence in fabricating Boca Chica as a tourism center, residential communities also engaged in their own spatial practices—practices that reasserted the durability of neighborhood histories, identities, and needs. Below I examine the efforts of one neighborhood to assert its sociospatial integrity against the tourism industry's overarching narrative of development. However, in reasserting "community," residents were obliged to renegotiate their internal differences, notably, deeply gendered evaluations of who did and did not count in the community-building project. This project of reimagining locality, though taking international tourism as its foil, was itself shaped by transnational experiences and processes that have recast the roles of women in Dominican society.

REIMAGINING COMMUNITY

A key social institution in Boca Chica and elsewhere in the Dominican Republic was the *junta de vecinos* (neighbors' association). Sponsored and partially subsidized by the state, *juntas* were neighborhood-based voluntary groups that represented the interests and needs of communities to the local *ayuntamiento* and to the state. In Boca Chica the *juntas* defined neighborhood identity and advocated on behalf of residents before local authorities. They were governed by elected officers—president, vice president, secretary, and treasurer—and the *juntas* of Boca Chica and Andrés were collectively represented by a coordinator.

I worked most closely with Junta La Unión, representing Bella Vista, the barrio in which I lived, comprising roughly four square kilometers.

Founded in 1968, La Unión was said to have been the first *junta* organized in Boca Chica and the model for those that followed. Weekly meetings, usually attended by twenty to thirty residents, were held in a building at the corner of my street, and its president, Chema Ortíz, lived on my block. Chema was a soft-spoken man of about sixty who had grown up in San Pedro de Macorís and in the 1970s had moved to Boca Chica, where he found work as a waiter at the Boca Chica Resort. After twenty years of working in hotels, Chema retired and took a part-time clerical job at the *ayuntamiento*'s office in Boca Chica. In 1994 he was elected president of Junta La Unión.

During my stay in Bella Vista, public service and quality of life issues dominated La Unión's agenda. One persistent problem was infrequent garbage collection, which had prompted some residents to burn their garbage, thereby compounding the problem. Other issues raised by La Unión and brought before the *ayuntamiento* included low water pressure, infrequent police patrols, nuisance noise from a nearby *colmadón*, and power outages in the wake of privatization. These problems were shared by other barrios in Boca Chica and Andrés, and there was a conviction among *juntas* that state authorities, lobbied by the TDA, focused their resources on the *zona turística* at the expense of surrounding areas.

As I left my apartment one morning in May 2001, I found a group of residents sweeping the streets and clearing rubbish from a vacant lot at the corner that was being used as a garbage dump. Clara, nicknamed "La Gringa," a middle-aged woman whom I had met earlier, encouraged me to join them. There were about thirty-five residents in all, the majority of whom were women, teenage girls, and children. Besides Chema, the *junta*'s president, only two other men were working.

Midway through the cleanup, a middle-aged man approached me and introduced himself as Miguel. He told me that he had returned to the Dominican Republic the month before after having lived in the Bronx for twenty years. Miguel had worked as an elevator operator in a luxury apartment building and, after having saved a nest egg, decided to return to Boca Chica and go into business with his brother, who owned a car repair shop along the highway. Miguel had been divorced two years earlier and his two U.S.-born children had remained in the Bronx with their mother. The neighborhood cleanup had been his idea, Miguel informed me. "We used to do it in the Bronx," he explained. "It brings people together."

Miguel told me that he had grown tired of the "rat race" in New York and that he had missed family, friends, and the lifestyle in Boca Chica.

13. Employees of Colmado La Fe, located in Bella Vista. Photo by the author.

He reiterated what others had told me: Bella Vista was one of the oldest and most closely knit neighborhoods in Boca Chica, and Junta La Unión had been the model for other associations.

When the work was completed, we reassembled at the *colmado* for refreshments. Colmado San Francisco was owned by Juana Guzmán and operated by two of her three sons. Like most *colmados,* San Francisco was a gathering place for local residents and, in the face of widespread unemployment and a rising cost of living, had become an increasingly important venue for low-cost socializing. Many *colmados* played popular music and provided chairs, if not tables, for their customers. In 2001 many *colmados* in Boca Chica installed electronic gambling machines, which increased their attraction for some. Because few foreign tourists and expatriates frequented the *colmados* (even those located in the *zona turística*), they were viewed by residents as particularly Dominican cultural spaces and contrasted to the tourism-oriented bars and entertainment venues.

A cultural marker of this contrast was the fact that the *colmados* tended to play bachata exclusively (never global pop, and only rarely merengue and salsa), a genre that was never played in bars, clubs, and other places serving tourists. Bachata, whose lyrics frequently addressed intimate, personal experiences (e.g., lost or unrequited love or separation resulting from migration), was viewed by many with whom I spoke as inappropriate for, if not inaccessible to, foreigners.

Like the *juntas, colmados* played an important part in producing networks of sociality and a sense of community identity. Since most residents of Bella Vista passed through Colmado San Francisco daily to make purchases, use its pay telephone, and socialize, it was an important venue for disseminating barrio news and gossip—a function strengthened by the fact that San Francisco, like other *colmados,* also served as gathering places for *motoconchos* who, by virtue of their itinerant work, were central figures in spreading information around town.

Miguel filled my plastic cup with beer. "You see, Boca Chica has an image problem," he began. "The people who come here—all they see is the bars, and the hotels and the discos, and the *tígueres* in the street. The tourists don't know that there are neighborhoods like this one and that there are people who work hard every day just like they do over there in the States."

Miguel introduced me to Belkis, secretary of Junta La Unión, and then cheerfully suggested that I be given the *apodo* (nickname) "El Gringo" to achieve symmetry with "La Gringa."

I sat with Belkis and La Gringa in front of the *colmado.* Belkis had also lived and worked in the United States. Leaving their two children behind in Boca Chica, Belkis and her husband had joined her mother and two brothers in Jersey City, New Jersey, in 1991, where she worked as a janitor at a chemical factory for ten years. A permanent resident of the United States, Belkis returned to New Jersey every year to fulfill her residency requirement, visit relatives, and work. "This is my country," she told me, "where I was born and where I want to live. But I can't earn enough money here in Boca Chica to survive. That's my problem."

Belkis's predicament was not uncommon. As Sherri Grasmuck and Patricia Pessar (1991) have demonstrated, many return migrants have found it difficult to convert skills as well as savings earned abroad into employment and entrepreneurial opportunities back home. Belkis had been unable to find work in the Dominican Republic that would pay wages comparable to what she earned in the United States. Unemployed, she remained reliant on remittances sent by her husband from New Jersey and on income that she earned as a garment worker during her annual return visits as a circular migrant.[8] This predicament was especially pronounced for women, who encountered few job prospects on their return and, often, pressure from husbands not to work (Pessar and Grasmuck 1991; Levitt 2001). For example, La Gringa, who had worked for fifteen years as a hairdresser in New York, decided to give up her vocation on returning to Boca Chica. "I needed a rest," she had told me earlier. "Let my husband work!"

Chema joined us, and I asked him about the *junta*'s activities. He explained that its focus was improving public services and, above all, the availability of potable water. "The problem that we have here in Boca Chica and Andrés is that we do not have the status of a municipality. We are between the capital and San Pedro de Macorís but don't get sufficient resources from either. We are the stepchild of both. All the government sees here is tourism, but this community existed long before the tourists came."

For this reason, Chema continued, the *junta* had to demonstrate to politicians and public officials alike that it was well organized and united and it enjoyed the support of residents. "When we do something like we did here today, cleaning the street, they see that there is more than tourism here in Boca Chica—all that you see down on La Duarte. A community also exists that has its own history, its own traditions, and is trying to improve itself." One project on the top of his list, Chema told me, was to resurrect the celebration of Boca Chica's patron saint, San Rafael, which had been discontinued some years before. As the gathering at the *colmado* disassembled, Chema invited me to attend the *junta*'s next meeting on May 12.

The street cleanup, like La Unión's other activities, addressed the persistent problem of poor public services—a problem exacerbated by Boca Chica's weak political status as the "stepchild" of the Distrito Nacional (National District). Equally important, La Unión's fostering of a sense of community integrity and common interests complicated and, at times, challenged Boca Chica's elite-mediated identity as a tourism center. In fact, La Unión's cleanup was staged only weeks after POLITUR, prompted by the TDA, had carried out a similar campaign—one, however, that was restricted to the *zona turística*. The cleanup might well have been Miguel's idea, modeled on community-building practices in the Bronx, but it underscored symbolically Bella Vista's neglect in elite discourses and policies and its resolve to represent itself as a community of interest.

This sense of locality and shared interests was not monolithic, nor did it go uncontested in Bella Vista's everyday politics of representation. Though a reaction, in part, to the disregard of locality by the internationally oriented tourism industry and the state, the notions of community practiced by residents were also inflected by transnationally mediated understandings of the interrelationship of power, space, and subjectivity and by changes in the Dominican economy and society.

The following Thursday La Unión met to plan celebrations for two approaching holidays, Día de las Madres (Mother's Day) on May 27 and the thirty-third anniversary of La Unión's founding on May 31. The meeting was attended by about thirty-five people, the majority (roughly 75 percent) of whom were women. Chema, joined by Belkis, the *junta*'s secretary, and Pedro, its treasurer, seated themselves at the table in front of the meeting room. Chema opened the meeting with the suggestion that the two holidays should be celebrated on the same day, May 27, which would save the group labor and money. He also announced that Presidente, a domestic beer company, had agreed to partially sponsor the festivities.

Chema explained that he had a two-part celebration in mind: a Mother's Day ceremony, which would publicly recognize mothers in the neighborhood, followed by a block party to celebrate the *junta*'s anniversary. The meeting then turned to a discussion of logistics—the purchase of a Mothers' Day cake, gifts to present to the mothers, and the preparation of food, which would be sold at the neighborhood party.

La Gringa rose to speak. "I know that we are speaking about Mother's Day, but I don't think that we should only give gifts to women who have children. Because not all of the women who work from day to day with the *junta de vecinos* are mothers."

Chema, looking somewhat nonplussed, deferred to the treasurer.

"*Claro*" (Of course), Pedro began. "But what we are doing here is planning for two separate things, Mother's Day and the anniversary. And each will have its own celebration."

La Gringa interrupted, "No, what I am saying is that we should give gifts to all of the women who participate, not to some and not others." "Look," she continued, pointing to two teenage women in the back of the room who were active in the *junta*. "Danilda and Sonia are young women. They don't have children. Well, not yet!" The audience laughed. "But they come to every one of our meetings, and they are good workers. They are not down on Calle Duarte in the discotheques and in the bars. They are here working with the community. If we give gifts to some of the women, to the mothers, then we should give gifts to them as well. That is what I say."

La Gringa's comments exposed a key assumption undergirding the proposed ceremony. As it was to be a joint celebration of the anniversary and Mother's Day, the presentation of gifts to mothers alone disregarded the contributions of nonmothers to the *junta* and to the community at large. Moreover, the matricentric ceremony also suggested that unmarried women, lacking agency in producing community, could only be recognized as being sexually at risk in the bars and discos on Calle Duarte.

In fact, the fear that Boca Chica's adolescent girls were prostituting themselves to foreign tourists was a leitmotiv in most discussions about community problems, often expressing male anxieties that were associated with other issues—for example, the encroachment of expatriate businesses into the local economy and the expansion of the tourism industry. Although some local women were involved in sex work, most sex workers came from elsewhere. La Gringa's declaration that the young women who worked with the *junta* were not on Calle Duarte affirmed a positive agency for women beyond the bonds of marriage and the household.

"Well, then," a man in the audience called out, "why not give gifts to everyone? What we are celebrating here on May 27 is el Día de las Madres. There also exists el Día de la Mujer (Woman's Day) in this country, but that's different. What, we're doing here isn't a—a feminist thing."

Talking erupted among the audience, and Chema raised his hand for quiet. "It's true that what we are discussing here is Mother's Day and that on this day we celebrate the contribution of all mothers in the country. But I think that we must also think of the children *(las niñas)*. Because here, in Boca Chica, we lose too many children to the street. I think that we should give presents to the mothers, and to the children as well."

Chema's suggestion yielded a compromise but one that subverted the sense of La Gringa's objection. Whereas she had displaced public recognition from the "facts of motherhood" to the contributions that all women made to the *junta* and the community, Chema's proposal returned emphasis to the mother-child dyad, that is, to recognizing the importance of "children" as extensions of their mothers while reasserting the hazards of unmarried female sexuality. However, at the time, Chema's ambiguous use of *las niñas* (girls) left it unclear as to whether he intended the gifts, and the recognition they would convey, to go to young women or to children more generally. The controversy seemingly resolved, discussion turned once more to logistics.

On Mother's Day members of La Unión (mostly the women) assembled at noon to decorate the building and coordinate the sale of food and refreshments. The food had been prepared by La Gringa and Belkis, assisted by other women from the neighborhood, notably Danilda and Sonia. Large palm fronds had been erected to form an arch over the entrance to the building. Two representatives of the Presidente Beer

Company assembled a refreshment stand in the middle of the road. Pedro arrived in a pickup and unloaded a stereo system and two huge speakers, which were placed in front of the building.

Inside, La Gringa and other women were wrapping the gifts that would be presented during the ceremony. The "mothers' gifts" were largely cosmetics and household items, such as napkin holders, makeup compacts, and fruit-shaped refrigerator magnets. Some had been purchased from the Escuela Laboral, a women's vocational arts school in Boca Chica. For the most part, the "children's gifts" were plastic toys.

"Which one is for you?" I asked Sonia in jest, pointing to the pile of toys.

"These are not for me," she replied. "I am a woman."

La Gringa responded in English. "I don't know why Pedro bought all these toys. It's a waste of money. They're for little children. But that's OK, we'll give them to the children."

When the preparations were complete, women and children began filing into the room, taking seats on the wooden pews. With the exception of the male officers of the *junta* and me, most of Bella Vista's men and teenage boys watched the proceedings from outside. On arrival, each "mother" and "child" were given a numbered badge in the shape of a heart. During the ceremony, the numbers were to be called, and the bearer of the corresponding badge was to approach the table to receive the appropriate gift.

Chema opened the festivities by recounting the history of La Unión. He then introduced the officers and praised their hard work over the years. A camera crew from Turivisión, a community-based television network, made its way up the aisle to a position at the side of the table.

"The *junta de vecinos* is a very important institution here in Boca Chica," Chema said. "And without the support and participation of the community, we would not be able to do the things that we do, such as celebrating Mothers' Day and the anniversary of our group." The audience applauded. Chema then thanked La Gringa and Belkis for their work in organizing the event. The two women stood and took bows.

"Without the *junta de vecinos,*" Chema continued, "we would not have the power to go to the authorities to resolve our problems and represent ourselves. Because here, in Boca Chica, everybody knows that we have many problems. Poverty, crime, children in the streets, without education and without work—lost ones. And unfortunately, we don't have the power and the influence that the hotel owners have, and the businesses down on La Duarte. For this reason, we must support the *junta de*

14. Gifts being distributed at Junta La Unión's Mother's Day celebration in 2001. La Gringa stands behind the flowers in the center of the frame. Photo by the author.

vecinos and the work that we are doing, not just here, but in all of Boca Chica and Andrés."

"Enough speeches!" a woman cried from the back of the sweltering room. The audience laughed and applauded.

Pedro then began a speech extolling the virtues of Dominican mothers in general and his own mother in particular but was cut short by calls for the speech making to end.

When it came time to distribute the gifts, La Gringa took a place behind the table where the gifts for the mothers and children had been stacked in two piles. Two children were chosen to present the gifts to their recipients. Pedro then began calling out the numbers. The first person to be called was an elderly woman who was ceremonially escorted to the stage by a little boy.

"I am very happy that you came today, Doña Mercedes," Chema said. "How many children do you have . . . and grandchildren?

Doña Mercedes smiled and then turned to the Turivisión camera. "I have five children, seventeen grandchildren . . . and great grandchildren? I don't know!"

The audience applauded, and La Gringa presented Doña Mercedes with a gift. Two adult women and a boy were called next, and each received the appropriate gift.

When sixteen-year-old Danilda's number was called, La Gringa first reached for a toy in jest and then handed her a "mother's present" instead. The teenager grinned, tore off the wrapping paper, and raised the tube of lipstick over her head for everyone to see. Although all the boys were given toys, on the arrival of each teenage girl, La Gringa held up a gift from each category and asked, "This one, *mujer* or *niña?*" to which the gathering responded accordingly. While the women in the room tended toward "*Mujer!*" for each girl who looked older than fifteen, the men and boys outside countered with shouts of "*Niña!*" When all the gifts had been given, the cake was distributed, and the gathering reassembled in the street outside.

By bending the improvised ritual to her own purpose, La Gringa reiterated the central and, to be sure, obvious role of women in the activities of the *junta,* displacing once more the ceremony's logic from the mother-child dyad, rooted in biology and domesticity, to one recognizing the contributions of all women. Moreover, by resisting the construction of teenage women as "children," La Gringa's actions argued that motherhood was not the exclusive road to womanhood and that *not* being a mother (and, by extension, a wife) did not predispose women to being lost to a life in the streets. Put simply, La Gringa's intervention disrupted the binary opposition between an *ama de casa* (housewife) and a *mujer de la calle.*

Afterward, as the men were gathering around the Presidente Beer concession, I overheard Pedro speaking with another man. He was peeved that La Gringa had altered the logic of the ceremony and claimed that there were "real mothers" who had not received gifts as a result. "When women go over there [i.e., abroad], they change," Pedro continued. "They become feminists. And when they return here, they want everything to change. Everything."

Pedro's claim that La Gringa's attachment to patriarchal family values had been weakened by her experiences abroad—in particular, her economic independence—was a view often expressed by men (see also Levitt 2001). As I discuss in chapter 3, women in Boca Chica were viewed by some Dominican men as having been corrupted by their encounter with foreign and, more to the point, "feminist" values through tourism and migration abroad—a view that was shared by male expatriates and tourists as well. In fact, changing attitudes about gender roles among Dominican women were less a result of their encounters with Western feminism than of their growing economic independence as wage earners both at home and abroad. Although greater participation in the labor force and economic autonomy has not led to economic prosperity, or even stability, for many women, it has weakened male claims to power as heads of households in both (Grasmuck and Pessar 1991; Safa 1995).

Junta La Unión's activities underscore the disputed status of locality under conditions of globalization and the heterogeneity of the discourses and practices through which it is constituted at various spatial scales. The Manichaean distinction between the *zona turística* and the *comunidad,* evocative of the settler/native opposition described by Frantz Fanon (1965), was challenged through the spatial practices of Junta La Unión and others. These practices reasserted the spatial and, indeed, political integrity of communities such as Bella Vista while contesting the stigmatizing tropes assigned to them by the discourses and practices of "all-inclusiveness." For residents of Bella Vista, Boca Chica was not a backdrop for tourism, a "natural resource" to be consumed at times and ignored at others, but instead a community of interests with a history that was not exhausted by the narrative of tourism development.

An even more extraordinary example of efforts to assert the interests, needs, and identities of neighborhoods against the insulated economy of the tourism industry was fund-raising roadblocks. Periodically, often on their anniversaries, some *juntas* established roadblocks on major roadways by extending ropes or chains across them, stopping non-Dominican pedestrians and drivers. The roadblocks had a carnivalesque atmosphere and often were accompanied by music. *Junta* members, often in costume, waylaid tourists and expatriates alike, asking for donations for *la comunidad.* Perhaps more appropriately viewed as a tourist tax, the roadblocks not only asserted popular sovereignty over space but also turned the logic of all-inclusiveness on its head: if the tourism industry *was* a self-sustaining enclave within which residents had little or no role, economic or symbolic, then tourists and others who transgressed its imagined frontiers were subject to a tariff.

Such assertions of the sovereignty and interests of locality, however, were not monolithic. In the case of La Unión's celebration, the efforts of its predominantly male leadership to assert locality threatened to subordinate women to the role of mothers and sexually at-risk children, which not only figured community agency as male but also reiterated the disciplinary logic of the tourism industry itself—one in which unaccompanied women were out of place and, thus, "delinquent." Rather than disrupt the asymmetrical division between the tourism zone and the community, the celebration risked reiterating it in sex and gender terms.

These gendered disputes about the significance of community cannot be reduced to a simple opposition, pitting putatively "local" interests against monolithically conceived "global" ones. To argue that place matters is not to reduce the spatial concerns of residents to a sentimental "sense of belonging" or to a static cultural repertoire that was being disordered in the face of transnational processes. As the case of La Unión demonstrates, residents drew on experiences and discourses at a variety of scales—local, national, and transnational. La Gringa's interventions were informed by her experiences and those of other women as wage earners and, in many cases, as heads of households abroad. These "social remittances," as Peggy Levitt (2001: 11) has termed "the ideas, behaviors and social capital" that return migrants bring back with them, influenced how residents imagined community and (re)produced gender. From this perspective, La Gringa's actions were at once local and global, as much a critical engagement with the international division of labor as a dispute about makeup and plastic toys.

AN INTERLUDE ON COLLABORATIVE RESEARCH

By May 2001, roughly midway through my fieldwork, I became concerned that my work to that point had focused too narrowly on Boca Chica and the tourism enclave. Although I had some contacts in Andrés (Minaya, for one), I had not spent much time there and knew little about how people not directly involved in the tourism economy viewed the issues that I was examining in Boca Chica. Since the *zona turística* was oriented toward foreigners, it was much easier for me to form relationships and sustain an everyday presence there than it was in Andrés and other primarily residential barrios. This problem, logistical in part, was somewhat alleviated when I bought a *pasola* (motor scooter), which made traveling between the two towns easier.

Moreover, in Boca Chica there were people to whom I had only limited access. For example, I had spoken informally with a number of merchants and police officers but had found it difficult to arrange systematic interviews. For people working ten hours a day, six and sometimes seven days a week, committing to a lengthy interview was a considerable sacrifice. Equally significant, there were some topics that residents were reluctant, if not unwilling, to discuss with an outsider of uncertain provenience, motives, and allegiances, for example, police corruption, relations between Dominican and expatriate merchants, or the sources of a household's income. Because ethnographic research is conducted on a social field where actors have varied and sometimes conflicting interests

15. A street in the commercial center of Andrés. Photo by the author.

vis-à-vis the researcher and each other, people have a stake not only in what is said but to whom it is said as well.

No small part of the challenge was communicating what I was doing and why. As a researcher from the United States, I was perceived by many to be a tourist, despite my protests to the contrary. As the image of research with which most people were familiar was that of a neatly dressed public official, armed with a clipboard and an ID card, the sight of me hanging about, seemingly idle, did little to persuade residents that I was not on vacation. Ethnographic research simply does not look like work.

As my presence continued over the months, many residents came to view me as something of a journalist, whose modus operandi seemed to best resemble my own. In fact, Boca Chica had often been the target of muckraking, often sensationalist investigative reports by the national news media, typically focusing on prostitution, HIV/AIDS infection, and delinquency. For this reason, some people—especially those with ties to the formal tourist economy—were wary of my work, concerned that I was writing an exposé for the foreign press.[9]

For these and other reasons, I decided to hire a research assistant, Milquella Reyes. I had met Milquella through a mutual friend and had interviewed her the month before. Milquella worked as the maître d' for a restaurant on the beach, and she was in the process of assembling her documents to apply for a job with a tour company in Juan Dolio, a resort area east of Boca Chica. Milquella was proficient in Italian and English and had spent her adult life working in Boca Chica and, it seemed to me, knew everyone in town. Thirty years old and the single mother of a fourteen-year-old son, she rented a house in an area of Andrés that was home to many unemployed sugar workers. She was smart, witty, and gregarious, possessed of an easy familiarity with people from all walks of life—qualities that made her ideal as a research assistant.

Milquella was born in San Juan de la Maguana and moved to the capital at the age of fourteen to live with her grandmother. Her father, who died when she was a child, had been a butcher, her mother a household worker. At sixteen, Milquella moved to Boca Chica to live with an aunt and found work as a waitress at Puerco Rosado, a restaurant then owned by an Italian investor and television host on the RAI network. In that same year, Milquella married a Spanish expatriate and the couple opened a pizza parlor. Outraged by her husband's womanizing and neglect of the business, Milquella left him after two years. The separation left her penniless. "I am a poor person—very poor," she told me. "I can't tell you how much I've lost in this world. When I left my husband, I left the house with nothing. Not clothes, not money, nothing. I did not want to take anything when I left, because I am a person who, when I make a decision, nothing else matters."

In 1989 Milquella's mother and sister came to live with her, and the family bought a plot of land in Andrés for 4,000 pesos where they built a modest wood-frame house. In the mid-1980s land prices were cheap in Andrés as the state-owned sugar company sold off or abandoned fallow properties. Following the death of her mother and the destruction of the house by Hurricane George in 1998, Milquella rented a house from a neighbor. When I met her in 2001, she had recently returned to her old job at Puerco Rosado and was selling Avon products to supplement her income.

During our interview, we had discussed topics ranging from changing gender roles and relations to the consequences of privatization and resort development. Though Milquella had not completed primary school, she was widely read and very well informed about national and international affairs. Milquella returned time and again to the impossibility, faced by many, of surviving on wages of only 2,000 or 3,000 pesos a month. The paradox seemed to both madden and fascinate her, and she explained to me the networks of credit and exchange that people formed with each other and with the *colmados* where they bought their necessities. Life in Boca Chica was like a shell game, she told me, a never-ending cycle of borrowing in order to repay.

"All that you see here in Boca Chica—the bars, the hotels, the good life. This is not the real Boca Chica. The real Boca Chica is a storm of misfortune." It seemed to me that Milquella was concerned that, as a middle-income professional from the United States, I would be unable to appreciate the anxiety, desperation, and hardships that consumed the everyday lives of the working poor—a disquietude that was voiced in the often heard reply to a greeting, "*Luchando por la vida!*" (I am struggling for life!). At one point during the interview, Milquella took a pen and pad from her bag and began outlining her monthly budget. "Look," she said, "this is the reality of Boca Chica."

RANGE OF MONTHLY INCOME IN PESOS	
Wages from Puerco Rosado	3,400
Tips	600–1,000
Avon Sales Commissions @ 30%	800–1,000
Miscellaneous Commissions	500–1,000
TOTAL	5,300–6,400 (US $323–$390)

MONTHLY EXPENSES FOR TWO	
Rent	2,000
Propane Gas	120
Potable Water	200
Groceries and Household Goods	2,000
School Fees	240
Health Care and Medicine	1,500
Transportation	660
Cell Phone Usage	200
Clothing	500
TOTAL	7,420 (US $452)

Although her expenses were not atypical, Milquella's income was well above average. Not only were service jobs in the tourism sector difficult to obtain, but Milquella was paid especially well because of her long-standing relationship with the restaurant's owner and her ability to draw customers. Moreover, the 10 percent commissions that she earned for brokering services to tourists (and the Avon commissions as well) were inaccessible to the majority of residents, who lacked foreign-language skills and related forms of cultural capital.[10] Indeed, what was remarkable about Milquella's household, in contrast to most, was that it survived on the income of one wage earner. I would later learn that Milquella, with help from a sister in Orlando, Florida, was also contributing to the health care expenses of a diabetic sister in the capital. When I pointed out to Milquella that her expenses exceeded her income, she laughed and replied, "In this country, needs are stronger than people"; that is, needs stretched beyond the abilities of people to address them.

Toward the end of the interview I asked Milquella what she felt should be done by the government to improve the lives of people.

> Here, in this country, there are only two solutions. One, increase the minimum wage. The other solution is to establish a national market for food. That would automatically lower all prices. Then, we would have an abundance of food. When there are no *plántanos* [plantains], for example, the national food staple, the price for *plántanos* increases to three, to four, to five pesos. And when there is an abundance in the market—one *plántano,* one peso. Everyone would have to lower the prices. And according to [the price] you buy, you must sell. If they buy cheap, then they must sell cheap. That's what the government must do. It must increase the production of food and create a national market. Before, in this country, we used to produce a lot—cacao, sugar, coffee, foods of all kinds. What the former president [i.e., Leonel Fernández] did, was saturate the market with foreign food [imports]. And for those products, you must pay in dollars. And that benefited no one—only the foreign companies.

It was clear to me that Milquella had a well-informed and sophisticated view of the economic polices that were reshaping Dominican society and that she would expect to play a role well beyond that of a data collector or proverbial "ethnographic consultant."

I discussed my proposal with Milquella over coffee, and she agreed to work with me. We agreed on a part-time, weekly wage of 1,000 pesos plus expenses. In addition, I would pay her 300 pesos for each interview that she conducted, 100 of which she would give to the interviewee as an honorarium. To ensure that her work with me did not interfere with her other work, Milquella organized her schedule and work tasks.

I told her that there were two ways that she could help me as a research assistant. First, I wanted her to conduct open-ended interviews with people who, I believed, would speak more openly with a local person who shared a common background and knowledge base. Included among these were merchants, police officers, and households in Andrés that were making the difficult transition from sugar-related livelihoods to ones dependent on tourism-related services. Before beginning these interviews, we met for two hours to discuss the topics that I wanted to pursue. For example, for residents of Andrés, I wanted to learn more about household economies, strategies for earning a living, and gender roles and relations. In some cases Milquella conceptualized and pursued her own lines of inquiry. For example, her focus on the problem of identity papers in an interview with a neighbor who was *sin papeles* and her analysis led me to appreciate not only the weak hold that many of the working poor had on citizenship rights but also the central role of identity checks in the policing strategies of state authorities.

Milquella decided where and when to conduct her interviews and in most cases with whom, and her improvisational skills were extraordinary. For example, when she encountered problems meeting with the onetime president of Boca Chica's *motoconchos* union because of his hectic work schedule, she interviewed him at his motorcycle stand on Calle Duarte at midnight. Although I had known Pelucho for many months and had an amiable relationship with him, he would never have spoken with me as candidly as he did with Milquella about police graft, his anger at local politicians, or his deep-seated disappointment at having never found stable and "respectable" work.

Second, I wanted to meet with Milquella weekly to verify information that I had learned elsewhere, to contextualize people and events, and to gain her perspective on my emerging analysis. At times we disagreed. For example, I had come to believe that *motoconchos,* with their rakish, hip hop style of dress and edgy lifestyle, could be viewed as a distinctive, masculine subculture that celebrated speed, movement, and risk—"urban cowboys" of sorts. Milquella disagreed. "No," she told me bluntly, "it's not that complicated. It's simply that they need work. Every day they are killed on the road. No one would choose to be a *motoconcho* if there were better alternatives." The truth, probably, was somewhere in between.

My conversations with Milquella, which deepened as our friendship grew, were a reality check for someone working in a discipline that has run the risk of crafting its own social worlds. For if the history of anthropology has taught us anything beyond the well-rehearsed disclosures of its colonial past, it is that the problematic nature of the relation between anthropologists and their subjects is not merely representational. Equally if not more significant, it is a problem of a deeply entrenched epistemological asymmetry, that is, a question of who gets to make sense of ethnographic data and "theorize" the world. From this vantage point, my collaboration with Milquella, as well as with others, shaped the directions of my inquiry and the texture of my subsequent analysis.

Milquella also lent credibility and social value to my role as anthropologist by publicizing our work through her extensive networks of friends and associates and by introducing me to people whom I did not know. Whereas I tended to conceal the notepads and other tools of the trade, Milquella flaunted them about town. I once encountered her on Calle Duarte en route to interview a retired National Police colonel with a tape recorder strapped prominently over her shoulder and a paper-choked clipboard cradled in her arms.

Milquella also developed her own interview technique that blended ethnographic methods with the stylistic flourishes of a Latina talk show host—a format that was, more than likely, both familiar and congenial to her subjects. Typically, Milquella began her interviews with a short introduction and as they progressed addressed comments to both her interviewees and a broader, imagined public. She described this approach as *más suave* (gentler) than a more formal interview style. Equally important, it was an approach that exposed rather than concealed her position as a researcher and, more precisely, her personal and political investment in the topics being discussed.

For example, Milquella's first interview was with her next-door neighbor, Josefa Sánchez, a mother of four whose husband had recently abandoned her.

MR: Here today we find a situation, a situation typical in this barrio and in the Dominican Republic. We are speaking today with a poor person, a very hardworking person, a humble person with a good heart. Let's begin by asking you your name. What is your name?

JS: Josefa Sánchez.

MR: Josefa Sánchez, what is your age?

JS: Forty-two.

MR: We are speaking with Josefa Sánchez, forty-two years old. Where were you born, your place of origin?

JS: In Santo Domingo. In the barrio, San Martín de Porres.

ML: What were your reasons for moving to Boca Chica?

JS: To find a better life. Here I found a small piece of land. My friend was telling me, "Oh, in Boca Chica you will find a little house." In that way, I could help myself.

16. Milquella preparing for an interview in front of her home. Photo by the author.

MR: Tell me, Doña Josefa, how was life in your place of origin?

JS: *Bueno*. In my place of origin, I lived a tranquil life. I supported myself in domestic work. Afterwards, I began to have my children. I took a man in, and he abandoned me. Now I live washing and ironing.

MR: Does that work distress you *(te tormenta)?*

JS: Yes, sometimes.

MR: Tell me something, how difficult is daily life here in Boca Chica, in the Dominican Republic for a humble working person?

JS: There isn't work.

MR: What are the reasons for you not having a job?

JS: Because I didn't have the capacity—I didn't study to get a job. And I had the misfortune of never receiving a *cédula de identidad,* in order to get a little job.

MR: Why is it that you never received a *cédula?*

JS: Because when my parents declared [my birth], it did not turn up. [The officials] told me, "Your birth certificate is lost, it did not turn up." And I am tired of paying *buscones* [persons paid to search for records] because they just say that they can't find the document. For that reason, I don't have it. And because of that, I support myself washing and ironing.

MR: This is a problem very typical for Dominicans, for the poor. A very serious problem. From the perspective of the state, Josefa Sánchez does not exist. Tell me Doña Josefa, can you calculate how much money you have paid *buscones* and lawyers to search for your papers?

JS: I paid one *buscón* 500 pesos. He put in a request, but he did not get it for me. He told me that nothing turned up. Then I found another man and gave him 800 pesos. That man deceived me. He told me to meet him at a house, and when I went there, he was not there. So I lost 800 pesos.

The problem of identity papers had been a pressing one for Milquella as well. She had only received her birth certificate in 1997, at the age of twenty-seven, after having spent weeks searching through records at the civil registry office in San Juan de la Maguana for the facts of her birth. The delay had cost her the opportunity to emigrate to Florida with her older sister. Moreover, in summer 2001 Milquella was having difficulty obtaining a Certificate of Good Conduct, which she needed to apply for a job in Juan Dolio. Milquella believed that the tortuous process of obtaining the chain of documents needed to establish full citizenship was deliberate and intended to exclude the poor from economic opportunities and rights, such as the vote.

Milquella then turned to a topic that was of concern to poor women in particular.

MR: Do you receive any help from the government—social assistance?

JS: No, nothing. Because I don't have papers.

MR: Do you receive help from the father of your children.

JS: He comes every three weeks and brings me 200 or 300 pesos.

MR: But at the very least, does he help you with clothes, medicine, and food for his children? When he brings you 300 pesos, is that it?

JS: That's it. There is nothing more.

MR: What is the name of the father of your children?

JS: Félix Valoy Quesada.

MR: She says that the father's name is Señor Félix Valoy Quesada. Can we call him an irresponsible father?

JS: *Así mismo* [That's right].

MR: Do you think that you can make him comply with the law of the country, and make the father of your children support them?

JS: I don't know what to say, because I put him before the law. And when the police found him, my husband told them that he couldn't [help]. And then he came here and insulted me. He told me that I shouldn't have done that and that I had no shame. And after that, I left him alone.

MR: Here we find a case very typical in the Dominican Republic. A law exists, Ley 2402, to make fathers support their children, but the police do not enforce it. And men can insult and intimidate the mothers of their children.

JS: *Así mismo.*

Doña Josefa's predicament was, indeed, common. When her husband was laid off from Ingenio Boca Chica in 1999, he found only sporadic work in construction and, soon afterward, abandoned the household to its own devices. Josefa began taking in laundry, earning roughly 1,500 pesos monthly and relying on relatives for support. From her son-in-law, a *motoconcho,* she received 500 pesos a month. Her two sons, ages eight and twelve, worked as shoeshine boys in Boca Chica, together earning about 20 pesos daily. As under- and unemployment among men rose, due, in part, to structural adjustment policies, women and their children were driven into the informal economy to support their households. With a monthly income of a little over 3,000 pesos, Josefa managed an *hogar imposible* (impossible household), as Milquella put it to me.

Milquella's comments on the irresponsibility of Josefa's husband and the lax enforcement of Law 2402 governing child support reflected her own life experiences and political commitments. Her own divorce had left her penniless, and she took great pride in her ability to support a household without the help of a man. Moreover, her solicitation of the name of the father exemplified a perspective that Milquella and her subjects often brought to the interview process. Each interview was an opportunity to expose an injustice that was at risk of remaining unrecognized; this act, to paraphrase Pierre Bourdieu (1977: 170–171), objectified previously unformulated experiences and made them public. "Can we call him an irresponsible father?" Milquella had asked. *"Así mismo,"* was Josefa's matter-of-fact reply.

In some of her interviews Milquella's subjects spontaneously broke

17. Milquella and her son, Ronny, at Puerco Rosado Restaurant in 2002, not long after she found work as a tour guide in Juan Dolio. Photo by the author.

stride and addressed an imagined public—the government, a neighbor, men in general—denouncing a wrong or expressing an opinion or belief. On some occasions Milquella herself turned the interview into a venue for publicizing a problem or an injustice. "If you could speak with President Mejía," she ended an interview with an unemployed man, "what would you tell him about your situation?" The man's response was a litany of needs and demands: jobs, lower prices, free medicine, potable water, and an end to the power outages.

Milquella's ethnographic practices, which I initially worried lacked rigor and direction, were not unlike the dialogic methods proposed by the Brazilian educator Paulo Freire (1970) for coproducing knowledge. For Freire, a critical analysis of the world could not be achieved by the transfer and "banking" of information among unequals, whether they be educators and students or researchers and their subjects. Instead, both participants in the dialogic encounter were invited to reflect on the problem at hand and, in the process, become critical "coinvestigators," jointly responsible for understanding.

In her interview with Doña Josefa, Milquella did not merely collect data; she also invited Josefa to reflect on *why* she had been not able to secure work and social assistance and why Ley 2402 did not work for poor women. The result of this dialogue led me to appreciate the importance of the issue of citizenship to understanding the politics of neoliberal economic restructuring and to recognize that the concept of participant observation was, at best, an awkward evasion of a far more complex and political process of ethnographic coinvestigation and mutual reflection.

3

Structures of the Imagination

The theater restores us all our dormant conflicts and all their powers, and gives these powers names we hail as symbols: and behold! before our eyes is fought a battle of symbols, one charging against another in an impossible mêlée; for there can be theater only from the moment when the impossible really begins and when the poetry which occurs on the stage sustains and superheats the realized symbols.

Antonin Artaud

People told different versions of the story of why Dolores went mad. I would often see her sleeping on a bench in Parque Central, opposite the Catholic church, nestled among plastic garbage bags stuffed with her personal belongings. At night I would see her wandering along Calle Duarte, barefoot and sometimes raving, accosting tourists in the bars and eateries and demanding a beer, a cigarette, or a few pesos. For Dolores never begged, and despite her apparent madness and the wretchedness of her condition, she carried herself with dignity, demanding and often receiving respect from all those whom she encountered.

Once I watched her invite herself to the table of a group of German tourists and nonchalantly help herself to one of their drinks. When a man in the party shooed her away, mocking her audacity and ragged appearance, she turned on him and planted her hands firmly on her hips. "*Vete al diablo!*" (Go to hell!), she exclaimed, glaring fiercely at the bewildered man. "Do you think that you are better than me, *alemán* [German]?" Abruptly, her anger dissolved into a mischievous grin as she circled the table, delicately sipping her Cuba libre, nose pitched in the air, parodying the tourists' pretensions. A crowd of waitresses and street vendors that had gathered to watch the scene laughed and exchanged comments until a member of the tourism police sent Dolores on her way.

Shortly after the incident, Milquella told me her story. Dolores had been born in Boca Chica and was regarded as the most beautiful woman in town. When she was nineteen she met a wealthy Italian businessman, many years her senior, who spent his summers in Boca Chica. (In an alternative version of the story, the husband was a rich Mafioso.) They married, and Dolores followed her husband to Milan, where she opened a women's clothing boutique. Every year Dolores would return to Boca Chica, stylishly dressed and carrying gifts for her family and friends. After a few years her husband died. According to Milquella, Dolores's in-laws did not want her to inherit her husband's wealth and slipped poison into her espresso. Dolores fell into a coma, was hospitalized for a month, and, after her release, descended into madness. When she returned to Boca Chica, Milquella explained, Dolores was abandoned, penniless and homeless, by her ungrateful Dominican family. In another version of the story, Dolores was said to have been the victim of *brujería* (sorcery), exercised by Dominican relatives who were envious of her success and good fortune abroad.

In *The Convict and the Colonel,* Richard Price (1998: 158) observed that in societies with histories of colonization, "the importance that madness and marginal people hold in the daily life of ordinary folk stems from the ways that they crystallize, in dramatic (often parodic) form, central aspects of colonial relations." Indeed, the story of Dolores expressed key aspirations, anxieties, and social tensions that shaped the lives of many people in Boca Chica: the profound disparities in wealth, resources, and opportunities between tourists and residents; the dream of migrating to a place where life is better; and the financial expectations and demands brought to bear on those who have migrated by those who have remained behind. In this respect Dolores embodied both the boundless hopes and the unspeakable uncertainties of the migration experience.

Milquella and others who told me the story of Dolores and her madness would always underscore the injustice of the actions of her Italian in-laws and the ungrateful, selfish behavior of her own family. In both versions Dolores's madness was recounted as a cautionary tale of unrealistic expectations and the naive belief in what some called *la gloria*—the dream of finding economic salvation abroad. Both versions attest, in Lévi-Straussian symmetry, to the dislocation of social relations that accompanies emigration under duress (Grasmuck and Pessar 1991).

In her encounter with the German tourists, Dolores's performances exposed the inequalities of the global division of labor while her demands for respect and distributive justice provided a moral compass—

a theater of justice for the poor that, as Price (1998: 162) put it, "is plain for all to see." Although she was often the butt of good-natured ribbing, residents of Boca Chica cared for Dolores. *Motoconchos* ferried her for free, vendors fed her, and few Dominicans would deny her request for a peso or two. An iconic figure in the asymmetrical landscape of the tourism economy, Dolores embodied absolute need, and to deny her requests for *un chin* (a little something) would violate the moral economy of the laboring poor—an ethic of generosity and reciprocity without which few could survive.

An equally prominent and didactic figure was sixty-year-old Papi, a sort of trickster who, in 2001, took to performing for tourists in the streets of Boca Chica. Barefoot and dressed in tattered clothes, sporting a dunce-style cap fashioned out of palm fronds and carrying a burlap sack full of homemade props, Papi improvised magic tricks and simulated the performances of circus clowns. During one performance, Papi attempted to juggle three limes while seesawing on a wood plank suspended over a beer bottle. Though tourists would ignore or mock him, Dominican and Haitian workers in the *zona turística* would gather around and cheer him on, bemused by his audacious attempts to stage entertainment.

During Semana Santa in 2001, Papi appeared on Calle Duarte blowing a whistle and carrying a stalk of sugarcane in imitation of the Haitian-influenced Gagá groups that paraded through the streets at this time of year.[1] Twirling the cane stalk like a baton, Papi danced his way through the throngs of tourists, now and then accosting one with a shout of "*Zafra!*" (a term that refers to the frenetic period of the sugar harvest) before demanding, in the fashion of the Gagá groups, a financial contribution. Street vendors, *motoconchos,* and other Dominican and Haitian bystanders laughed and exhorted the tourists to pay the Gagá. A group of Haitian hostesses from La Noria nightclub fell in line behind Papi, mimicking his hip-twisting dance steps and imitating the sound of the *vaccines,* the long bamboo tubes played by Gagá members with their voices. When the old man blocked the path of three tourists with his baton and a shout of "*Zafra!*" the Haitian hostesses gleefully shouted, "*Peye sòti! Peye sòti!*"—Haitian Kreyòl for "pay to pass."

As the spectacle unfolded, two young POLITUR officers approached Papi and the Haitian dancers, waving their night sticks for them to leave the area. A squabble ensued. The hostesses argued that Papi's performance was appropriate during Semana Santa and that they had every right to be there. The policemen countered that the Gagá improvisation was a nuisance and was disturbing the tourists. When one of the officers quipped that Gagá processions should be confined to the Haitian *bateyes* and not performed in the *zona turística,* the dispute escalated to a debate about whether the Gagá was part of Dominican culture.

"I am Haitian," Lourdes yelled at the policeman in Spanish, "but I was born here. I am as Dominican as you! So don't tell me that the Gagá isn't Dominican."

The officer hesitated, as if baffled by her transnational reasoning. "It doesn't matter," he said curtly. "What I am telling you is that this is making problems."

Among the crowd that had gathered there was agreement that, whatever the Gagá's origins, Dominicans also participated in the Gagá processions and that they were, in fact, a tradition in Boca Chica during Semana Santa. A *motoconcho* commented to me that the POLITUR officers were from the capital and did not know about these things. In the pandemonium, Papi slipped away.[2]

One day I encountered Papi sober in a *comedor* (luncheonette) not far from where I lived. He told me that he was originally from San Pedro de Macorís and that he had worked all his life at Ingenio Cristóbal Colón on the outskirts of San Pedro. As he got older, he explained, he could no longer bear the backbreaking work and the searing heat of the refinery, so he moved to Boca Chica to live with his sister, a housekeeper at the Boca Chica Resort. However, as he had no livelihood and was unable to contribute to the household, his sister asked him to leave. Papi took to the streets, surviving on food handouts and donations for his performances.

Like Dolores's impromptu performances, Papi's antics gave cultural expression to changes and dislocations in the political economy that had accompanied, in this case, the decline of the sugar industry and the meteoric rise of tourism. For, like Papi, many unemployed workers and their families had migrated from agricultural regions to Boca Chica and other tourism zones, lured by the prospect of participating in tourism's transformation of the nation's "natural" resources and culture into commodities that could be consumed by foreign tourists. Like a bricoleur, Papi pieced together a semblance of entertainment from his past and present worlds—a hat crafted from palm fronds and a stalk of sugarcane. As an object of labor, whose transformation into a fetishlike commodity had been the object of Papi's labor for decades, the stalk of cane was well suited to serve as a ritual baton, invoking a reciprocal accounting between tourists and residents—"payback" for surplus value unaccounted for.

The Haitian hostesses, some of whom had been born in the *bateyes*, affirmed the ritual significance of Papi's performance by arguing that tourists too should be subjected to the logic of reciprocal exchange governing the Gagá. If, in the ideology of luxury tourism, local residents and their hybrid cultural practices were antithetical to the disciplined atmosphere of tourism, then the Gagá procession was a spontaneous "revolt of the local," as Daniel Miller (1997) put it—a reassertion of the symbolic currency of everyday life and of the unruly diversity of the social. And like other impromptu and quotidian cultural performances, the improvised Gagá procession incited a public debate concerning, in this case, the status of Haitian cultural identity in the face of the power-laden, official transcript of Dominican national identity.

These and other cultural practices disrupted, subverted, and, often, parodied the dominant discourses and tropes of the tourism industry and, more broadly, neoliberal narratives of economic progress. For both Dolores and Papi exposed, in the theatricality of their daily lives, the glossy promises and glossed-over consequences of structural adjustment policies. These small acts catalyzed and collectivized structures of feeling, ethical dispositions, and forms of critical consciousness that animated the politics of the working poor—a "mothers milk ideology," as George Rude (1995) put it. Insinuated into the fabric of everyday life, they spawned and disseminated notions of social ethics and justice that formed the seedbed for collective forms of social protest.

One night, for example, I was returning to Boca Chica from Andrés on the public bus. Sitting across from me was an elderly man, barefoot and toothless and dressed in tattered clothes. Pressed between his knees was a plastic pail of fish. When the fare collector circulated to collect the 3 peso fee, I gave him a 20 peso note; the old man, a 5 peso coin. When the collector returned to give change, he handed 2 pesos to me and 17 to the old man. The fisherman rose as if to protest and then, puzzled, glanced at his open palm, the collector, and me. Other passengers looked on with curiosity. The woman sitting next to him smiled and asked, "What's the matter? Sit down, *abuelito!* [little grandfather]." As I left the bus, I remarked to the collector that the fare to Boca Chica had gone up, letting him know that I knew that he had reversed our change. The collector grinned and said, "He needs it more than you."

The collector's reversal was both a practical act of redistribution and a symbolic performance of economic justice, violating the insulated tourism economy and the power relations on which it rested. The fisherman's faltering reaction had provoked an exchange of glances among the passengers as we made sense of the event, settling in the ambiguity of the moment on a shared, yet mute, recognition that justice had been served. "Sit down, grandfather," the woman had said, as if to reassure him that hierarchy did not always work and that the privileged did not always hold all the power.

Such practices engendered powerful, albeit often fleeting, signs of "ripe powers," as Artaud (1958: 28) put it, points of reference in the structuring of subaltern consciousness. The fare collector's decision to give the larger amount of change to the old man should not be dismissed as anecdotally interesting but systemically inconsequential: the redistributive ethos that informed it also governed other exchanges in the lives of the laboring poor, providing a safety net for those at the bottom of the late capitalist food chain. A few days later I encountered my friend Minaya on the beach. He had somehow heard the story of the fare collector and admonished me to pay closer attention.

It would be simplistic to call such small acts expressions of class consciousness or solidarity in the orthodox Marxist sense. Although these cultural practices expressed a worldview, a consciousness that was crafted within the economic order—the organization of productive relations—it was a *situated* worldview composed of meanings, sensibilities, and dispositions that were mediated, or better, refracted, by the social division of labor and the commingling hierarchies of difference that both structured and reproduced it in time and space. This was a subaltern consciousness that was hybrid, protean, and contingent and one that was produced not by the formal relation of capital to labor but rather *through* the sensuous and situated conditions of everyday life under capitalist exploitation. In short, it was a *cultural* consciousness of justice for which class struggle was a central but not exclusive modality of expression and practice. Indeed, the fare collector's act simultaneously indexed and undermined hierarchical distinctions between labor and capital, residents and foreign tourists, as well as between the policed tourism enclave and the "sociocultural environment" that was devalued in the industry's ideology—distinctions that, taken in their totality, underpinned the wider organization of productive relations and political power.

These disparate practices of resistance found wider collective expression in public protests and events (such as Junta La Unión's activities), as well as through the production of community-based mass media. If the proliferation of new technologies has led to a stretching of the "cultural imaginary" for people in places such as the Dominican Republic, this expansion has been channeled through, and shaped by, the contingencies of space and time (Appadurai 1996).

MEDIATING LOCAL KNOWLEDGE(S)

Boca Chica's overdetermined reputation as an international tourism pole, oriented to the fabrication of pleasure for foreign tourists, was also challenged by Turivisión, a community-based television station broadcast by the region's cable provider, Economitel. A Dominican-owned telecommunications company, Economitel provided cable television services to Boca Chica, Andrés, and surrounding communities. In addition to broadcasting national networks such as CDN (Cadena de Noticias) and Color Visión, Economitel carried a variety of international networks, such as CNN, MTV, German DTV, and Italian RAI International.

Not long after establishing cable TV service in the area, Economitel acceded to requests from community leaders to provide a venue for locally produced programming that would be responsive to community events, culture, and other programming priorities. Channel 3, which had hitherto broadcast foreign-produced content, was turned over to community control. Fomerio Rodrigues, a resident of Andrés who had studied communications in Venezuela, was hired to be the program director of the fledgling community-based venue.

Turivisión occupied three small rooms in Economitel's offices in Boca Chica (studio, control room, and reception area) and operated on a shoestring budget, enlisting young people from the area to work as volunteer technicians and reporters. In addition, it sold airtime to independent producers, which included Christian evangelists, local political officials and activists, and a variety of talk show hosts. In 2001 the monthly fee charged for a one-hour-per-week program slot was 2,000 pesos (US $122), sizable but within the reach of middle-income producers. Turivisión also produced and broadcast low-budget television commercials for both tourism- and nontourism-related businesses, which contributed to the channel's modest operating budget. Although there were no reliable estimates of the number of Economitel subscribers in Boca Chica and its environs, the relatively inexpensive subscription fee of 200 pesos per month (US $12.50) placed cable service within the means of most middle- and low-income residents who owned television sets. In addition, some residents established their own "pirate" connections to Economitel's network.

Given the neglect of the area by the national print and electronic

18. Fomerio Rodrigues (right) and two technicians in the control room of Turivisión. Photo by the author.

media, Turivisión was the principal source of local news and entertainment for most residents. For example, call-in talk shows, such as *Ser Útil* (To Be Useful) and *Rumbo al Progreso* (Road to Progress), cohosted by Héctor Peña and José Beato, community activists and officials with the Partido de la Liberación Dominicana (PLD), or Dominican Liberation Party, served as public forums for airing and discussing national and local issues, ranging from debates over elections and economic development policies to crime, infrastructural needs, and the privatization of Ingenio Boca Chica. Guests on these shows included local businesspersons, labor representatives, elected officials, and others who were significant in the region's political, economic, and cultural life. Turivisión played a critical role in the shaping of community opinion and identity and in producing a key sector of Boca Chica's public sphere.[3]

Rodrigues, who coordinated production and scheduling, also hosted a popular daily program, *Revista de la Comunidad* (Community Magazine), which documented community events and history—funerals, weddings, public meetings, and protests—and produced human interest stories of importance to the community. For example, days after Milquella introduced me to Rodrigues, he invited us both to appear live on *Revista de la Comunidad* to discuss the research that we were doing and its relation to community concerns. Our appearance on Turivisión buttressed my credibility as an anthropologist and served to quell competing rumors about my activities. On the day of the interview I presented Rodrigues with a copy of my book, *Black Corona,* in part to establish my credibility. On the following day I was surprised to see Rodrigues promoting the book, along with locally produced wood carvings and paintings, on Turivisión's equivalent of the Home Shopping Network.

Despite its name, Turivisión produced little programming about tourists or the tourism industry. Rodrigues told me that the station's primary mission was to produce content about everyday life in Boca Chica and surrounding communities, which, he felt, was obscured, if not distorted, by the community's reputation as an international tourist destination. "Even among many Dominicans," Rodrigues said, "the impression is that there is nothing here but tourism—just sun, the beach, and, of course, prostitution. What we are doing here is demonstrating to the world and to the country that there is a community here—a community that has had a long history before tourists arrived. And that here in Boca Chica and Andrés and in La Caleta, there are many people working and struggling—professionals, artists, and others who are making important contributions to the development of the country. Not only tourism."

In the national media Boca Chica was typically treated as a bellwether of the impact—positive or negative—of international tourism on Dominican society. With few exceptions, the majority of reports about Boca Chica that appeared in the print and electronic media during my time there focused either on international tourism (e.g., whether it was increasing or decreasing) or on social problems said to be linked to it, such as prostitution, HIV/AIDs infection, and crime. This focus on Boca Chica (as opposed to Juan Dolio, La Romana, and other resort areas) was due in part to its reputation as the *balneario* (bathing resort) of the capital, making it a lightning rod for the airing of anxiety, ambivalence, and, sometimes, resentment.

For example, in an article published in the major daily newspaper *Listín Diario* titled "In Boca Chica, Children Are Prey to Prostitution," an investigative reporter claimed that each of the "stages" on the way to prostitution could be identified. According to residents, he wrote, children arrived in the *zona playera* at the age of four or five to beg from tourists or to collect bottles for which they could get deposits. After becoming familiar with the area, the children were then said to branch out into careers selling flowers or working as "mules" for drug dealers or as sex workers, robbing their clients in the process. "Some," he continued, "then become '*fisgones*,' which is to say, they will do anything for money [see chapter 3]. The *fisgones* devote themselves to fulfilling the requests of anyone they encounter: if someone wants a young woman, they find one; a homosexual, they also find one; or, if necessary, they allow themselves to be used sexually. Many of them become infected with AIDS." The story concluded by identifying the final stage of corruption, that of the Sanky Panky, "who searches for tourists in the hope of marrying one and moving abroad" (October 25, 2001, 7).

The report, typical of Boca Chica's coverage in the national media, underscores the ambivalence with which many people, both those in the media and residents, viewed tourism. On the one hand, and consistent with elite discourses, many residents spoke about tourism in the abstract as an almost magical force that generated prosperity and modernized the nation. On the other hand, and in more concrete contexts, tourism was frequently portrayed as a corrupting force that undermined the nation's sovereignty and threatened the nation's cultural values, especially among children. As Jean Comaroff and John L. Comaroff (2001: 21) have pointed out, anxieties surrounding the violation of children have become "metonymic of threats to social reproduction" and, specifically, of "the affluent North siphoning off the essence of poorer 'others' by mysterious means for nefarious ends" (see also Pérez 2004). *Listín Diario*'s narrative of the evolution of child corruption not only elided the responsibility of capital, both foreign and domestic, but also constructed Dominican children and, by extension, Dominican society as powerless in the face of tourists' desires, providing an example of the dominant corruption narrative that many residents believed distorted and occluded Boca Chica's history and culture.

The opinion that Boca Chica was rendered invisible and mute in mass-mediated portrayals of the area as a tourism center aggravated widely held perceptions and beliefs that the needs and interests of the area were neglected, if not ignored, by state authorities in favor of the interests of *los hoteleros* (the hotel owners) and, more generally, native and expatriate elites who owned tourism-related businesses. For example, residents told me that in the wake of Hurricane George, which devastated the area in 1998, government relief efforts focused primarily on the *zona turística*—the resort hotels in particular—while neglecting Andrés and the popular barrios of Boca Chica.

Accusations of favoritism shown to the hotel interests were frequently

19. Children performing folkloric dance at the graduation ceremony of Boca Chica's Escuela Laboral (Vocational School). Photo by the author.

made by residents with respect to the deployment of police and the provision of infrastructure such as water, electricity, and paved roads. As an employee of the *ayuntamiento* put it, "When the tourists come here, what they see is the *zona turística,* where everything is clean and organized and where there is security. This is good, because we need the tourists, and they should get what they pay for. But if you leave the tourism zone and go to Andrés, or to Altagracia on the other side of the highway—there, everything is different. There is no electricity, there is no potable water. The children are always sick because the water is contaminated. But the tourists don't see that. That is Boca Chica too, but it is the community that tourists don't see."

Indeed, much of Turivisión's field-based news reporting addressed people who were, as Rodrigues put it, "invisible," without "a mechanism to represent themselves to society." Typically, also, the language adopted by video crews when discussing and reporting stories conveyed a sense of discovering or uncovering *(descubriendo)* subjects and places that were unknown, hidden, or otherwise obscured by Boca Chica's overdetermined identity as a tourism zone. Moreover, it was often noted by Turivisión staff and by others that Andrés, Boca Chica, La Caleta, and surrounding settlements lacked a distinct and coherent spatial and political identity. It was believed that, because many of the neighborhoods surrounding Boca Chica were "unauthorized communities," or squatter settlements, they were underserved and ignored by government authorities. Many of Turivisión's field reports served to shore up the area's spatial integrity by representing its landscape visually and by producing a viewing audience, or public, that cut across its dispersed settlement areas.

For example, one day Rodrigues invited me to accompany him, his seventeen-year-old cameraman, and a young reporter named Sucre (who also hosted a Christian evangelical program) to tape a story about a Dominican man who had returned home after living in exile for many years to find that much of his family's estate had been illegally occupied by squatters, who were under the protection of high-ranking army officers. For Rodrigues, the story was important because it exposed an everyday abuse of power that, though not uncommon, seldom made it into the national media. Moreover, Rodrigues explained, the man's family had been prominent in opposing the Trujillo dictatorship.

We climbed into Rodrigues's SUV and headed west toward La Caleta, a community straddling Autopista Las Américas near the international airport. Despite its distance from Andrés–Boca Chica (about five kilometers), La Caleta was regarded as part of greater Boca Chica, and many of its residents were employed in Boca Chica's tourism industry. For an hour we searched in vain for the entrance to the man's property.

Frustrated, Rodrigues decided to improvise an alternative story in the vicinity. Rodrigues told us he had heard that there was an underground cave, fed by a natural spring, that passed under the highway and emptied into the sea. We found the mouth of the cave at the bottom of a gully—a craggy opening about three meters high and fifteen meters wide. The cameraman began taping as we descended to the cave's entrance.

"Friends and viewers of Turivisión," Sucre began, "we are about to discover a natural wonder that is right here in La Caleta. A cave, a mysterious cave, that we have discovered here today, almost by accident." Sucre paused as he negotiated the side of the gulley. Rodrigues guided the cameraman from behind.

"Here we are at the mouth of the cave. You can see that it is not very high. You can see that I have to bend down to enter, and if you were driving along the highway you would not see this natural wonder. I don't know what we will find inside—maybe bats or maybe even snakes—but friends, come with us to find out."

Once inside, we descended for another twenty meters to a flat shelf where there were three crystal-clear pools, feeding into each other. A group of teenagers were sitting by one pool, drying themselves with towels.

"This is incredible," Rodrigues said, directing the cameraman to pan across the pools before zooming in on the teenagers. "People don't know that this exists right here in La Caleta," he exclaimed. "This is a natural wonder."

"*Buenas tardes, jóvenes* [Good afternoon, young people], we are here with Turivisión," Sucre said to the group. "Channel 3 in Boca Chica. Tell our viewers why you have come today to this place of great beauty—this natural wonder that is hidden beneath the highway in La Caleta?"

The teenagers grinned awkwardly.

"What is your name?" he asked a young woman.

"Yahaira Sánchez."

"Tell us, Yahaira Sánchez, why have you come here today?"

"To swim."

"Of course! To swim in the cool water, the pure water. And tell me, Yahaira, what do you think of this natural wonder—this dark and mysterious cave beneath the highway? Speak to our viewers out there who want to know about this incredible place."

"I like it."

"Where do you live, Yahaira?"

"In the capital."

"Friends of Turivisión," Sucre said, turning to the camera, "these young people have come all the way from the capital to enjoy themselves at a natural wonder that few people—perhaps, no one—in Boca Chica, or in Andrés, or in La Caleta know exists, right here under the highway."

Rodrigues directed the camera to a pile of beer cans and rubbish in one corner. Sucre continued, "Here, you can see in this obscure corner of the cave, garbage that has been left by someone. Not by these young people, because you can see that the garbage has been here for some time. Clearly, there is a need for the authorities, maybe the secretary of tourism, maybe POLITUR, I don't know, to take measures to preserve this cave in its natural beauty for the generations to come."

Rodrigues signaled the cameraman to cut, and we climbed back up the gulley to the side of the highway, where Sucre would conclude the story.

"Everyone knows about the beautiful and famous beach in Boca Chica. A beach and coral reef that thousands of tourists from all over the world visit every year. But tell me, my friends, did you know that right here in La Caleta, under the highway that we use every day, is a natural wonder as beautiful, as refreshing as the beach in Boca Chica?

"This is Sucre Campos reporting to you for Turivisión. The channel of the people of Andrés, Boca Chica, and La Caleta."

20. Sucre greeting bathers inside the subterranean cave at La Caleta. Photo by the author.

The improvised report on La Caleta's cave asserted the significance of local geography, beyond the confines of the *zona turística* and the purview of the secretary of state for tourism. Sucre's repeated, though perhaps hyperbolic, appeal to the irony that such a natural wonder was "unknown" reiterated the perception that the elite geography of the tourism industry occluded alternative constructions of nature and social space in the national, as well as the transnational, imaginary. His repeated reference to the cave's location in La Caleta not only stressed the latter's integrity and its ties to Andrés–Boca Chica but also proposed that there were economies of pleasure that were unmediated by the state and the tourism industry. This was suggested by Sucre's comment that the state should—but clearly did not—preserve the cave and by his expression of surprise that teenagers from the capital would choose La Caleta's cave over Boca Chica's world-famous beach.[4]

Other programming demonstrated a similar concern with the temporality and topography of everyday life and events and with constructing narratives that emphasized the particularity of local history and culture. This particularity had to be unearthed, if not recovered, in the face of dominant representations of Boca Chica as a "tourists' paradise," on the one hand, and the site of vice and fractured values, on the other.

Much of the news reporting was done in the manner of cinema verité: uninterrupted shots with minimal in-camera editing and few commentaries or interviews provided by reporters on the scene. Typically, the reporter's role was limited to holding the microphone and facilitating access and movement of the camera operator. In part, this was due to practical considerations: generally, crews consisted of only a driver, a camera operator, and a reporter. Moreover, tapes were often broadcast immediately on return to the studio, with little or no studio editing. However, Turivisión's style was also informed by Rodrigues's ideas concerning the form and function of community media.

"Boca Chica is a small community, and we are small too," Rodrigues explained. "Generally, our viewers know the context, more or less, to understand what is happening, without much explanation and without commentaries. But—and you could say this is my philosophy of television—we also want the report, the people who are involved in the report to speak for themselves, to speak directly to the public in a manner that provokes debate. What we want to do is facilitate a dialogue between the story that we are reporting and the community, our viewers."

As a media student in Venezuela in the late 1970s, Rodrigues had been influenced by Third Cinema, a movement among politically radical, post–coup d'etat Argentine filmmakers associated with the Grupo Cine Liberación (Chanan 1997). Against first cinema (the Hollywood film industry) and second cinema (art, or auteur, cinema), group members Fernando Solanas and Octavio Getino wrote a manifesto in 1969, *Hacia un tercer cine* (Toward a Third Cinema), that stressed the eminently political relationship between the process of filmmaking and its audience and elaborated the role of cinema in the cultural and political decolonization of the developing world. Solanas observed in 1978:

> We realized that the most important thing was not the film and the information in it so much as the way this information was debated. One of the aims of such films is to provide the occasion for people to find themselves and speak about their problems. The projection becomes a place where people talk out and develop their awareness. We learnt the importance of this space: cinema here becomes humanly useful. (Quoted in Chanan 1997: 1)

Rodrigues's insistence on the openness and dialogic character of the production process—central tenets of Third Cinema—enabled the camera's subjects to take an active role in Turivisión's reports, and the latter frequently directed the camera and the development of the resulting narrative. As in the case of the "hidden cave" report, seemingly unimportant

21. Rodrigues interviewing a Dominican return migrant whose land has been occupied by squatters. Photo by the author.

events were approached as key opportunities to unsettle *doxa* about Boca Chica and its people; as Solanas and Getino put it, "every image that documents, bears witness to, refutes or penetrates the truth of a situation is something more than a film image or purely artistic fact; it becomes something which the system finds indigestible" (quoted in Chanan 1997: 2).[5]

For example, following the death of a *motoconcho* in a highway accident, Rodrigues and his crew decided to not only report the facts of the accident but also document the man's wake and burial in its entirety. After the program aired, I asked Rodrigues why the cinema verité footage had been given so much airtime—two hours.

"Here in Boca Chica, in the entire country, *motoconchos* provide a service that is very important—that is critical. Without them, the country would not function. But in a strange way, they are everywhere but nowhere in the mind of the public. That's why it's very critical to show that they are valued by the community. Because most *motoconchos* are young men, like the one who died on the highway, who are without work, and who are trying to support their families—to feed their children."

On the day of the wake Rodrigues dropped the cameraman, reporter, and me off at the home of the deceased *motoconcho* in Andrés. A crowd of about one hundred had gathered in front of the wooden house, many under a large plastic tarpaulin that had been erected to provide shade for the mourners. Eusebio filmed the gathering for a couple of minutes, panning one way and then the other across the crowd. At that point a relative of the *motoconcho* led the camera into the house. Maria, the reporter, and I waited outside. In the resulting footage, the camera recorded the line of mourners sitting and standing along the walls of the room where the coffin was displayed.

"This is the mother," a female relative of the deceased said to the camera, as she directed Eusebio to a grieving woman. The relative continued, at times tugging Eusebio by the arm, until all of the relatives in the room had been introduced. A male relative then directed Eusebio to the coffin and opened its hinged window to expose the face of the dead man. The face was bloated and cotton had been stuffed in the mouth and nose. Eusebio zoomed in on the face and then zoomed out to film the family members who had gathered around the coffin for the camera.

When Eusebio returned to where we were waiting, Maria plugged a microphone into the camera and asked a coworker and witness to the accident to explain how it had occurred. Manolo, the witness explained, had been trying to cross the highway in the rain when he was struck by a bus. His body, hurled into the air, had fallen fifty meters away.

"How old was Manolo?" Maria asked in a matter-of-fact tone.

"Twenty," the witness replied.

"Did he have a wife, children?"

"Yes, a wife and one daughter."

"Why do you work in such a dangerous profession?"

"Because there is no other work."

Maria ended the brief interview without commentary and unplugged the microphone, freeing the camera to follow the funeral procession, which had just left the house. Four pallbearers, followed by a crowd of mourners, carried the casket down the unpaved street toward a waiting hearse. As they approached the corner, where a dozen or so *motoconchos* had gathered with their motorcycles, words were exchanged and the procession made a detour to the *motoconcho* stand. At the request of the drivers, the pallbearers laid the casket across the seats of three motorcycles and opened the coffin's porthole to expose the dead man's face.

"Start the engines," one man called out. "Bring the keys," another shouted to the crowd that had gathered around the makeshift shrine. Moments later the owners of the three motorcycles appeared, keys in hand, and started their engines.

The drivers revved their engines as the dead man's coworkers approached the coffin's window and spoke their final words. Following suit, dozens of cyclists who had surrounded the procession raced their engines, producing a deafening roar. After five minutes or so, the coffin was removed and carried to the hearse. Escorted by about fifty *motoconchos* and their passengers, the funeral procession made its way along the highway to the cemetery. After the interment we returned to the studio where the unedited tape was immediately broadcast.

Turivisión's production of Manolo's funeral and the improvised ritual illustrate the radically local uses to which new technologies can be put, as well as their potential for being appropriated at the grassroots. Rodrigues's philosophy of dialogic television, coupled with the contingencies of low-budget production, yielded media practices in which the camera's subjects participated in their representation and in shaping the logic and content of the narrative. For example, the cameraman's compliance when filming the family of the deceased allowed the latter to represent their network of kith and kin, integrating the camera and audience into the mourning process and into the social networks that it affirmed. Moreover, the presence and complicity of the camera, it appeared, had prompted the man's coworkers to improvise a commemorative ritual, stretching the narrative from one about an accident to one that valorized a livelihood disparaged in the media and persecuted by the police. For despite the critical importance of the services they provided, *motoconchos* were portrayed by elites as a nuisance, if not a menace, to society, and officials in Boca Chica often accused them of being prone to crimes such as robbery and drug dealing—crimes that registered elite anxieties linked to both their mobility and the breadth of their social networks. Maria's terse interview with the dead man's coworker cut through this discourse to establish a simple proposition: for young men, there was no other work and this fact was no "accident."

The procession's ritualized detour elevated the tragic death of an individual to a symbol of the struggles and aspirations of many, collectively expressed by the racing of the engines. In fact, engine noise was a central complaint against the *motoconchos* by elites in Boca Chica, who charged that the *motoconchos* were a sonic violation of *el ambiente turístico*. This persistent complaint had been used, in part, to justify banning *motoconchos* from Calle Duarte from dusk to dawn. In defiance of this policing of the town's ambience, *motoconchos* traditionally removed their muffler casings during Semana Santa to amplify the volume of their engines. Introduced into the improvised ritual, the racing of the engines was a sonic assertion of their right to earn a living and operate within the manicured space of tourism.

Turivisión's cinema verité reporting also bore witness to protests that typically went unreported in the major media and unnoticed by wider publics. For example, in June 2001 I accompanied Rodrigues and his crew to tape a spontaneous demonstration that had erupted in Altagracia, an unofficial settlement located north of the highway and about three kilometers from Boca Chica's town center. It was not uncommon for residents to alert Rodrigues by telephone to events that were unfolding in town, as an interested means to bring them to the attention of the public.

Like other unofficial communities, Altagracia had been founded as a squatter settlement on public lands in response to the influx of migrants from the capital and other areas of the country. Over time, more permanent concrete structures had been constructed and businesses established, which required infrastructural improvements in electricity, garbage collection, and, above all, potable water. In the case of Altagracia, local authorities had installed a water conduit to service the area, but it remained unconnected to the water source. Instead the settlement was being served by an improvised plastic pipeline and communal tap, which was inadequate for the population. Moreover, residents contended that the water was contaminated and causing illnesses.

When we arrived, two dozen or so residents were gathered around a ditch where, it appeared, work on the pipeline had stalled. A fiery barricade blocking the settlement's main access road had been erected out of rubbish and burning tires. Eusebio, Turivisión's most experienced camera operator, set up his video camera and approached the crowd. Rodrigues and I followed behind. The mob grew rapidly when Eusebio began taping and formed itself in front of the camera.

"*Agua! Agua!*" (Water! Water!), the crowd shouted in unison, as women pounded five-gallon buckets and jerry cans with sticks. Eusebio panned the camera across the trench and then raised it to the crowd. A young man stepped forward and into the frame.

"Here, in Altagracia, people don't have water," he said, glaring into the camera lens. "It's been three months since they buried the pipes here, and there still is no water. And this is all because of politicians!" His words incited renewed chanting, and a second man, shirtless, stepped forward and pointed his machete at the ditch. The crowd quieted.

"We, the people of Altagracia, are hungry because without water we cannot cook. Here there are many poor people who cannot bathe. One tank of water costs 50 pesos. The poor cannot—I cannot afford to buy water." Eusebio panned the crowd once more. "This pipe must produce water," the man continued. "If it does not give water, then it will give blood! Just as in the capital. So says the entire barrio." The crowd roared, and the women raised their buckets into the air. Eusebio followed the shirtless man as he blended back into the crowd, directing the camera at the machete dangling from his wrist.

Although protests, often accompanied by violence, had occurred in Santo Domingo and other areas of the country during 2000–2001, typically provoked by the daily power outages, Boca Chica and Andrés had remained relatively calm. Because of the presence of the resort hotels and tourism related-businesses, residents of Boca Chica (though not Andrés) were generally shielded from the punitive blackouts that were visited on more economically marginal barrios. However, mass demonstrations in the capital and elsewhere—in which the protesters sometimes erected burning barricades to shut down public streets and commerce—were closely covered by the media. In some cases these protests led to armed confrontations with the authorities, producing casualties on both sides. The shirtless man's allusion to events in the capital was thus a clear threat of insurrection.

"Say something, Doña Carmen," a teenager called out.

An elderly woman, white-haired and toothless, presented herself before the camera. "My name is Carmen Morales. I am eighty-four years old, and I have lived in Altagracia for six years without water. Now there is a pipe, but they say that the water won't come until 2004, in three years."

The elderly woman's testimony served to vouch for the permanency of the settlement as well as the duration of the water problem. As the crowd became increasingly at ease with the camera and with its own defiant message, the identities of the public officials responsible for the problem began to emerge.

"These pipes have been in the ground for four months, but they aren't functioning because, here, there are lying politicians—from the president of the *junta de vecinos* to the *regidora* (city councilwoman). All the politicians. An engineer from here said that there could be water now. But the president of the *junta de vecinos* says that it will come in 2004, when they finish the project. And we won't go along with that."

A young woman added, "This problem is the fault of one man, who says that he is the president of the entire barrio and that the water will come when he says so. If there is no water this week, then there will be blood. So says the entire barrio."

The crowd led the camera to the existing water tap, which emptied into a cement basin in the ground. Eusebio zoomed in on the trickle of water flowing from the two-inch PVC pipe. "This is the little water that we have," a woman explained. "And it is dirty. It is contaminated. This water is making people sick. Children have rashes on their bodies because of this water. In Boca Chica there is water. Then we must have water too!"

The young woman, joined by others, began to fill her pail as if to prove that this was the water they used. Abruptly, a scuffle broke out between two of the women as they jostled to gain access to the pipe. Laughing, other women joined the fray, while the men struggled to pull the women apart. When the brawl ended, a man stepped into the frame to explain.

"I would like the entire world, the entire country, to see what is happening here with the water in the barrio of Altagracia. This is a live experience that you are seeing, the situation that we have in the barrio. The women fight because there is only one pipe for everyone to use. And the people need water to cook and wash. This we do not accept. So says the entire barrio!"

The commentary, provoked by a theatrical reenactment of social discord engendered by scarcity, informed its imagined audience of the gravity, immediacy, and social meanings of the problem. Indeed, the significance of both the problem and its solution was crafted as the protest unfolded through its dialogic engagement with the camera and its anticipated audience—the "entire world," the nation, politicians, and potential allies. Through these practices of protest, in all their theatricality, residents improvised a language and a logic of defiance, solidarity, and pressing and non-negotiable needs as testified to by Doña Carmen. Artaud (1958: 27), comparing theater to the plague, observed, "Like the plague, it re-forges the chain between what is and what is not, between the virtuality of the possible and what already exists in materialized nature." Similarly, the residents of Altagracia performed rebellious possibilities and imagined solidarities within the formidable constraints of their everyday needs, engendering in situ oppositional forms of consciousness.

Within an hour the crowd had grown to more than one hundred, and Eusebio zoomed out to capture its immensity. In the midst of this long shot, seven members of the National Police, armed with shotguns and dressed in camouflage, arrived off camera in a pickup. Eusebio panned the camera to capture their arrival. The sergeant in charge glanced at the camera as he left the truck, then stepped toward the mob.

The protesters explained their situation to the sergeant, interrupted now and then by shouts of *"Agua!"* from the crowd. Glancing every so often at the camera, the officer told the crowd to form a "commission" of five or six persons to go to Boca Chica and explain their predicament to the colonel in charge.

"We don't want a commission," a woman shouted. "We want water." The chanting resumed with renewed vigor. While the sergeant negotiated with the mob, a *regidora* representing Boca Chica arrived in a Jeep Cherokee. She approached the mob, raising her cell phone high over her head to quell the clamor.

"Calm yourselves, please. Calm yourselves." The crowd settled down. "We don't want to create a problem on top of the one that we already have. Yes, we want water. We want water. And we want to reach an agreement with Chicho and with the engineer to connect the water." The crowd cheered and then jeered at the mention of the *junta* president's name.

The shirtless man, machete in hand, stepped back into the frame. "The people of Altagracia do not want more talk from politicians. We want water. And if the water does not come, then . . ." The proposition was left unfinished as he turned his back on the politician and the police.

"Let us do something good," the *regidora* continued, staring into the camera, "not something bad. Let's form a commission and go and speak with him. Let's turn on the water but not by burning tires, not by throwing stones. Not by violence."

A heated discussion ensued as some protesters, mostly women, insisted that they wanted water and not the talk of politicians. Gradually, some in the crowd gave in to the idea of the commission, and six spokespersons—all of them men—left on motorcycles for the police station in Boca Chica, followed by the politician and the police. The camera crew remained, recording the testimonies of women, who described the illnesses that had been suffered by their children and the difficulties that they encountered doing household chores. Most men wandered off with the departure of the delegation.

"We want water, not talk," an elderly woman told the camera, as she loaded a donkey with empty plastic jugs. Another approached the camera. "You see," she said, pointing to the woman and the donkey, "the commission has gone to talk to the politicians, but we are left here to find water for our children. If they have water down there," she said, pointing toward Boca Chica, "then we should have water too!"

The protest in Altagracia highlights Turivisión's role in creating an alternative public sphere, one that challenged Boca Chica's overdetermined image as a tourism center and served as a venue for expressing and disseminating alternative and, in this case, oppositional views regarding the community's identity and needs. For at stake in the protest was precisely the priority, given by the authorities, to the development of infrastructure in the *zona turística* at the expense of unauthorized barrios such as Altagracia. The contrast repeatedly drawn by residents between their own lack of water and how things were *allá* (there), in the *zona turística,* underscored this sociospatial asymmetry. More broadly, the protest was also a demand for economic justice—a demand that was being echoed in barrios across the nation in protests against the privatization of power and other public resources.

However, beyond the demand for water was a demand for visibility and representation in the symbolic economy of the region—one in which the problems and needs of poor barrios were invisible and their residents rendered muted in elite discourses about crime, vice, and corruption. The refrain "We, the people of Altagracia," that prefaced the testimonies of many before the camera was also a demand for visibility, voice, and, indeed, publicity—to bring an *unofficial* community to the notice of public officials and render "indigestible," as in Third Cinema, the status quo.

If the camera bore witness to events in Altagracia, then the frame provided a stage on which residents not only voiced their demands for social justice but also performed their outrage and anger and the consequences of scarcity. The improvised altercation among the women at the water pipe theatrically displayed the social repercussions of scarcity to an audience that could not imagine them; it had to be dramatically reenacted. Indeed, it was this ambiguity, this blurring of the division between the real and the imagined, that conveyed the desperation, tenacity, and uncompromising nature of their demands. For if scarcity could lead to social conflict and even violence in Altagracia, then the threat that "the pipes would give blood" was to be taken seriously by those beyond it.

The presence of the camera influenced not only the development of the protest but also the behavior of the public officials who, mindful of the camera, were not unaware of the publicity that it would bring. The recommendation to form "a commission," made by the police and reiterated by the *regidora* was probably aimed as much at deflating the media event as at resolving Altagracia's problem. Turivisión's modus operandi, in part imposed by the properties of the technology, ensured minimal editing and a short time lag between production and broadcast, situating both the protest and its audience in a near–real time political space. In short, both protesters and officials were negotiating with publics that stretched well beyond the barrio of Altagracia.

As the crew was packing its equipment, I asked a woman who had been vocal in the protest whether things would have been different had Turivisión not been there. "Of course," she replied. "There would have been fewer people in the street, and the police would have been rougher *(más bruto)*. They carried themselves well, because the authorities did not know who was watching the television."

Although the story did not reach the national media, Turivisión's broadcast of the protest in Altagracia on three consecutive afternoons intensified public discussion of the water problem, and Channel 3 pursued the topic on call-in talk shows. Within one week of the protest, the water conduit in Altavista had been completed and was in operation.

It would be wrong to interpret Turivisión's coverage of the protest in Altagracia, or its programming in general, within the framework of a simple binary opposition between the local and the global, or the grassroots and the elite-oriented media. Though the media philosophy espoused by Rodrigues and other producers valorized a dialogic engagement with everyday events and experiences and, in particular, those of the poor and disempowered, Turivisión's diverse programming implicated a more complex set of mediations and power relations. If, as in the case of Belizean television, the introduction of cable television weakened the role of local elites as "retailers of metropolitan [i.e., British] cultural capital" (Wilk 2002: 180), then the emergence of Turivisión could be viewed, in part, as a reassertion of the mediating power of elites within the space and discourses of locality. For example, nearly all of Turivisión's call-in political talk shows were hosted by supporters of the PLD, which, during the period of my fieldwork, was out of office. Though much of the political commentary and discussion broadcast on such programs as *Ser Útil* and *Rumbo al Progreso* stretched beyond party politics, during certain key debates, both venues energetically argued PLD positions against the governing Partido Revolucionario Dominicano (see chapter 6). Moreover, monthly production fees, although modest, tended to exclude producers who lacked disposable income.

Moreover, the interests and modes of self-representation documented during Altagracia's protest were themselves fractured, notably, along gender lines. Whereas men tended to express their protest through speech—and, as it turned out, in the language of negotiation and compromise—women, skeptical of "talk," stretched their politics of representation to include the inexpressible, that is, to meanings embodied in conflict, in the diseased bodies of their children, and in the materiality of their everyday labor. For the women of Altagracia, the problem of water was inextricably embedded in the asymmetrical division of household labor and could not be washed away so easily.

Below I tease out some of these complexities in the social relations and sites of media production, directing attention to changing gender roles and relations and their mediation through Turivisión's first venture into fictional drama.

LA NEGRITA Y EL TURISTA: STAGING "THE REAL" IN BOCA CHICA

Not long after the protest in Altagracia, Rodrigues approached me with a project that he said he had been thinking about for years. He wanted to produce a *telenovela,* a televised soap opera, that would be for and about the people of Boca Chica. As we sat in the control room, Rodrigues pointed out to me that though *telenovelas* were wildly popular in Boca Chica, all of the ones shown on Economitel were imported from Mexico, Brazil, and Colombia and did not adequately reflect the lives, experiences, and dramas of Boca Chica's residents. Moreover, he explained, the majority of the imported *telenovelas* depicted the lives of elites and rarely reflected the sociocultural diversity of the societies that they portrayed. A locally produced *telenovela,* Rodrigues said, would provide a unique opportunity to present the story of Boca Chica "from the inside" and in a format that would be both entertaining and educational.

The plot that he had in mind, Rodrigues assured me, was based on a true story—that of a teenage woman named Maria who had once worked as a housekeeper for his family in Andrés. The woman had appeared at his doorstep one morning looking for work. Maria explained to him that she was from a small pueblo in the countryside, in the Cibao Valley, and had fled from an abusive husband who did not provide for her newborn infant. On the advice of friends, Maria had decided to leave her husband and look for work in Boca Chica, where, she believed, the tourism economy afforded more opportunities. It was, Rodrigues told me, an archetypal narrative.

While working in Rodrigues's household, Maria met and became involved with a Canadian tourist, who would often pick her up after work. One day, and without notice, Maria did not appear for work. Concerned, Rodrigues made inquiries about Maria in her old neighborhood but found no clues to her whereabouts. Then, he explained to me, two months later, a young man appeared at his door asking for Maria and claiming to be her husband. Not knowing where she was, Rodrigues could only wish him well.

Rodrigues told me that the story had remained with him as a kind of a mystery. A young woman—a teenager—courageously leaves an abusive husband in the countryside to seek her fortune in Boca Chica. Then she becomes involved with a foreigner from a wealthy country and disappears. The story, Rodrigues explained, captured many of the problems, aspirations, and social tensions of the contemporary context: migration from the countryside, domestic abuse, changing gender relations, and the dream, shared by many, of migrating *afuera* (abroad) to a place of opportunity. To dramatize this latter point, Rodrigues had decided to solve the mystery: the *telenovela* would end with Maria marrying the tourist and moving to Toronto. In the last scene, as Rodrigues envisioned it, Maria's contrite husband would confront her at the airport as she was boarding a plane to a new life, baby in arms and a new husband in tow. With tears in her eyes, as Rodrigues saw it, Maria would make the choice to leave. He had chosen the title *La Negrita y el Turista* (The Young [Black] Woman and the Tourist) for the drama.

Notwithstanding my scholarly interest in the project, I reckoned that Rodrigues wanted me to participate in the production of the *telenovela* because I had studied cinema in college. I asked Rodrigues whether he had written a screenplay. He replied that there would be no screenplay; the dialogue and plot development would be improvised by amateur actors who would perform, as he put it, "their own lives and experiences." For Maria, or "la Negrita," Rodrigues had in mind a friend's teenage daughter who had been raised by grandparents in the countryside. For the abusive husband, he would find a *tíguere,* or at least someone who could affect the behavior and mannerisms of one. And for the Canadian tourist, he said, almost in passing, he had chosen me.

I protested that I had no acting experience. He said that it would be better that way. The prospect of appearing in a *telenovela* that would be aired in my research area was troubling, to say the least. On the one hand, it had taken me many months to establish my identity as a researcher and, however successfully, broadcast the purpose of my project; to be recast as a tourist in a soap opera was not only alarmingly ironic but also risked undermining my credibility as an anthropologist. On the other hand, I was uncomfortable with the plot and, in particular, Rodriquez's gloss on the ending. The narrative of a poor young woman from the countryside who, abused by her Dominican husband, is "rescued" by a foreign tourist not only offended my gender and racial politics but also reiterated tropes vaunted by many male expatriates and tourists—that Dominican women were docile, that Dominican men were macho and abusive, and that foreign men had the wherewithal and will to be caring and responsible husbands for their Dominican wives. The story was, in short, an inversion of Dolores's story and a narrative counter to my own.

I discussed these misgivings with Rodrigues, and he assured me that the ending would be open ended and that the actors, through their improvisation, would decide the twists and turns of the plot. What was important to him, he explained, was the drama surrounding the decision to stay or migrate and the social, economic, and political conditions that had imposed it.

I then discussed the proposition with Milquella, who was mischievously delighted by the awkward prospect and encouraged me to participate. For my part, I worried that declining the invitation would sour my relationship with Rodrigues and Turivisión. In addition, as Milquella reminded me, few people in Boca Chica were losing sleep at night coming to grips with my identity. I also figured that, however contrived the plot seemed to me, it addressed central problems, conflicts, and aspirations that preoccupied many people. From this vantage point, the *telenovela* project was a Geertzian dream—an opportunity to "look over the shoulders" of people performing and interpreting their lives.

While Rodrigues set himself to casting, I continued my life as an anthropologist, focusing my attention on a controversy surrounding the proposed construction of a port facility and FTZ near Andrés (see chapter 6). A few days later Rodrigues called to tell me that he had assembled a cast and wanted to conduct screen tests the next day to ensure that everyone was up to his or her part. The tests began at nine o'clock the next morning in a vacant lot next to Economitel's office. Turivisión's staff had assembled a motley assortment of props for the screen tests. In addition to cast members and their friends, the event attracted two dozen or so onlookers from the area: *motoconchos,* Economitel employees, and students from a nearby school.

Rodrigues called the assembly to order and introduced the cast. He then sketched the general outline of the plot, reiterating the improvised nature of the dialogue and the elasticity of the plot. La Negrita was to be played by Fernanda, an eighteen-year-old high school student. For the husband's role, Rodrigues had chosen Flavio, a nineteen-year-old *motoconcho* and flaneur. In the first screen test, la Negrita, having recently given birth to a child, was to be confronted and chastised by her carousing, macho husband for not having prepared dinner and cleaned the house.

Flavio entered the imaginary casita, closing the door behind him. "*Negra,* what is there to eat? I'm hungry. Where is my food?"

Fernanda remained silent, nursing a virtual infant.

"Wait," Rodrigues interrupted. "Flavio, you have to be more forceful, more *tíguere.* When you enter the house, throw open the door as if you were drunk and angry. And shout."

Sonia, a woman in her thirties who had been cast as the mother of la Negrita, laughed along with the other spectators. "Flavio, it's easy. You *are* a *tíguere,* just be yourself."

Flavio grinned self-consciously and then flung open the door. "*Niña,* where is my food!" He glared pop-eyed at Fernanda and threw up his arms. "*Diablo!* Look at this house, it's a pigsty. Get my food!" he shouted, standing over her menacingly.

"There is no food," Fernanda replied. "There is no money."

"What!" Flavio yelled, giving her a glancing slap to the shoulder. "I gave you 500 pesos yesterday. What did you do with that?"

The spectators gasped. Fernanda affected tears. "I bought medicine for the baby." Flavio paused, not sure what to do next, and then looked to Rodrigues.

"Perfect," Rodrigues said. And when we do the real scene, we will do it in a casita in Andrés, or Altagracia, with a dirt floor and . . ."

"Wait, Fomerio," Sonia called from the sidelines, smiling and wagging her finger to indicate "No." "This is not reality. This is *not* reality. What Dominican woman would accept that?" There was a murmur of agreement from the women in the crowd. "She's right," said a high school student, "that isn't reality."

Rodrigues smiled awkwardly. "Sonia, la Negrita is a young woman from the countryside, innocent and uneducated, she doesn't know . . ."

Sonia laughed and stepped forward. "Fomerio, *yo soy del campo!*" (I am from the countryside!), she replied, pressing her index finger into her chest. "And in the countryside, the women are not like that!"

There was loud laughter. Rodrigues smiled, shaking his head from side to side. "OK, no problem, let's do it again. This is only a test." "But

22. Rodrigues discussing the plot of *La Negrita y el Turista* with the cast and crew. Sonia, soon to be codirector of the *telenovela,* stands at the far right. Photo by the author.

this time," he said, turning to Fernanda, "be stronger, more combative." Fernanda nodded her assent.

Flavio threw open the door. "*Negra,* what are you doing? Where is my food?"

Fernanda scowled at him. "There is no food. And there is no medicine for the baby. Where is the money that you promised me?"

Flavio stepped toward her. "*Diablo!* Don't talk to me about money." He again slapped her on the shoulder. "In this house, I am the man and you do what I tell you to do. Now . . ."

"*Coño!*" Fernanda shouted, raising one arm to defend herself and cradling the infant with the other. "Don't touch me! This is my mother's house, not your house. Get out of my house. If you touch me, I will *kill* you!" Flavio paused, glanced awkwardly at the camera, and then stormed out, slamming the invisible door behind him.

The crowd applauded and broke into uproarious laughter. Sonia slapped Flavio on the back of the head as he swaggered past her. "Be careful *tíguere,* Dominican women are dangerous—dan-ge-rous."

"*Claro,*" Flavio replied, laughing and readjusting his baseball cap.

A good-natured dispute broke out between the women and the men in the crowd, many of whom were high school students and friends of the cast, as to which version of the scene better captured Dominican "reality." A middle-aged man, an Economitel employee who had been watching, argued that the final version of la Negrita was more characteristic of women in Boca Chica than of women in the countryside. His comment implied that Boca Chica's women had been influenced by foreign ideas about gender roles, a claim often made by men about Dominican women in Boca Chica and abroad. One of Fernanda's girlfriends challenged him, arguing that Dominican women had changed and would no longer tolerate such abuse, let alone from a man who was not providing for his family.

"Wait," Sonia added, "what do you know of the countryside, Vladimir? You are from the capital. Today even women in the countryside make their own money. We are independent!" The man smiled, shook his head, and returned to work.

The screen test, as would others to follow, provided a public forum in which cast members and spectators performed and debated themes and roles that were as prominent in their everyday lives as they were in Rodrigues's skeletal narrative. Sonia challenged the portrayal of la Negrita as a passive victim of male abuse, as framed in the plot, and also the race- and class-distorted constructions of rural backwardness and subjectivity. Against this elitist and essentialist notion of *el campo,* Sonia presented herself, a black woman from the countryside and household head who plainly did not conform to the stereotype. Moreover, Sonia challenged (as had Fernanda in her final enactment of la Negrita) the socioeconomic assumptions underpinning male power: the "myth of the male breadwinner," as Helen Safa (1995) phrased it. "This is *my* house," had been la Negrita's response to her husband's demand. Like the "joker," or facilitator, in Augusto Boal's *Theater of the Oppressed* (1985), Sonia's interventions contributed to transforming the protagonist, la Negrita, from a passive subject of oppression to an agent capable of exercising her own will and desire.[6]

Questions of gender and agency came to dominate discussions as the screen tests continued, transforming the narrative from one about female abuse, rescue, and migration abroad into one about changing gender roles in Dominican society. For example, in the next screen test, la Negrita sought her mother's advice about her future and her marriage. In the original plot la Negrita was to leave the countryside against her family's wishes, and this was to be a central dramatic tension in the story, a variation on the corruption theme, expressed in elite and especially in male discourses. In Sonia's improvisation of the role, the mother advised la Negrita to leave the abusive husband and, offering to care for the infant, told her that she should seek financial independence. "Go and make a life of your own," the mother said at the end of the scene. "Make your own money. It's better that way."

Sonia's assertion of control over the treatment of women's gender identities and roles not only registered widespread, albeit contested, changes that were taking place in Dominican society as women achieved a modicum of economic independence through entry into the labor force at home and abroad (Levitt 2001); it also mirrored aspects of her own life history. Sonia had married an Italian expatriate at the age of nineteen and, until his death, managed a restaurant that he owned in Boca Chica. When her husband died, she converted the restaurant into her residence and a hair salon and, with the help of a cousin and her eldest daughter, ran a successful business. In spite of himself, Rodrigues's project had begun to come to terms with "the real Boca Chica."

In the next week's screen tests I was to have my debut in a scene in which the tourist, after having long hidden his feelings from his maid, la Negrita, confesses his love for her and his desire to marry. For this sequence, Rodrigues had suggested that we use my apartment, located just across the highway from Turivisión's studio. Encouraged by the progress to date, Rodrigues had also decided to discontinue the screen tests and begin production. Moreover, rather than tape the *telenovela* in its entirety prior to broadcast, the production team had decided to air each episode on its completion, which would leave the plot open ended and allow viewers to phone in comments and suggestions on the evolving drama to Rodrigues's show, *Revista de la Comunidad.*

I was in a panic. As the crew set up the lights and equipment in my apartment, I sat at the kitchen table and surrounded myself with my laptop, newspaper clippings, and the few books that I had brought with me. I displayed Frank Moya Pons's classic text, *The Dominican Republic: A National History,* prominently within what I imagined the frame would be. Rodrigues, standing in the doorway, gave the signal to begin.

Fernanda, playing la Negrita, walked into the kitchen, opened the refrigerator, and began assembling ingredients as if to prepare a meal.

"How is your baby, Maria?" I asked. In the evolving plot, the infant's health had become a central issue motivating la Negrita's life-bending decisions.

"Better," she replied, not facing me. "I sent the medicine that you bought to my mother."

"Maria," I continued, trying to sound conflicted. "There is something that I must tell you—something very personal, something difficult for me to explain."

"Yes?" she replied, turning toward me.

Rodrigues interrupted the shot. "Esteven, this is too formal too. We have to find another way to do this—to create the drama that occurs at this moment."

Eusebio, the cameraman, spoke up. "Fomerio, the majority of tourists who come to Boca Chica are not like this, reading books and *Listín Diario* and working on a computer. This is not the reality of Boca Chica." For the production team, *la realidad* had become the language and benchmark of success.

"*Claro!*" agreed Sonia, who was now serving, de facto, as the production's codirector. Rodrigues listened, frowning in thought.

Eusebio continued, "He should be more cheerful, and with vices—smoking, drinking beer, a womanizer who . . ."

"With a prostitute!" Sonia proffered.

Rodrigues smiled, liking the idea. I winced. The revamped plot was discussed at length and with considerable enthusiasm. Sonia suggested that that the scene begin with the tourist drinking beer and reading the sports pages of an English-language newspaper. Sonia's concept led to more discussion and to a new plot that recast the tourist as a directionless, morally weak, and disillusioned soul and la Negrita as a strong-willed, principled woman who would define the terms of the ensuing relationship. In the plot reversal the emphasis had shifted from la Negrita's rescue from poverty and abuse by the tourist to her redemption of the latter from a life of moral turpitude—a *Flying Dutchman* set in the tropics.

In the taping of the revised scene, la Negrita was again preparing lunch when a scantily clad prostitute (played by Sonia) appeared from the bedroom and ordered her to make coffee. An argument ensued when la Negrita challenged the woman's right to boss her around. The tourist, moved to action by his undisclosed feelings, evicted the prostitute and approached la Negrita to have a talk. The tourist confessed his feelings to his housekeeper, but she resisted, responding that she would only consider his proposal if he changed his ways *and* promised to support her baby. La Negrita then recounted the story of her first marriage and her escape from the countryside, concluding firmly yet compassionately, "I could love again but only a man who respects me and provides for my child." The scene ended with la Negrita exiting the apartment, leaving the tourist, head resting in his hands, to mull over his life and desire.

Over the next few days, more scenes were taped. In one, Maria sought the advice of her English teacher, a fellow Dominican, on her decision to

23. La Negrita (Fernanda) discussing her decision to emigrate to Canada with her English teacher, played by Sucre. Photo by the author.

emigrate; in another, her estranged husband confronted her after work and, promising to mend his ways, pleaded with her to return to the Cibao Valley. Both scenes highlighted la Negrita's agency—first, in self-improvement, and, second, in resisting the sweet talk of an abusive husband. With the first episode nearly complete, Rodrigues set himself to organizing the taping of la Negrita's exodus from the countryside, a flashback that would be filmed on a bus.

However, production of the *telenovela* came to an abrupt halt when Fernanda withdrew from the project under pressure from her family. Her parents, she later told me, had decided that such public exposure was unsuitable for a *señorita* and one who was engaged to be married. I was relieved since I had come to believe that it was also unsuitable for an anthropologist. Reality had become too real for both of us.

Through the staging of *La Negrita y el Turista,* those involved in its production worked through social issues, problems, and tensions that were central in the lives of area residents as much as cast members. Migration abroad, the copresence of poverty and consumption-driven tourism, the status of local culture, identity, and commitments in the face of globalization, and, perhaps most significant in this context, changing gender roles and relations in Dominican society were all live issues that informed and de-formed the drama's evolving plot.

But the production of *La Negrita y el Turista* also exposed and mediated ruptures and antagonisms among its diverse participants that had their origins in gender, racial, and class differences and in differently lived experiences. Rodrigues's initial narrative resonated with both conventional male attitudes concerning sex/gender roles and identities and elite conceptions of racial and class subjectivity. Cast as a black woman from the countryside, la Negrita was, from this perspective, ignorant, naive, and a passive recipient, for better or worse, of modernity and the patronizing desire of a tourist. It was the familiar elite narrative of the migrant from the countryside who, faced with the tempting yet perilous challenges of modernity, risks moral corruption and begs rescue. However, Sonia had recalibrated the moral compass.

Production stalled as Rodrigues searched for a replacement to play the role of la Negrita. In the meantime, the production crew pieced together a trailer from fragments that had been already taped. Happily, the scene in my apartment was not included; Fernanda felt that it was too intimate. Adding to the urgency, I was due to leave the country in two months. I decided to take matters into my own hands in the hope of finding an older replacement. I asked a friend whom I had known for more than a year to consider playing the part of la Negrita.

Mabel, originally from San Francisco de Macorís, was twenty-eight years old, a divorced mother of two, and worked as a bartender at a popular restaurant on the beach. The bar where she worked was a favorite spot for North American engineers and others involved in the construction of the AES power plant across the bay, and I had often discussed the AES project and other issues with her. Inquisitive, smart, and opinionated, Mabel took a particular interest in politics and was alive to gender issues. Mabel's participation, I reasoned, would complicate the narrative and cast the protagonist as a mature adult. She tentatively agreed to play the part, and I arranged for Rodrigues to interview her at her workplace. It was a brief encounter. As we were leaving, Rodrigues told me that he did not feel Mabel was appropriate: she was too mature in age, attitude, and life experience.

I was disappointed, as well as concerned that Mabel would take Rodrigues's summary rejection as an insult, one in which I was complicit. I visited her the next evening at her apartment to discuss the rebuff and took the occasion to conduct a formal interview that I had been meaning to do for months.

Mabel lived in a studio apartment with her eighteen-year-old sister, Ruthie. The studio was in a newly constructed complex that had been intended for tourists but, with the 2000–2001 slump in tourism, had been rented out to local residents at a considerable discount. Mabel's two children lived with her aunt in San Francisco de Macorís. Though she sent half her wages each month to provide for their care, her aunt incessantly demanded more. Two years earlier Mabel had married a lawyer from Bermuda. When the man became "controlling" on their wedding night, she left him. Mabel was torn between two equally undesirable alternatives: she could remain in Boca Chica, where she could not earn enough money to send for her children; or she could emigrate with her children to Bermuda and join her domineering husband. For as long as I had known her, she had vacillated between these two sets of gendered constraints.

SG: I'm sorry about what happened with Fomerio.

MI: To me, it's not important. It's simply that he wants a young woman *(una negrita)*. He does not want a woman with experience. It doesn't matter.

SG: But what do you think about the project. About the story that he wants to make?

MI: I think that it's a good thing to make a story, a *novela,* about Boca Chica. But it's not reality. To make a work like that, one must make it about the reality of women in Boca Chica. About the woman who finds a tourist on La Duarte to better her life.

SG: I don't understand.

MI: Listen, for a woman who works as a housekeeper for a family to then find a tourist. No, it's not possible. They must make it as it really is in Boca Chica. Understand?

SG: More or less.

MI: How do I tell you? Here there are more—Let's suppose something. Ruthie lives here with me, and Marlene [Mabel's niece] moves to Boca Chica from her town in the countryside. Ruthie begins to educate her about how things are down on Calle Duarte. How women earn money, how the police are, how to find a tourist so that he'll pick her up *(se la lleva)*. How to make progress. But no woman is going to begin here by washing and ironing and end by marrying the patron of the house.

SG: I agree. Because, in reality, things don't happen that way.

MI: Exactly. One has to begin with reality. How she was prostituting herself, how things were in reality. How she found a tourist at a discotheque or in a bar. That he took her from there and set her up and then took her to his country, even though she had a Dominican husband who was not taking care of her child.

SG: It's like a fantasy, the way the story is now.

MI: You could say that. But it would be good. Because it would be a colorful story. But it has to begin with the reality of Boca Chica. The reality of women.

SG: But what is that reality?

MI: Look. It is very difficult for a woman who comes to Boca Chica from the countryside to find a job, to support herself, washing and ironing. It's very difficult. When a woman comes here from her town, the first thing that she thinks about is how to grab *(atrapar)* a tourist for money and improve herself. That's what I think.

Mabel's critique of the nonreality of the plot underscored the impossibility of making a living wage by washing and laundering clothes and the unlikelihood that a tourist would marry his maid and provide for her children. Both were improbable, if not impossible, roads to economic progress. In fact, the majority of poor and racially marked women who migrated to Boca Chica eked out a living by working in the tourism sector, typically informally and not infrequently as sex workers. Moreover, I think, Mabel objected to the plot's implication, reiterated in elite discourse, that "leaving with tourists" was a moral choice made by women over and against other viable livelihoods. Reality in Boca Chica was more complex and daunting and could not be represented by such binary moral accounting.

At the time of my interview with her, Mabel was grappling with this grim economic reality. Marlene, her seventeen-year-old niece, had recently come from San Francisco de Macorís to live with her. Mabel wanted to enroll her in a computer school in the capital but did not have money for tuition and, besides, was struggling just to make ends meet. Mabel told me that on more than a one occasion she had seen Marlene and Ruthie loitering on Calle Duarte and that she was worried that both women would be drawn to sex work. This was a reality more real than any *telenovela* could be.

In the end, *La Negrita y el Turista* was never completed. By the time I left the field in late August, Rodrigues had turned his attention to other projects. Turivisión, however, did broadcast the trailer composed of a montage of clips, which provoked considerable speculation about the plot, the "reality" of life in Boca Chica, and my role there. Ironically, days before I was to leave Boca Chica, a POLITUR officer whom I had been trying to interview called me over to his table in a restaurant. In the past the lieutenant had been cold, dismissive, and wary of my overtures.

"*Turista!*" he chimed, gleefully patting me on the back. "This one," he said to his colleagues, "is the protagonist in the *telenovela* that Fomerio is making." There was a round of well-meaning laughter, and they invited me to join them for a beer.

Turivisión's work must be viewed as a complex engagement with, and mediation of, multisited and multilayered networks of cultural meanings, social relations, and arrangements of power, stretching from the quotidian gender politics of households to the political and symbolic economy of the global order of things. Through Turivisión's activities, local cultural producers—surfing the wave of global media—reproduced and renegotiated the significance of community, investing it with meanings that bypassed, appropriated, and, at times, contested the power-laden structures of representation in which they were embedded.

But the project of producing the realities of community against the hegemonic narratives of the tourism industry and the national media was itself channeled through local power relations, webs of signification, and, as Faye Ginsberg (1994: 13) has put it, "the lives of motivated social actors and processes of everyday life." Nowhere was this more aptly demonstrated than in the disorderly production of the *La Negrita y el Turista,* whose unstable, evolving narrative not only embodied changes in sex/gender identities in Dominican society but also realized a performative social field within which alternative sex/gender, racial, and class subjectivities could be imagined and negotiated. For despite the narrative's initial conformity to power-invested constructions of identity, its production provoked participants and observers to resist and revise its order of meaning in light of their everyday experiences, social relations, and political commitments.

To be sure, local gender norms and power arrangements exerted a formative constraint on the narrative's development, notably, through the intervention of Fernanda's parents, who cast her in a role as *señorita* (a term connoting sexual innocence) that was the antithesis of la Negrita's hard-won independence and agency. Moreover, the adoption of the popular *telenovela* genre imposed conventional definitions of what counted as drama, centering frequently on male contests over access to female sexuality. From this point of view, the dramatic focus of Rodrigues's narrative rested as much on which of the two men would control Maria's sexuality as on her own life-altering decisions. That Mabel could praise the project as good entertainment while rebuffing its gender-biased assumptions underscores the layered and contextually specific nature of the process of media reception.

As the case of Turivisión demonstrates, a nuanced understanding of the influence that accelerating developments in global telecommunications technologies are having in places such as the Dominican Republic must be grounded in the analysis of the disparate and multilayered social networks and relations of media production, circulation, and reception and their context-specific temporal and spatial forms. If, as Arjun Appadurai (1996) has brilliantly argued, technological developments in electronic media have transformed the imagination into "a collective, social fact," increasingly emancipated from spatial constraints, then the case of Turivisión, embarrassingly "local," provides evidence that the imagination remains embodied in the social and in the hierarchical and multiscalar relations of power that fashion it through time and space; that is, the medium, at once technological and social, continues to be the message.

Moreover, the prickly symmetry between the story of Dolores wandering through the social space of rumor, gossip, and myth and the technologically mediated drama of la Negrita suggests not only that both have been formed and de-formed by ineludibly "real" and embodied social structures but also that the electronic media have yet to win their monopoly over the practice of the imagination. I suspect that the story of Dolores will outlive the story of la Negrita. Whatever the case may be, it remains an ethnographic question.

4

Sex Tourism and the Political Economy of Masculinity

Jimmy's Bar and Grill was set back about twenty yards from the beach, nestled among palms. It was the last remaining example of the weekend *cabañas* built by affluent *capitaleños* in an earlier era. The bar was owned by Jimmy Ryan, an expatriate from Boston who had lived in Boca Chica for more than twenty years. Since the late 1980s Jimmy's Bar had been a popular meeting place for male tourists who traveled to the island to meet Dominican women. On any given day about two dozen men would stop to drink, to socialize with other Americans, or to ask Ryan's advice about hotels, car rentals, and other traveler's concerns.

Jimmy's Bar was also a gathering place for Dominican women who were looking for male clients for manicures, massages, and sex. In the 1990s it gained considerable notoriety through tsmtravel.com, a California-based web site dedicated to "travel and the single male." The web site provided its paid subscribers with up-to-date information and travel reports relating to sex workers worldwide. Advertised as a "TSM-friendly" place, Jimmy's Bar attracted first-time as well as well-traveled male tourists from North America and, to a lesser extent, Europe.

One night, just before closing, three regulars at Jimmy's place began a conversation about the "nature" of Dominican people. Bill, a tall, lanky expatriate in his late fifties, began the conversation by declaring that Dominicans lacked ambition and had no respect for education. An article on public school reform that had appeared the day before in *Listín Diario* provoked his remarks. Frank and Mike, the two other men in the bar that night besides Jimmy and me, were North American tourists. Frank, a New York–based computer programmer in his mid-thirties, had been visiting the Dominican Republic for eight years and had a steady Dominican girlfriend in Boca Chica whom he supported with a monthly allowance. Mike, a middle-aged merchant marine, had been visiting the Dominican Republic for three years and stayed for as long as six weeks each trip.

Storytelling dominated the conversation as each man provided an account of an experience that illustrated Dominican ignorance, corruption, and lack of ambition. Such talk was common among expatriates, who were ever alert to any slight that seemed to question their sense of innate superiority and entitlement. Jimmy, a taciturn man in his sixties, listened to the stories from behind the bar, nodding his head in agreement and now and then offering a gloss on their meaning based on his experience in the country. In contrast to most expatriates, Jimmy spoke Spanish and had a keen interest in Dominican culture and politics. When Frank had finished one such story, Jimmy turned to Bill, bemused.

"Bill, how many years have you lived in this country? As long as I've known you, I've never heard you speak a word of Spanish." The others looked to Bill, expecting to hear an outrageous response. Jimmy reached for a bottle of Havana Club and filled everyone's glasses.

"You know why I never learned Spanish after eleven years in this fuckin' country?" Bill replied. He took a swig of rum and rose to his feet. "I'll tell you why," he said, jabbing his wiry finger into the air. "Because they don't understand what you're saying anyway. It's like talkin' to a fuckin' brick wall. All the Dominican knows is money."

"You're right about that," Jimmy said flatly.

"Let me tell you what happened just the other day," Bill continued. "I took my car to the mechanic to get some work done on the brakes. Now what this guy did was buy used parts, put them in the car, and then he wants to charge me for *new* parts. I said, 'No way José! Show me the receipt. I wanna see the fuckin' receipt for those parts.' So he shows me the receipt. And what the dumb bastard did was change the '1' to a '2' so that he could charge me 2,000 pesos instead of 1,000 for the parts. You believe that? Well I paid him the fuckin' money, and I told him, 'You wait and see. I'll be back.'

"So I went down to the police station and told them that this fuck had just ripped me off. And those dumb bastards were just sitting there, grinning. They're not gonna do nothing. And do you know why? Because '*No hablo ingles.*' That's what that sergeant . . ."

"Reyes," Jimmy proffered.

"Right, Reyes. That's what he tells me. So I said, 'OK, you *no hablo ingles?* Then I'm gonna see if you speak Spanish.' So I called my wife and told her to come down to the station."

Bill turned to me and explained. "My wife's Dominican and her whole family is police—father, brothers, cousins, everybody. They're all high up in the police.

"So my wife comes down to the police station and gets right on the phone and starts talking in Spanish like a fuckin' machine gun—*badada!* And when those fucks heard her say 'General López,' they started shittin' in their pants. You see," he looked at me, jabbing his finger, "the only time a Dominican does anything fast is when they think they're gonna get fucked. And those guys were gonna get *fucked,* I shit you not."

Frank interrupted, "Now hold it, Bill. You put them in a car, and they drive like fuckin' lunatics." He grinned and waited for Bill to respond through the rum.

"That's right, they drive like fuckin' nuts."

"Let him finish the story," Mike protested.

Drunk and distracted, Bill took a few moments to collect his thoughts and then continued. "Anyway, the next day at 9:00 in the morning, somebody rings my bell, and it turns out that it's the brother of the prick that ripped me off. He gives me my money back, every fuckin' peso, and he tells me that the police have his brother in jail. And he wants *me* to go down there and tell the police to let him go." Bill raised his eyebrows in triumph and peered at me. "See, they're not gonna let that prick out of jail unless *I* tell 'em to."

"Did you go?" Mike asked.

"Yeah I went. And you should have seen 'em, 'Oh, Señor Bill, I'm sorry about what happened, we made a big mistake . . . ' Apologies up the kazoo. And do you know what? They were all speaking English, every last one of them. I shit you not."

Like many of the stories these men told each other, Bill's narrated the mastering of social differences—cultural, linguistic, political—through the exercise of control over women. In Bill's account it is his Dominican wife, or more accurately, his putative control over her, that empowered him to expose the nature of Dominican people and put them in their place in the global order of things. And Bill was not alone. Each year tens of thousands of North American and European men, the majority of them white, traveled to the Dominican Republic in search of women over whom they could exercise sexual and domestic discipline as potential husbands, "boyfriends," or clients in the sex tourism industry.[1] Through the social practice of this form of heteronormative masculinity, what I will call imperial masculinity, these men collectively constructed and naturalized ideologies of racial, class, ethnic, and sex/gender differences that both registered and reinscribed the sociospatial hierarchies of the global division of labor.

I argue that for these men, the real and fantasized subordination of women provides the imagined prototype and concrete field of social practices through which social distinctions and hierarchies are interpreted, naturalized, and eroticized (O'Connell Davidson and Sánchez Taylor 1999). In the minds of these men, as Ann McClintock (1995: 24) noted of their Enlightenment predecessors, "the imperial conquest of the globe [finds] both its shaping figure and its political sanction in the prior subordination of women as a category of nature." To be sure, heterosexual men constitute a diverse category with racial, class, and cultural differences that influence male gender identities. Rather, my focus is on a field of cultural practices, and their structural supports, that subject women to homoerotic fantasies of control and domination that mimic and reiterate broader, indeed, global, relations of political and economic power.

I am not arguing that gender asymmetry is primary in a historical, political, or psychological sense when considered in relation to other structures of social inequality. The issue that I raise and consider here concerns the manner and extent to which the symbolic coherence and practical articulation of increasingly global social hierarchies rely on imagining and exercising this heteronormative model of masculinity. For I would like to suggest that it is the eroticization of these social distinctions, on the model of sexual control and discipline, that contributes to their durability, flexibility, and perceived naturalness in hierarchical social systems. One might say that in the cult of imperial masculinity hierarchy *feels* good. "You see," to recall Bill's words, uttered with no small amount of satisfaction, "the only time a Dominican does anything fast is when they think they're gonna get fucked. And those guys were gonna get *fucked*, I shit you not."

On the other hand, I highlight the ways in which women who participated in sex work transgressed and reworked race- and class-inflected gender norms relating to their labor power and economic futures while disrupting the heterosexual norms and relations desired by male tourists and expatriates. Beyond approaches that treat sex work as principally a "survival strategy" and then consider the degree to which it is coercive or disempowering to women, I direct attention to the cultural practices through which women violated social norms and institutions implicated in regulating and disciplining their gender identity, sexuality, and labor within Dominican society and the global economy. In Boca Chica sex work was reducible neither to "sex" nor to "work" but instead embraced disparate practices through which women renegotiated and contested hierarchies that were secured *simultaneously* in terms of gender, sex, race, and class.

Marjolein van der Veen (2001) has recently pointed out that much of the literature on prostitution in the radical feminist tradition (e.g., Pateman 1988; Barry 1995) has tended to treat the selling of sexuality as the defining feature of persons engaged in sex work, which results in a reductionist view of the "self." "The selling of sexuality," van der Veen writes, "becomes the defining feature of that person: a sex worker is defined by that particular identity rather than by the multiple, other identities she may have as mother, sister, daughter, artist and so on" (2001: 35; see also Pettman 1997). I share this view and, for that reason, use the label "sex worker" with caution and reject the tendency to view sex work either as essentially work or as essentially dehumanizing.[2]

The question of the relationship between sex and gender asymmetries and the structuring of hierarchical social systems has been at the center of feminist research and theory building in anthropology and other disciplines (Rubin 1975; Collier and Rosaldo 1981; McKinnon 1989; Truong 1990; Ong 1991; Ortner 1997). Feminist scholars have argued that the widespread, if not "universal asymmetry," in how the sexes are culturally evaluated can be understood neither as a necessary consequence of biology (e.g., women defined as *natural* child bearers) nor as secondary effects of other social processes, such as capitalist class formation (Rosaldo 1974: 17). Instead, researchers have argued that, since sex and gender relations are implicated in the structuring and reproduction of all social systems, women's subordination must be analyzed in relation to wider, yet context-specific, processes of social stratification (Collier and Rosaldo 1981).

In her landmark essay, "The Traffic in Women," Gayle Rubin (1975: 209–210) defined the scope of this task: "A full-bodied analysis of women in a single society, or throughout history, must take everything into account: the evolution of commodity forms in women, systems of land tenure, political arrangements, subsistence technology, etc. Equally important, economic and political analyses are incomplete if they do not consider women, marriage, and sexuality."

It is to Rubin's phrase "equally important" that I want to direct attention. For although feminist and, more recently, Queer theorists have taken up the challenge to analyze systemic arrangements of power in relation to sex and gender relations, other students of social inequality have been less disposed to reworking their analyses of social hierarchies in light of the structural implications of sex/gender systems.[3] For example, although it is recognized that elites in stratified social systems typically exclude women or assign them subordinate status, sex/gender hierarchies and, more to my point here, masculinity are seldom treated as a critical, if not indispensable, condition of possibility for the mobilization and exercise of male power.[4] And though it may be begging the question to point out that in most, if not all, stratified societies studied by anthropologists men exercise the lion's share of formal political power, the fact that they are men, a politically constituted and exercised category, deserves critical analysis. As Catherine MacKinnon (1991: 160) put it in a related context, "The question is, what are they?"

My central premise is that heteronormative masculinity (i.e., what heterosexual men believe themselves to be, possess, and represent) is a power-laden social and semiotic architecture within which men fashion, interpret, and negotiate their relations with each other and the social world. Furthermore, this currency of male sociality, comprising culturally constituted beliefs, values, and structures of feeling, as well as concrete social powers and prerogatives, plays a critical role in mobilizing, coordinating, and "naturalizing" male power in hierarchical social systems. Masculinity, to quote Foucault (1990: 92) in a related context, can be viewed as a "moving substrate of force relations which, by virtue of their inequality, constantly engender states of power." From this perspective, masculinity, as practiced ideology, is always already available to lend structural meaning and support to racial, class, imperial, and other hierarchical orders.

To what degree do systems of inequality based on such social differences as race, class, ethnicity, and national identity (or some combination of them all) depend on, if not presuppose, the symbolic as well as political organization of male social power, that is, a sex/gender system that not only privileges but also must reiterate and mobilize heteronormative masculinity? Put differently, to what degree do the political articulation and reproduction of social inequality require the mobilization of heterosexual men *as such?* By investigating the question of masculinity as such, I direct attention to the discourses, practices, and structures of male sociality that serve to model, shore up, and naturalize relations of inequality under conditions of global economic restructuring.

To be sure, the relationship between economic restructuring and sex/gender hierarchies stretches well beyond the frontiers of tourist enclaves such as Boca Chica. In the Dominican Republic neoliberal economic development policies, monitored and enforced by the World Bank, the IMF, and other financial institutions, have given rise to development strategies that rely heavily on the naturalization of gender and other social differences (Báez 1989, 1991; Ong 1991; Safa 1995, 1999; Hernández 2002). Over the past three decades the Dominican economy has shifted from one based on agricultural production and manufacturing for domestic consumption to one based on tourism and the labor-intensive processing of exports in free trade zones. Both the tourism and export-processing sectors of the Dominican economy rely heavily on the exploitation of women's labor and, as a result, have set in motion social forces, both structural and symbolic, that provide a key macroeconomic context for the analysis of Boca Chica's sex tourism industry and the exercise of imperial masculinity.

DOCILE BODIES AND EROTICIZED POWERS

> I am a single mother with a 12-month baby. I work in the Zona Franca operating a sewing machine. I have beautiful ideas and dreams of my future. I am a very unlucky lady. I fell in love and I thought that he loved me. But I was deceived, abandoned and left pregnant. I would like to find a man who will truly love me. He can be up to 50 years old. It is all right if he is divorced and has children. My only crime is that I am poor.
> —Yesenia, 22 years old.
>
> Ad placed with a U.S.-based Internet "introductions" service

The rapid growth of the tourism industry in the Dominican Republic relied on the mobilization and reconfiguration of social hierarchies and ideologies based on gender, class, and racial distinctions. As many researchers have pointed out, the international tourism industry constructs, commodifies, and markets exoticized and deeply gendered images of non-European host societies that stress the passivity and enduring "otherness" of their peoples (Enloe 1989; Truong 1990; Bolles 1992; Mullings 1999; O'Connell Davidson and Sánchez Taylor 1999). These representations, rooted in the centuries-old fantasies of male European travelers and colonizers, construct tourist destinations such as the Dominican Republic as sites of hedonistic license and consumption that recapitulate the historic prerogatives of imperial elites among colonized peoples (Kempadoo 1999).

This gendered iconography of space constructs non-European host societies as submissive and erotically feminine and finds structural support in the sexual division of labor in the tourism industry. As Vivian Kinnaird, Uma Kothari, and Derek Hall (1994) have noted, women hold the majority of tourism-related jobs, typically low-skill and low-wage, such as chambermaids, kitchen staff, and other service personnel. This gendered division of labor reflects both the international tourism industry's conflation of pleasure-producing services with women's labor and dominant gender norms within host societies that relegate women to domestic service occupations. Thus the tourism industry not only constructs the tourist experience in gendered and racialized terms—as an encounter with a docile, obliging, and feminized Other—but also mobilizes, affirms, and reconfigures patriarchal ideologies and power relations within host societies to form a division of labor that accentuates wealth and power differentials between "hosts" and "guests" (Mullings 1999). In the Dominican Republic these patriarchal and racialized discourses and practices, operating at the local, national, and transnational levels, enabled and lent meaning to the social practices of masculinity among male tourists and expatriates.

Another deeply gendered development associated with economic restructuring policies in the Dominican Republic has been the meteoric growth of export-processing industries in FTZs. These zones are industrial enclaves, or estates, that offer investors duty-free import and export of goods and a variety of tax and regulatory incentives that facilitate labor-intensive assembly operations. Typically, FTZs are self-contained, spatial enclaves that are dominated by foreign investment and produce goods designed for export that require high inputs of cheap labor. In 1970 the Dominican Republic opened its first FTZ with the objectives of generating foreign exchange and jobs. By 1992, promoted by the United States Caribbean Basin Initiative and by World Bank and IMF structural adjustment demands, 403 companies, employing more than one hundred thousand workers, were doing business in thirty-one FTZs, all heavily subsidized by the Dominican government (Sagawe 1996).

The rapid expansion of the export-processing sector in the Dominican Republic has led to profound changes in the social and spatial organization of the labor force and in the sexual division of labor (Safa 1999; Hernández 2002). On the one hand, as Laura Raynolds (1983: 163) has pointed out, "fully 80 percent of export processing jobs and firms are located in the greater Santo Domingo metropolitan area or in the provincial capital cities of Santiago, San Pedro de Macorís, and La Romana." This has produced a concentrated pattern of urban job growth and stimulated rapid rural-to-urban migration. For example, the population of San Pedro de Macorís, a city just to the east of Boca Chica, almost doubled, from 42,000 to 80,000, in the decade following the establishment of its FTZ.

On the other hand, the expansion of export-processing industries has led to a rapid and unprecedented incorporation of women into the labor force in low-paying and labor-intensive manufacturing jobs in FTZ industries. Between 1970 and 1994 female participation in the Dominican labor force increased from 25.3 to 36.4 percent. By 1994 women accounted for 58 percent of the labor force in the export-processing sector, and 65 percent of all women working in FTZs were employed by garment and textile companies (Raynolds 1998). Workers in the non-unionized export-processing industries tended to be poorly paid and unskilled, subjected to compulsory overtime, and entitled to few, if any, benefits (Pantaleón 2003). The average monthly wage paid by FTZ industries to new workers in 1995 was 1,678.69 pesos (US $130.41). Representing an hourly rate of 34 cents, this amounted to about a third of the wage level required to stay above the poverty line, defined by the Dominican government as 4,743.33 pesos per month.

The expansion of this low-wage female labor force has been shaped by gender-biased practices and ideologies that devalue and exploit women's labor in both Dominican society and the globally oriented export-processing sector. As Raynolds (1998: 161) writes, "Companies profit from Dominican patriarchal traditions, that limit women's alternatives and make them disproportionately responsible for home and family. Women's restricted employment ensures that they will accept low-waged and unconventional jobs, particularly if this work permits them to forgo migration and remain near their families." Managers of FTZ industries typically exclude women from administrative and supervisory positions and assign them instead to repetitive and fast-paced assembly-line tasks on the grounds that women are better suited *by nature* for work that requires patience, manual dexterity, and acquiescence to highly regimented working conditions (Ong 1991; Freeman 2000).

Moreover, women working in export-processing zones were routinely subjected to sexual harassment and abuse. A 2002–2003 study conducted by the International Labor Rights Fund (ILRF) in conjunction with Fundación Laboral Dominicana (Dominican Labor Foundation) concluded that more than 40 percent of the women surveyed in FTZ factories producing goods for the U.S. market had been subjected to sexual harassment (Pantaleón 2003: 3). The majority of the abused women were between the ages of nineteen and twenty-five, and 43.7 percent of the sexual aggressors held supervisory positions in the factories.

Thus the rapid development of the tourism and export-processing industries have both shaped and been shaped by practices of gender subordination that situate Dominican women within the global economy as "natural" subjects of labor and sex/gender exploitation. Whereas the export-processing sector appealed to the "natural" qualities of women to mobilize and devalue their labor, the tourism industry fabricated experiences of pleasure and consumption that relied, symbolically and structurally, on power and wealth differentials figured in gendered and racialized terms.

TECHNOLOGIES OF MASCULINITY: SEX TOURISM AND THE INTERNET

Many of the men whom I met in Boca Chica had become aware of the sex tourism industry there through Internet web sites that catered to male travelers interested in prostitution. Although there were a variety of U.S.-based web sites devoted to male sex tourism, tsmtravel.com, boasting six thousand paid subscribers, was by far the most popular and sophisticated one in 2001.[5] TSM hosted "travel reports" about prostitution around the world, message boards, and "adult entertainment" photographs and video clips submitted by subscribers.

The development and social uses of web sites such as TSM highlight the role of new technologies in mediating transnational social hierarchies and, more to the point, recapitulating and reiterating an imagined geography of difference, rooted in enduring imperial power relations and representational schema. TSM enabled its members to identify economically vulnerable populations of women around the world and to exploit that vulnerability through the naturalized, pleasure-seeking economy of heteronormative masculinity (Hughes 1996). Like pornography, these web sites conflated desire with domination.

A popular feature of TSM, and similar sites, was its detailed travel reports, submitted by subscribers and often accompanied by photographs and maps. The reports provided up-to-date information on sex tourism destinations, such as Thailand, the Philippines, and Brazil, and included detailed data on transportation, hotels, sex worker venues and prices, and social, political, and economic conditions. For example, a July 1999 travel report alerted TSM subscribers to the favorable exchange rate in Quito, Ecuador:

> During my recent trip to Quito, the big news was the exchange rate: over 11,000 Ecuadorian sucres to the dollar. Quito is now undoubtedly one of the better TSM values in the Western Hemisphere. . . . I made one discovery not mentioned in previous posts. There is a bar/brothel located about a one-minute walk from the Hotel Embassy at Almagro 208 @ Pinto in what appears (from the outside) to be a residential house. . . . The price there for 15 minutes of sex is only 30,000 sucres (less than $2.75).

TSM's message boards and real-time chat rooms enabled members to communicate with each other and post queries concerning travel destinations, such as brothel locations in Manaus, Brazil, or airfares between Bangkok and Manila. Subscribers, using screen names such as "Miami Pete" and "Badboy," also took advantage of the message boards to announce travel plans and coordinate meetings with other members at predesignated locations and times.

The adult entertainment photo section was divided between images culled from Internet pornography sites and amateur photographs taken by TSM members during visits to sex tourism destinations. Frequently, the photographs were incorporated into travel narratives and captioned. TSM's galleries underscore not only the relationship between the production and consumption of pornography and the practice of sex tourism but also the complicity of both in the collective construction of heteronormative masculinity through the exercise of control, "scopic" as much as physical, over the bodies and sexuality of women (Dworkin 1981). Significantly, male sex tourists played an increasingly prominent role in producing and distributing pornography through Internet web sites in general and through personal web pages dedicated to single male travel.

Web sites such as TSM provided men with up-to-date information about the economic vulnerability of women—women of color in particular—and also enabled the formation of technologically mediated structures of male sociality focused on the "self-imagining" of heteronormative masculinity on a global scale (Appadurai 1996). Male sex tourism positioned women as subjects of gender-based labor exploitation; it also figured them within an electronically mediated masculine imaginary as eroticized subjects of sexual control and consumption (O'Connell Davidson and Sánchez 1999).

THE NIGHT ECONOMY

After dark, economic activities in Boca Chica shifted from the beaches to Calle Duarte. Dominican residents who did not have economic interests on Calle Duarte or in its environs shunned the area at night and rarely patronized tourist-oriented businesses, which were viewed by most as *feo* (ugly), *de mala fama* (disreputable), and overpriced. Instead residents supported Dominican-owned restaurants, bars, and clubs in Andrés and *colmadones* located in Boca Chica's popular barrios.

Midpriced hotels lined Calle Duarte and the cross streets extending north to the highway, the majority of which were owned by foreign expatriates. With the exception of the all-inclusive resorts, hotels in Boca Chica permitted guests to bring women (though rarely men) to their rooms at no extra charge, provided that the latter had *cédulas*. The practice of checking and, in some cases, collecting the *cédulas* of sex workers was directed more at ensuring the security of tourists than at confirming the age of the female guests.

However, not all of the hotels in Boca Chica indulged sex tourism. Gabriel Zapata instituted policies that discouraged male sex tourists from staying at his beachfront hotel. Zapata did not allow guests to entertain nonregistered visitors on the hotel's premises, which undermined the practice of male sociality and bonding central to single male travel. In contrast to other small and midsized hotels, Hostal Zapata cultivated a customer base of Dominican Americans, *capitaleños,* and international tourists seeking a "family-friendly" and affordable alternative to the resort hotels.

Although researchers have directed attention to male sex workers in the Dominican Republic, few men in Boca Chica were self-identified or socially recognized as sex workers, or Sanky Pankies.[6] In part, this was because Boca Chica was not a popular destination for single female tourists, and those single women who did visit Boca Chica tended to stay at the all-inclusive resorts. But equally important, men who worked with female tourists, sometimes receiving money for sex, were able to claim an identity (such as *guía,* or guide) that stretched beyond the narrow and stigmatized identity reserved for female sex workers (Kempadoo 1999; Herold, Garcia, and DeMoya 2001). Although same-sex sex tourism existed in Boca Chica, it was clandestine and repressed by the local authorities and hotel managers.[7] For example, most hotels prohibited tourists from having same-sex local guests in their rooms. In short, the privileging of heteronormative masculinity, locally and within the international tourism industry, constructed sex work as female and heterosexual.

Sex work among adults is not illegal in the Dominican Republic, and the authorities in Boca Chica tolerated it.[8] Although the town had no system for licensing sex workers, women were required to carry *cédulas* that confirmed their identity, residence, and age. Local authorities described their policing strategies as targeting women who were "criminals" or minors under the age of eighteen. Periodically, units of the National Police and POLITUR conducted sweeps of Calle Duarte and its environs, checking identity cards and arresting women without them. Prosecution of sex workers intensified in 2000–2001 under pressure from the secretary of state for tourism and the Asociación Pro-Desarrollo Turístico de Boca Chica, a tourism advocacy group largely controlled by the resort hotels (see chapter 2).

Shortly before dark, women from Andrés, San Pedro de Macorís, and elsewhere—as many as two hundred on weekends—would begin to arrive at the bars and discotheques on Calle Duarte to socialize with male tourists. Sex workers received payment of between RD $400 and $800 from their foreign male clients. Generally, sex workers operated independently rather than under the control of *chulos*. However, women often worked in concert with men—*fisgones* and *motoconchos*—who procured clients for them in return for a commission, typically 25 percent. Such arrangements were opportunistic and did not imply durable bonds or commitments. An added expense for many sex workers was the protection money they paid to the police in return for being allowed to work free from harassment and arrest.

Women typically established informal arrangements with the owners of bars and discotheques that enabled them to meet clients at these locations in return for soliciting customers and selling drinks. In more formal arrangements, women worked as unpaid hostesses, receiving customer tips and an employer-issued ID badge. Frequently, women from the same town or barrio clustered at the same venue, which increased their security and enabled them to pool transportation, room and board, and other expenses. Such arrangements provided varying degrees of protection from police harassment and arrest since the National Police and

24. A *motoconcho* taxi and passenger traveling along Calle Duarte. Photo by the author.

POLITUR were reluctant to encroach on tourism-related enterprises. Moreover, it was widely reported that businesses involved in sex tourism paid the National Police in return for impunity.

These working arrangements engendered a hierarchy among sex workers, based on their social status and the value assigned to their services. Women not connected to a bar or similar venue were viewed by sex workers and clients alike to be of the lowest status and the poorest paid. These women, disparaged as *mujeres de la calle,* were also the most persecuted by the authorities. At the opposite extreme, hostesses affiliated with bars and discotheques were considered to be "higher class" and deserving of more remuneration. This hierarchy tended to correspond to evaluations of skin color and social capital, with lighter skin brokering more status, security, and control in transactions with clients and in relations with the police. Moreover, women working as hostesses at high-status venues, such as the Zanzibar Bar or Laser Discotheque, were able to inhabit broader and more ambiguous working identities and, thus, to avoid the stigma of being labeled *cuervos* (prostitutes). In short, the status of women involved in sex work was roughly proportional to their "epidermic capital" and to the degree to which their sexuality was mediated by male power and authority, whether of the club owners or of the police (Trouillot 1994). Women attached to high-status venues were perceived by both male clients and the police to be less settled into sex work than their lower-status coworkers and, consequently, less disposed to crime, drug abuse, and HIV/AIDS infection.

For example, twenty-eight-year-old Giovanna Pérez, a divorced mother of two, began working with tourists as a hostess at the Zanzibar Bar and Café in 2000. Giovanna commuted from the capital on weekends to supplement wages that she earned as a cook. While at the Zanzibar, Giovanna developed a reputation for being "difficult," and she argued frequently with the bar's owner and customers. After one such altercation, Giovanna was fired and banned from the Zanzibar and the discotheque next door—the premier venues on Calle Duarte.[9] Giovanna then began working at the Madhouse, a German-owned bar with a coarse and raucous reputation. After a quarrel there with a group of German men, Giovanna and a coworker were arrested and jailed for a weekend. Though Giovanna continued to work at the Madhouse, a sergeant in the National Police began regularly shaking her down for 200-peso "gifts."[10]

A few weeks after her arrest Giovanna told me, "If I were working at the Zanzibar, this would not have happened. Because, there, the police do not dare ask for money. A woman like me [she held her hair, gesturing to its straightness] should not be working in a place like this. Not a place like this. But because of that stupid man [the Zanzibar's owner], I am here. I was betrayed." Not long after my talk with her, Giovanna disappeared. Rumor had it that she had gone to Sosúa to work. In Boca Chica it was the tourism industry that was the sex workers' pimp.

Boca Chica's massage parlors served as another venue for sex workers. In 2001 there were four parlors scattered throughout the town. One of them, Pattaya Massage (named after Pattaya beach in Thailand, a sex tourist destination), was located near the highway in a commercial building. Pattaya was managed by Sonia, a former masseuse. Her Swiss husband had financed the business, but after the couple separated, Sonia operated the parlor on her own, ferrying six to eight women daily to and from the capital. Employment in the massage parlors was viewed by workers and their clients as being more reputable and skilled than sex work in other venues, and women received significantly greater compensation: 2,000 pesos (US $125) for a "sensual massage," 800 pesos of which went to the house. Boca Chica's other massage parlors were also reputed to employ women from the capital, who were considered, as Sonia put it, "more refined and responsible." Pattaya's clientele included foreign tourists, expatriates, and, occasionally, Dominicans.[11] Sonia enforced condom use (a poster promoting safe sex was displayed over the bar) and saw herself as an advocate on behalf of her employees.

There was considerable awareness among sex workers and others working in the *zona turistíca* that condoms prevented the transmission of HIV/AIDS and other sexually transmitted infections (STIs). Condoms were prominently displayed in pharmacies, *colmados,* and the stalls of street vendors, and in my conversations with sex workers and their clients, I was given the impression that they were used.

In the mid-1980s Dominican government and nongovernmental organizations (NGOs) embarked on a campaign to reach out to and inform sex workers about HIV/AIDS and STIs and safe sex practices using peer educators (Kempadoo 1998). In 1989 two Dominican NGOs, the Centro de Orientación e Investigación Integral (COIN) and the Comité de Vigilancia y Control del SIDA (COVICOSIDA), joined together in a campaign to develop a network of peer-led *Mensajeros de Salud* (Health Messengers) to work in centers of the female sex industry (Moreno and Kerrigan 2000). Influenced by Freire's philosophy of education among equals, the peer educators worked in cities and tourism centers, providing information about HIV and STI transmission and training sex workers in negotiating with clients and in the social marketing of condoms (Family Health International 2005).

By the mid-1990s the organizing efforts of COIN's Health Messengers had led to the publication of a newsletter produced by sex workers, *La nueva historia: Periódico de la noche* (The New History: Newsletter of the Night), and to the founding of a theater company that held training sessions and performances for sex workers, clients, and operators of sex venues on safe sex practices (Kempadoo 1998). In 1995 COIN held its first congress on sex work to promote awareness in Dominican society and among government officials of the causes of prostitution and the problems faced by sex workers. In 1996 the Movimiento de Mujeres Unidas (MODEMU; Movement of United Women), an independent organization of sex workers, was formed to organize and advocate on behalf of sex workers (Kempadoo 1998).

There was some evidence to indicate that the educational and empowerment efforts of COIN, MODEMU, and related organizations had made an impact on safe sex awareness among sex workers and others in Boca Chica. Some people whom I knew had encountered COIN's Health Messengers in the late 1990s and were aware of the organizing activities of MODEMU. Sonia, Pattaya's owner, was familiar with MODEMU from reports that had appeared in the media and knew two Health

Messengers who worked in the capital. Giovanna had attended meetings about safe sex practices at a nightclub in the capital where she had once worked. Other residents knew of the condom distribution and HIV/AIDS awareness campaigns that had taken place in Boca Chica in the late 1990s, though some had the impression that these had been government sponsored. More generally, the activities of COIN and MODEMU provoked public deliberation and debate throughout the Dominican Republic about the socioeconomic origins of sex work and about the violence, discrimination, and other problems facing sex workers.

MAKING MEN

It was 7:30 in the evening when I arrived at Delmonte's, an American-owned restaurant not far from the Coral Hamaca Beach Hotel. I had earlier scheduled an interview with its owner, Kenny Bruno, a plumbing contractor from Boston who had married a Dominican woman and settled in Boca Chica. In addition to his restaurant, Kenny operated a lucrative mail order cigar business. Delmonte's sat on a terrace overlooking the beach. Steps from the terrace led down to the sand, where an additional dining area serviced daytime customers.

I sat at a table on the terrace and asked the waiter for Kenny. He informed me that Kenny was in Cuba, where he often went to buy cigars for his business. I decided to stay and have dinner. It was a warm, clear night, and there was enough moonlight to make out the figures of teenagers playing in the water below. Three boys were taking turns jumping off each other's shoulders into the waist-deep water, to the delight of a group of girls who watched from the beach, laughing and shouting encouragement.

Save for four middle-aged white men who were sitting at a table on the other side of the terrace, the restaurant was empty. The men were dressed in golf clothing and were wearing the red plastic bracelets that identified them as guests at the Coral Hamaca Beach Hotel. They talked quietly over their beers about baseball, sailboats, and Fort Worth, Texas, where two of the men had lived. Every so often, one of the men glanced expectantly toward the bar inside.

As I was giving my order, a cheerful, chubby Dominican man arrived with two young women. His keys rattled in his hand as he waved to the Americans. He had on the pale green shirt worn by the drivers of tourism taxis. The four men twisted in their chairs to watch the girls approach, grinning pop-eyed at one another as the driver sat the girls at the table. The driver introduced the two girls as Belkis and Maria. The men grinned and greeted them but did not introduce themselves.

Both girls appeared to be no older than eighteen. Maria was petite and wearing a white miniskirt, red tank top, and white platform sneakers. Her hair was pulled back tightly into a ponytail. Belkis was tall and wearing a low-cut, shiny blue dress that clung to her full figure. When one of the men gawked theatrically at her exposed thigh, she laughed nervously and covered her mouth.

"Hey, Stu," a second man blurted. "Ain't she too young for you?"

"I'm drinkin' beer, Bob, I don't give a shit," Stu replied with a southern drawl. He pointed to Bob's empty beer bottle. "Hey, you're getting behind there, big boy."

The cab driver laughed, slapped his knee, and signaled to the waiter to bring more beer. The two girls quietly ordered Cokes.

Stu leaned toward Belkis and placed his hand on her thigh. "And how old are *you,* young lady?" He grinned and cut his eyes to his friends. Belkis didn't understand. She covered her mouth, laughed quietly, and then looked to the taxi driver for help. The driver questioned her and reported, "She is sixteen years old."

"Woowee!" Stu blurted. "Ain't this some place? You can't beat this."

A third man, who was sitting next to Maria, joined in. "Hey, Stu, you gotta speak the lingo if you want to get anywhere down here." He turned to Maria. "*Que e-dad* you got, honey?" he said, badly mispronouncing *edad* (age).

The table erupted in laughter. The cab driver clapped his hands with glee, "Very good!"

Confused, Maria looked to Belkis, grinned, then clapped her hands as well.

For the next twenty minutes, the four men and the driver talked among themselves while the girls sipped their Cokes in silence. When they finished their drinks, the driver handed Belkis a bag that he had stowed under the table, and the two girls disappeared into the restaurant. Ten minutes later they returned in bikinis.

Their reappearance was greeted with whoops and hollers from the table. Stu got up from the table and wrapped one arm around each of the girls. "Hey, big boy, you gotta get a picture of this. Get out your camera!"

Bob unpacked his camera, and each of the men took turns posing with the girls. When the picture taking was over, Belkis and Maria stood awkwardly beside the table, unsure of what to do next. The cab driver talked for a moment to Belkis and then announced to the Americans that the girls wanted to go swimming.

"Sure, why not," Stu replied. "I can handle a wet bikini!" The table laughed again as Belkis and Maria, holding hands, scurried down the steps to the beach below. The men stood, whooped and hollered once more, and angled to get a better view of the disappearing figures. "Boy, that Maria's got a nice bottom," Stu muttered.

"Ain't this paradise?" Bob asked.

"Well, if it ain't, I sure don't know what is," came the response.

I got my check and left. The next day Kenny returned from Cuba, and I went back to do the interview. The Americans from the night before had also returned and were sitting inside the restaurant with Belkis, Maria, and two other women. I asked Kenny about them.

"Who, those guys?" he asked, half waving and half pointing to their table. They waved back. "They're the highest-ranking military officers in the D.R. [Dominican Republic]. They come here all the time."

"Why?" I asked.

He was distracted. The restaurant was filling up quickly. Kenny caught the waiter's eye and then pointed to a table of impatient-looking Germans.

"No, I mean, what are they doing in the D.R?"

"They're here to monitor Cuba. You know, the situation there."[12]

As the above vignette suggests, sex acts occupy a small portion of the time that male tourists spend in Boca Chica. Indeed, the men spend more time interacting with each other than they do with women—which highlights the degree to which masculine self-identification relies on male-centered cultural practices and forms of sociality (Sedgwick 1985; O'Connell Davidson and Sánchez Taylor 1999). Striking in the above case, as in many of the ritualized interactions between tourists and sex workers, is the general lack of interest, an almost studied indifference, on the part of most men in the women they have come to meet. During the two hours or so that I watched the Americans at Kenny's restaurant, they spoke few words to Belkis and Maria and made eye contact with them only furtively. Their interactions with the women (groping and gazing at their bodies, asking their ages, and posing for photographs) were theatrically performed in a manner so as to incite the collective participation of the men (through laughter, whooping and hollering, and catching each other's eyes) and enable the alignment of a shared male gaze—one whose conditions of possibility rested on the very real, yet contested, economic power of male tourists to position

Dominican women as docile bodies within the global political and sexual economy.

Teresa DeLauretis's (1990: 115) observations concerning the "nonbeing of woman" capture well the subject positions assigned to Belkis and Maria in this ritual of masculinity: "The paradox of a being that is at once captive and absent in discourse, constantly spoken of but of itself inaudible or inexpressible, displayed as spectacle and still unrepresented or unrepresentable, invisible yet constituted as the object and the guarantee of vision; a being whose existence and specificity are simultaneously asserted and denied, negated and controlled."

It is this imagined and indeed paradoxical state of nonbeing that was the elusive target of the masculine gaze as it was constituted and exercised through the practices of male sociality. Male socializing in Boca Chica revolved around a surprisingly narrow set of ritualized spectacles through which men fantasized the nonbeing of women and, in turn, imagined themselves to be all powerful subjects. Much of this socializing occurred at night in the many restaurants, bars, and clubs that lined Calle Duarte. For example, by 10:00 P.M., the Zanzibar Bar and Café was usually packed with male tourists and Dominican women, some employees and others not.

Like other bars and clubs in Boca Chica, the Zanzibar employed attractive young women to serve as hostesses. These hostesses were not paid wages but received tips from customers. In addition, some of the hostesses also "left with tourists" after work for "short-time," paid sex or for longer liaisons. For café and bar owners, the hostesses attracted and retained male customers by dancing provocatively and by striking up conversations and erotic poses, which not infrequently parodied and poked fun at tourists' fantasies concerning the "natural" qualities of Dominican women.

I sat at the Zanzibar's high mahogany bar next to Divina, a twenty-two-year-old who had begun working as a hostess the week before. Divina was from San Pedro de Macorís and had come to Boca Chica to find work to support her newborn son. She was living at the time with her brother, who worked as a *motoconcho* and rented a small house in Andrés. Previously, Divina and her widowed mother had worked at a textile factory in the San Pedro FTZ. However, with the birth of her son, their combined wages were no longer enough to support the household.

Divina was leaning against the bar, watching the tables outside. In contrast to the other hostesses, she dressed casually, often in blue jeans, sandals, and a neatly pressed T-shirt. Serious in demeanor, she did not dance or flirt to attract customers but was otherwise very conscientious about doing her job as a hostess. I had met Divina the day before, when Milquella and I had lunch at the Zanzibar. Milquella knew Divina's brother and offered to try to get her a job at the restaurant where she worked.

I greeted Divina and asked how things were. She made a sour face and said that she was not making any money. She told me that her mother had called that morning to tell her that her baby had a fever. She was concerned that the infant might have a dangerous strain of the flu that people were calling the "Kosovo flu." She needed money to buy medicine. I asked her how much she had earned the night before. She replied that she had made 150 pesos (about US $10) in ten hours. "*Mucho trabajo, poco dinero*" (A lot of work, little money), she added dryly. There was a flurry of activity outside, and Divina left to attend to a group of young Italian men.

The bar was now full, and the sound system was blasting merengue star Elvis Crespo's latest recording, "Suavemente." High-status venues such as the Zanzibar tended to play global pop that was familiar to their customers, seldom merengue and never bachata. Hostesses in skin-tight miniskirts flirted through the crowd, shaking their hips and singing along with the record. The tables that had been set up in front of the bar, blocking the public street, were fully occupied by clusters of North American and European men.

Divina was now sitting at a table with six Italian men who were dressed in jeans, polo shirts, and Nike sneakers. She appeared livelier than before and was talking to a thin man with gold-rimmed glasses and a pockmarked face. While the others looked on, he questioned her and then translated her replies into Italian for his friends. Each response was greeted by excited laughter and rapid talking. As I approached, I heard the man ask her in Spanish, "Which men are the best in bed—the strongest?" He clenched his fist and raised it into the air like a trophy. The others grinned and gaped at her expectantly. "*Italianos!*" one man blurted. The men laughed and looked at each other, then to Divina for a response.

Divina laughed. "I don't know," she replied. "I don't have the experience. All men are the same." There was a pause for translation and then laughter as the men protested her reply.

I sat down at a table with three middle-aged American men whom I had met earlier at Jimmy's Bar and Grill. Rubin, a recently divorced lawyer from Manhattan, was on his third trip to Boca Chica in the past

25. Hostesses at the Zanzibar Bar and Café taking a break. Photo by the author.

year. He had learned about Boca Chica through TSM's web site. On this trip he had brought along Martin, an old friend from Harvard law school who lived in Los Angeles. They had met the third man, Roger, in Boca Chica. They were sitting with Ana Maria and Gladys, two sisters whom the lawyers had met the night before at a casino in Santo Domingo. The two women talked quietly to each other, musing on the spectacle around them.

Rubin spoke some Spanish and presented himself to me as an expert on Dominican women and culture. "That's the one I want," he said, grinning widely and watching Divina. He caught her eye, and she approached the table, thinking that he wanted to order a drink. The Italians watched with concern. Rubin put his arm around Divina's waist and then looked to us, as if to make sure that we were paying attention. "This is the best girl in Boca Chica," he pronounced. "Look at her!" he added, eyeing her figure. "I want you to be my girlfriend," he told her. Divina laughed and pulled away.

Another hostess intervened, laughing and shaking her forefinger in Rubin's face. "No, America," she said in Spanish. "She is not for you. She doesn't leave with tourists." Divina left, and the other hostess remained.

"I like this one better," Martin commented, putting his arm around the woman's waist. "She's got bigger tits." The hostess sat on his lap.

"You're nuts," Rubin replied, making a face. "She's hard core. All she wants is your money. Let me tell you, I know this country. The best girls are in the *campo*. The women here in Boca Chica are all hard-core whores.

"But that one," Rubin continued, eyeing Divina, "you could marry her. She's not corrupted yet. She'll cook and clean for you and never give you any trouble as long as you take care of her. That's the way Dominican women are—the good ones."

"But why the countryside?" I asked. "What's the difference?"

"Because life there is simple," Rubin explained. "Everything is natural—the air, the food, the lifestyle, everything. They grow their own food, and they don't need money to spend on fancy clothes and makeup and all that bullshit. And the Dominican believes in strong families. That's why you see them all with babies."

Emboldened, Martin joined in. "The countryside is about survival for these people. And if they meet an American, and they like him, they'll do anything for you. They won't look at another guy. Because these girls hate Dominican men. A lot of guys who come here don't know that. Dominican girls don't want to be with them. They call them *tígueres* because the Dominican guys treat their women like shit."

Rubin knew that I was an anthropologist and that I intended to write a book. He looked at me and continued. "That's why me, personally, I like the dark-skinned girls the best. I'm not prejudiced like some of the guys who come down here and don't know anything." He kissed Ana Maria on the cheek. "See, they're not as corrupted with the consumer mentality and the fast life. Most of them are originally from *el campo*." Ana Maria smiled and asked Rubin for another rum and coke.

Like Rubin, many male tourists imagined the countryside to be a place bereft of the troubling complexities of modernity (and, above all, feminism) and uncorrupted by capitalist commodities; a place where everything was natural and people, good and simple. Like the imagined heart of darkness in Africanist discourse, *el campo* and its inhabitants existed for these men as an "impossible nullity," a void where, as Christopher Miller (1985: 27) put it, "the head, the voice—the logos, if you will—is missing." In this racialized fantasy, women from the countryside made good wives and mothers because, living closer to nature, *their* nature, they lacked *logos* and thus agency. It was this impossible nullity, this nonbeing of woman, that was the elusive focus of male sex tourists as they collectively worked to fashion and inscribe masculinity within the imagined void of the natural women. From this perspective, "nature" was viewed as pre- or extrasocial, as a place where sex could be imagined as passivity and a gender identity imposed from without.

"Which men are the best in bed?" the Italian had asked, raising his fist like a phallus. *"Italianos!"* another had confirmed triumphantly. Divina's response was moot since this had been a conversation among men and about men in which she was positioned as a prop, or, better, a tabula rasa on which to both fantasize and inscribe phallic power and agency.

Similarly, Rubin's performance relied on the collective though putative power of men to situate and, indeed, bond women within this masculine imaginary, enabling him to construct and enunciate the fantasized distinction between the Dominican "whore" who possessed agency and the docile and domesticated woman of the countryside, who was the ideal wife and mother. Within the imagined frontiers of the countryside, blackness, poverty, and marginality appeared to these men as natural differences that both signified and facilitated male power over women. Through their efforts to situate Dominican women as docile subjects of sexual control and domestic discipline, these men constructed and, more to the point, *performed* male gender identities that indexed and articulated complex constructions of racial, gender, economic, and geopolitical difference and power (Butler 1993; see also Allison 1994). Far from being a "free play" of signification, as Kath Weston (2002) has pointed out, this performativity was rooted in, and conditioned by, relations of political and economic power.

Of course, the specific configuration of distinctions and valences that adhere to constructions of white male heterosexuality (a diverse category in and of itself) differs in significant ways from the masculine identities that were performed by, say, African American or Latino male tourists. Although there were relatively few nonwhite male sex tourists through 2001, their numbers were increasing. I spent one evening at the Zanzibar Bar and Café with three African American men from Chicago. They were all TSM members, and, although they socialized occasionally with white American men at Jimmy's Bar and Grill, they tended to spend most of their time among themselves. Curtis, a forty-four-year-old policeman, had come to Boca Chica with his nephew and a friend from the job.

Late in the evening, when his nephew asked whether he intended to take a hostess back to his hotel, Curtis replied, "Man, these girls are too dark for me. They're country broads who came over here from Haiti. I didn't come all the way here to bang no black chick." His words are disturbing, but their meaning is clear. From Curtis's perspective, race and geography carried values different from those that they held for white men like Rubin. Dark skin signaled proximity, affiliation, and perhaps rural backwardness rather than the idealized and eroticized landscape of *el campo.* Racial distinctions did figure in how African American sex tourists constructed and exercised their masculinity, but masculinity was supported by different fantasies of sexual difference and control. White men wielded a form of epidermic capital in their relations with Dominicans and Haitians that was unavailable, if not repugnant, to African American men. Although Curtis's comments were by no means representative, the African American and Latino men whom I encountered tended to be oriented toward the capital and the urbane experience rather than the more insulated and, indeed, fetishized *zona turística.*

In this sense Boca Chica's *zona turística* was a stage, a theme park where men rehearsed and reiterated the privileges of economic, racial, and geopolitical power through the eroticized fantasies and rituals of women's subjection. A number of male tourists remarked to me that Boca Chica reminded them of Disneyland, an observation that gestured to the sophomoric sensibilities of adventure, risk, and competition that men cultivated through sex tourism and the thematic structures of the masculinities they worked to construct.

Jonathan Rutherford (1997: 27), writing on the relationship between British masculinity and the culture of imperialism, described the upper-middle-class Victorian ideal male as a "perpetual adolescent": "The figure of the boy in all the great adventure stories of the era represented the repressed longing of these men for all they had been forced to renounce—maternal love, their own bodies, sexual desire." Though this is a tenuous comparison, male sex tourists celebrated and described their homosocial bonds and activities in ways that stressed an adolescent-like freedom from responsibility (e.g., jobs, families, and ethical norms) and the pressures of Western feminism, as well as an unbridled pursuit of adventure and pleasure. I have heard more than one man describe his experience in Boca Chica as like being a kid in a candy store.

Bars and restaurants, for example, the German-owned Austria and Madhouse bars, the Dutch-owned Route 66, and Kenny's "American-style" restaurant, cultivated a customer base of tourists and expatriates based on national and linguistic identities. These establishments were typically marked with flags and other symbols of national identity and offered specialty menu items (e.g., Philadelphia steak sandwiches, schnitzel) and imported beers that appealed to men as subjects of nation-states. A travel report posted by a TSM member on the group's web site captured both this nationalist sentimentality and the puerile

26. Tourists at the Laser Discotheque on Calle Duarte. Photo by the author.

sense of adventure and competition that men commemorated through sex tourism.

> The Italians [in Boca Chica] were retreating to their homeland, with their supplies running out, and they knew that the Americans were cumming *[sic]* in force with big American guns and plenty of ammo. They did not want to be there when our reinforcements rolled into town. So in came such TSMers as Jody, Irving, NY Guy, Omega, Allan F., Worm, Joker, Canuck, Newt, Parrot Head, Ricky, Freddy (he's Danish but we let him hang out with us anyway). . . . There were others but I cannot remember their names. (TSM trip report, September 10, 1999)

This excerpt, replete with militarized, sexual euphemisms, underscores not only the degree to which the practice of heteronormative, male gender identity implicates national and other imagined differences (at once phallic, economic, and geopolitical) but also the homosocial, if not homoerotic, character of the practices themselves, both on the Internet and in the field. "We are," as Eve Sedgwick (1985: 38) observed in a not unrelated context, "in the presence of male heterosexual desire, in the form of a desire to consolidate partnership with authoritative males in and through the bodies of females" (see also Mosse 1985). Moreover, the appropriation of militaristic, often Vietnam-era language suggests the degree to which wider, imperial structures of feeling and practice served as models for honing this form of heterosexual masculinity. For example, a male tourist once referred to a visit that he was making to Andrés as a "mission in the vill." Another referred to bar-hopping as "a fire mission." In Boca Chica men propped up and exercised their nationalisms through the real and imagined subjection of women and, in the process, cultivated platoonlike forms of camaraderie and sentimentality.

Women who did sex work typically ignored, parodied, and disrupted these practices of homosociality, as well as the attempts of male tourists to render them docile nonbeings. In social gatherings, for example, women often carried on parallel conversations among themselves in Spanish, which critically evaluated and often ridiculed the actions, conversations, and, indeed, sexual prowess of male tourists. I witnessed one incident that illustrates this point. Three Canadian men were sitting with their Dominican "girlfriends" at a restaurant in Boca Chica when one complained that his girlfriend was pestering him to buy things for her baby. Unbeknown to him, his girlfriend was following the conversation and translating it, along with a caustic commentary, for the two other women. Provoked to action by her friends, the woman reached into her purse, pulled out a bottle of pills, and threw it at the man. "You can buy Viagra, but you can't help my baby!" she shouted in Spanish. "*¡Vete al Diablo!*" (Go to hell!). The woman stormed out of the restaurant with her friends, leaving the man red-faced and the Dominicans within earshot reeling with laughter. (Apparently, he had sent her to the pharmacy to buy the pills.)

Moreover, women often performed displays of sexuality that deconstructed naturalized stereotypes of their own sex/gender identities and parodied the sexual pretensions of male tourists. I once witnessed a hostess circulate among the tables at the Zanzibar Bar and Café holding an imaginary penis, which she lashed at dumbfounded tourists to the delight of her coworkers. In this and other performative venues, hostesses and sex workers also performed same-sex acts, such as kissing and fondling, which, directed in part at male tourists, transgressed heteronormativity and challenged assumptions about their availability. Some women openly acknowledged their bi- or homosexuality, and there was considerable discussion among those who worked in tourism-related jobs about sexual identity. Lourdes, a Haitian hostess at the Zanzibar, once confronted a North American tourist for not leaving a tip. When he rudely dismissed her request, she slapped him in the face and fiercely set upon him, restrained only by her coworkers. Another hostess, known to be the offended woman's lover, approached the bewildered tourist, laughing.

"Do not mess with her, America," she told him in English, "she is a lesbian. You better give her the money." The tourist paid the tip and left, hounded by the jeers and laughter of the hostesses.

These performative practices, however, should not be viewed through a binary lens, contrasting sex tourist with sex worker, or heterosexual with homosexual. As Weston (2002) has pointed out, overemphasis of performative repetition can risk dehistoricizing the contexts of performance and privileging the visual (often, the commodifiable) over other registers of practice and experience. In the case of sex workers, their cultural practices gestured to and engaged not only each other but also other power-laden fields of sex/gender subjection and regulation, including domestic arrangements and the wider social division of labor. These wider arrangements of power, rooted in the spatiotemporal order of the political economy, provoked certain forms of practice but also conditioned their venue and content. For example, for many sex workers, consumption of both images and commodities constituted an important mode of practice for contesting racialized constructions of their sex/gender identity, agency, and class position. Women frequently pointed to gold jewelry, cell phones, and other commodities as symbols of their success and independence from men. Although sex workers modified the meanings of these images and commodities through use, their appropriation was nonetheless channeled through durable networks of media and markets, which exercised cultural force.

Here, I would like to focus attention more squarely on the women who were involved in sex work and consider how the latter interpreted and negotiated their own positions and interests as women and workers within the political economy of sex tourism. I contend that sex workers not only challenged the real and imagined prerogatives of male tourists; equally important, through their struggles to make ends meet, they also contested the heteronormative structures of power and meaning that underpinned the broader, global division of labor.

LUCHANDO POR LA VIDA: STRUGGLING FOR LIFE IN THE GLOBAL ECONOMY

Noella was born in a small town near Santiago and orphaned at an early age. Her maternal grandmother raised her along with five siblings, and the family eked out a living growing yucca and other produce. At the age of twenty-six, while visiting a sister in Boca Chica, Noella met a Dominican man who convinced her to relocate there with her two children. When the relationship ended, Noella began working as a hostess at the

Zanzibar Bar and Café and doing occasional sex work to support her household.

I met Noella in 1998, during a preliminary fieldwork visit to Boca Chica. I bought her a beer and, after I assured her that I was not looking for a companion, told her about what I was doing. A few days later I asked if I could interview her, and she declined. (I later learned that she had thought that I was a journalist.) Instead I would visit her regularly at the Zanzibar and, when she was free, talk to her about Boca Chica and the organization of sex work. Over time, Noella introduced me to other hostesses who, when business was slow, would often join me at my table for a beverage. Noella gave me the *apodo,* which would stick among the sex workers, of *padre* (father, as in priest), an allusion to my apparent celibacy.

In general, women involved in sex work were quite candid about their lives and their struggles to make a living. This was due, in part, to the fact that it was assumed that male foreigners already knew the general outline of nightlife on Calle Duarte. However, more significant, sex workers consistently characterized their activities as work, pursued in the context of uncompromising needs and impossible alternatives, and, for that reason, expressed no indignity or embarrassment, at least to me. Noella once said to me, bluntly, "Look, I know that I am a prostitute *(una puta),* but if I have to open my legs to put food on my table and see that my children go to school, that I will do." Among informal workers and, more generally, poor people, there was little, if any, moral censure attached to sex work. The vast majority of people were living too close to the edge of catastrophe to indulge in moralizing. For example, I never heard the word *puta* or *cuervo* used by anyone to disparage or disgrace a woman.[13]

When I returned to Boca Chica in summer 1999, Noella told me that she was getting married to an Italian man whom she had met two years before. Paulo was fifty-four years old and a factory worker in Milan. He had been sending her money each month to help pay her rent of 3,500 pesos (US $215) and other living expenses, which amounted to about 3,000 pesos per month. I interviewed her on the day that Paulo was scheduled to arrive in Boca Chica. Later in the week the couple would go to the capital to apply for a three-month marriage visa for Noella. When I met her at the Zanzibar, Noella told me that she was having second thoughts about marrying Paulo. I asked her how she felt about leaving her country and moving to Italy.

"In this country there is nothing," she replied. "You have to leave here to help yourself. I just have to go because I can't work like this all the time. One day, they'll replace me. I can't go on struggling all the time, here, in the streets, walking home at night at 4:00 in the morning. It's not possible. If I find a man who wants to marry me and live in peace, I will not tell him no."

Paulo had told her that he would get her a job at the factory where he worked and which, Noella told me, would pay much more than the factories in the FTZs. She also had discussed moving to Italy with a girlfriend who had married an Italian and was living in Genoa. Her friend had reassured her that the schools and health care system in Italy were good and that her two children would benefit.

"Sure, I'm afraid," Noella continued, "but since I am not the first or the last to go, I have to get myself together and go. One must struggle for life *(luchar por la vida)*. I already know this country. I want to know other countries to see how life is there. I believe that if I go to Italy for those three or four months, I will know better if I like it there. I want to see how they treat me. If they don't treat me well, I will return to my country, the Dominican Republic."

I went back to the Zanzibar later that evening. Noella was sitting at a table with Paulo and her two children, whom I had not seen before. She was wearing her ID card but not working. She was a customer. The other hostesses fawned over them and served the children hamburgers that they had bought at a nearby food stall with their tips. Noella caught my eye and smiled. Paulo waved.

Noella did not go to Italy. Two weeks later she told me that Paulo had become jealous and possessive after she received her visa. Once in Italy, she reasoned, she would be at his mercy. "Maybe he won't find me a job at his factory. And maybe he won't send for my children." Shortly thereafter, Paulo left Boca Chica and Noella returned to her job at the Zanzibar. Noella's decision not to migrate to Italy was rooted in the credible fear that Paulo, by exploiting her visa status, might hold her hostage in his household and not allow her to pursue *paid* work and provide for her children. The fear of migrating abroad only to be disciplined as an *ama de casa* was behind the decision of many women not to marry foreigners, even when it might have improved their standard of living. Stories abounded of women whose insecure visa status reduced them to virtual prisoners of their husbands. In fact, few sex workers shared the domestic fantasies of male tourists. Contrary to popular opinion among many Dominicans and tourists, *la gloria,* the dream of emigrating abroad with a foreign man was not uppermost in the minds of all, or even most, sex workers as they strategized their livelihoods. Noella's decision was more than likely a more typical and "real" ending to *La Negrita y el Turista,* Turivisión's aborted *telenovela.*

Moreover, Noella's decision ensured that she would remain relatively free to pursue alternative strategies for socioeconomic mobility. For example, Noella had enrolled her fourteen-year-old daughter in a school to learn English, which, she believed, would prepare her for a front desk job in tourism. Also, in the event that the family migrated to the United States, where she had relatives, Noella felt that her daughter's English skills would give them a head start. Sex workers had to and did carefully weigh their pressing needs for income in the short run against the need to establish a modicum of economic security and independence for their families in the face of rapidly changing local and global economic circumstances. Income, security, *and* independence thus figured prominently in how these women led their lives.

For example, many of the women whom I interviewed had previously worked in factories in the FTZs but reported that low wages, taken together with poor working conditions and workplace abuse, had forced them to leave—a pattern of high turnover that is characteristic of FTZ-dependent economies (Ong 1991). Women pointed out to me that because factory work did not provide a living wage, an economically viable household required a second wage earner, traditionally a spouse. For this reason, women viewed subproletarian factory work as presupposing a stable relationship with an employed man. Given the high rate of un- and underemployment among Dominican men, this was not only a difficult condition to fulfill but also a domestic arrangement that tied a woman's future to a man's economic stability and, sometimes, abusive control. "To survive in the factories," one woman told me bluntly, "you must have a husband. And I don't want one." Thus women often assessed the relative merits of domestic and paid work arrangements in terms of the resulting control that men would hold over their lives and those of their children, whether as husbands, factory bosses, or boyfriends (see also Safa 1999).

Ivelisse explained to me why she had begun an expensive cosmetology course at a private school in the capital:

> I am studying because I want to find a man. A man who is good, is intelligent and can help me make a future. . . . I'm not looking for a man to keep me because, at this point in life, women must have training *(preparación).* They must have a profession; have their own businesses, their own lives. An ignorant woman thinks that if she finds a man with money she has everything.

> Or if she finds a foreign man. But that's ignorant because the man may give her nothing, and, in that case, the woman must have her own life.

Like Ivelisse, many involved in sex work cultivated fluid and manifold links to both the formal and informal economies, which, to varying degrees of success, provided economic security through occupational flexibility. Some women pursued occasional sex work while employed full time in low-paying, service sector jobs in Boca Chica. Others worked in the FTZs surrounding the capital and in San Pedro de Macorís and traveled to Boca Chica on weekends to supplement their wages—often to address a financial calamity, such as a family illness or death or job loss. For these reasons and others, the category "sex worker" fails to adequately capture the complexity of the relations of power that oppress them or, for that matter, the resourcefulness and fortitude with which the women struggled for life in Boca Chica.

It would be simplistic to reduce women's involvement in sex work to an economic survival strategy—to "merely the result of economic logic, rational choices, and free market mechanisms" (van der Veen 2001). Involvement in sex work and the tourism economy enabled some women to exercise modes of agency and subjectivity and patterns of consumption that they associated with middle-class urbanity and economic independence. For example, many women took pride in having access to new technologies, such as cell phones, pagers, and email accounts at local cyber cafés. Exposure and access to current global trends in fashion and popular culture through cable TV stations (e.g., MTV and Spanish-language networks such as Univisión), the Internet, and women's magazines (e.g., *Essence* and *Latina*) were often described to me as important benefits associated with working in the *zona turística*. This concern with style was evidenced by the considerable amount of attention and resources that many women devoted to beauty products and services. Noella estimated that she spent an average of 2,000 pesos (US $120) per month at the beauty parlor. More generally, women often described their work in the tourism zone as a process of "developing" themselves *(desarrollarse),* with the implication being that of becoming modern, savvy, and cosmopolitan. For poor and, especially, racialized women, these cultural practices laid claim to commodities and prerogatives that were ordinarily reserved for middle-class women.

Perhaps more significant, women involved in sex work challenged normative gender roles and forms of sexual regulation that enforced women's subordination and heteronormativity. Indeed, many women came to sex work only *after* having already rejected domestic and paid work arrangements that were exploitative and subjected them to abusive male authority and rigid, heterosexual social norms. For this reason, it is impossible to disassociate the economic strategies pursued by sex workers from the cultural practices through which they contested and transgressed normalized race, class, and sex/gender identities. As Judith Butler (1997: 272) put it, "Both gender and sexuality become part of material life, not only because of the way in which they serve the sexual division of labor, but also because normative gender serves the reproduction of the normative family."

To be sure, the success with which women were able to pursue these varied forms of struggle—at once economic, social, and semiotic—was conditioned by a wide variety of factors, including familial resources and responsibilities, education, and their perceived racial, class, and ethnic identities, which, for sex workers as for others, bore on their life chances. Ivelisse, for example, was from an economically stable, urban family and was a high school graduate and light-skinned *(trigueña)* by Dominican standards of racial classification. Her life prospects contrasted sharply with those of Noella, born in a poor, rural family, uneducated, and *morena.* Moreover, for all women, sex work involved life-threatening risks of exposure to HIV/AIDS and other STIs, client and police violence, and powerful social stigmas. Nevertheless, many women who were involved in sex work did so with a critical understanding of the interplay among political economy, gender, and sexuality.

This claim contradicts male tourists' interpretations of how sex workers were negotiating their positions within the tourism sector. Many men maintained a dual and contradictory evaluation of women's identity and agency: they were either demonized as "whores" who cared only about money or romanticized as sensual and devoted partners who could be controlled and, therefore, made ideal wives. The result was a Hegelian tension in their accounts between the desire to dominate, on the one hand, and the desire to sustain the fantasy that it was their masculinity, not their money, that was the source of their power, on the other. Like Hegel's master, male sex tourists wanted women to recognize their desirability as *essentially* men.

A 1995 article published in TSM's web-based newsletter, titled "White Sands, Blue Skies, Dark Women," wrestled with this seeming paradox:

> There are countries where the women are less expensive, and countries where the brothels are fancier or more conspicuous. . . . But I can't imagine that there are any countries where the women are better in bed than the

> women of the Dominican Republic. Perhaps it is as simple as this: Dominican women love sex and they love American men. Yes, you have to pay them. Everyone needs to make a living. But once you have paid them, you will begin to feel as though they paid you and that they are trying to get their money's worth by trying every possible position and configuration, by having you as many times as they can, and by begging for more. Don't be surprised if they ask you to stay and live with them. (November 1995, 5–6)

This fantastic reversal, mimicking the inverted logic of the rapist, denies the agentive quality of women's involvements with male tourists; instead it argues that the latter's economic power over women is an effect of their *natural* appeal as men and the culturally unmediated sexual drive of Dominican women. As one male tourist explained to me, "For Dominican women, sex is like breathing." By naturalizing their relationships with sex workers, male tourists denied their coercive character and, in the process, elided the gender, racial, and economic inequalities that make them possible.

Sex workers challenged this naturalization of sex work by insisting on a strict accounting of the value of their labor power and by disrupting tourists' fantasies regarding their "natural" sexuality and the equally naturalized myth of male desirability. For example, Rachel, a part-time hotel employee, told me that she was once invited by a German tourist to spend a week with him at a luxury hotel in Juan Dolio, a resort area east of Boca Chica. Rachel told the tourist that, if she were to go, he would have to pay her the wages that she would lose from her job and also pay her sister to take care of her two children during the trip. The tourist protested, she told me, maintaining that he was in love with her and that the trip itself would cost him a fortune. "I told him," Rachel said, 'The hotel is *your* business. But you must pay me for my time and for my children.' That is what I told him."

Boca Chica is just one site within a global tourism industry where regulatory norms regarding sex and gender differences are materialized through, as Butler (1993: 2) put it, their "forcible reiteration . . . in the service of the consolidation of the heterosexual imperative." The reiterative practices through which these norms were exercised ranged from the mass-mediated discourses and images produced by men *for* men on the Internet to the everyday performances of masculinity by men *with* men in the streets and bars of Boca Chica. These practices found their coercive force and conditions of possibility in a political economy that situated Dominican women as "natural" subjects of sexual subjection and labor discipline within a global and "hypermasculine" division of labor (Nandy

1988). It was the naturalizing function of this ideal of male sexual mastery that accounted for both its reiterative force and its capacity, as a discursive and institutional field, to articulate and lend stability to complex and, often, mutually antagonistic systems of social hierarchy. As Linda Singer (1993: 59) has pointed out, "What increases the ideological potency of sexuality as a mechanism of social control is that regulation ultimately becomes translated into the currency of self-regulation, because sexuality has already been constructed as that which is or belongs to the realm of the private, i.e., as opposed to the social. The regulatory force is represented and enacted through a currency not of coercion but of desire, in a way that encourages its individuation or personalization."

Nowhere was this power-evasive reduction of the social to the "private" and of coercion to putatively self-regulated desire more sordid than in the testimonies of sex tourists themselves. In a TSM travel report, a man claiming to have enlisted two women to act as procuresses opined on this dialectic of power and desire:

> I don't think my two friends have a portfolio of girls—they just go out looking in their town of Andrés and when they see a good looking girl they ask her if she wants to make some pesos. Most times, I believe, they say, "Sure, why not." Women in the Dominican Republic are very good at sex. It's as simple as that. From the highest born to the lowest, women are taught how to please a man. It's the only power that they have in this culture, so they learn it well. Mao said something like, "power springs from the barrel of a gun." He clearly never met a Dominican female. Of course, if he had, he would have just said to hell with the revolution and gotten a blow job. (August 2, 1999, 2)

By obscuring political economy under the sign of the phallus, male sex tourists not only essentialized sex and gender identities; they also eroticized social hierarchy by imagining and experiencing its constituent forms of social power as personal sources of pleasure. Why, to paraphrase the writer, fight a revolution when you can find pleasure dominating a woman? It is in this sense that the practice of imperial masculinity serves at once to depoliticize and articulate social hierarchies by actively imagining their inequalities to be *natural* sources of male power and pleasure, on the one hand, and homosocial bonds and sentiments, on the other.

Among male sex tourists, racial, class, and ethnic distinctions were interpreted and negotiated through this lens of male power and desire. Many men viewed dark skin color as a sign of pastoral simplicity, domesticity, and sensuality, and dark-skinned women were imagined to be uncorrupted by modernity and, above all, by Western feminism. For others, lighter skin tones evoked the trope of the exotic, Carmen Miranda–like mulatta, a well-traveled icon of licentious sexuality in the service of male bonding (see Kutzinski 1993). By contrast, Haitian women were reputed to be assertive and aggressive "professionals" and were viewed as both threatening and lacking in feminine qualities. One Canadian man put it to me this way: "The Dominicans and the Haitians are completely different. The Haitians are all hardened pros, and they'll rip you off. The Dominican girls aren't like that. It's not in their culture." The lack of feminine subservience among Haitian women, imagined as a cultural trait, altered the value of their racial identities, situating the trope of blackness within a symbolic field of danger and rebellion (see chapter 5).

Male sex tourism in Boca Chica provides insights into the role of heteronormative masculinity in constructing, naturalizing, and eroticizing social hierarchies grounded in a variety of claims about human differences. As a normative ideal and social practice, imperial masculinity transposed power differentials and social distinctions tied to race, class, and ethnicity, as well as sex/gender, into the symbolic economy of the heterosexual, male body—a homoerotic economy of desire and consumption that found its structuring principle in the real and imagined subjection of women. To be sure, heterosexual masculinity is neither stable nor monolithic. In the Dominican Republic, as elsewhere, it was the complicit exercise of disparate structures and discourses of male power by state authorities, global corporations, and domestic and foreign men that situated Dominican women at the bottom of the global division of labor. Indeed, it was precisely the capacity of heteronormative masculinity to bond men erotically across these differences that accounted for its peculiar service in the structuring of the global economy.

5

Race, Identity, and the Body Politic

An illegal person cannot produce a legal person.

Major General Manuel Polanco Salvador, chief of the Dominican army

Gérard Avin died on August 28, 2001, one week before I left the field. I wanted to go to his funeral, but, amid the rumors and confusion surrounding his death, I had lost touch with the people who were making the arrangements. I found out about his funeral after the fact. Miriam, the caretaker of the building in which I lived, approached me as I was packing and told me that she had heard that a memorial service had been held in Andrés only the day before. She had also heard that Gérard had been buried in a cemetery on the outskirts of Boca Chica. If so, I thought at the time, it was not without irony, for Gérard had often described Boca Chica as his "prison," and for as long as I had known him he had been trying desperately to leave.

I first met Gérard in summer 2000 at an American-owned restaurant in Boca Chica. He sat next to me at the bar and ordered a beer. He was slender and about 5 feet 8 inches, wore his hair in short dreadlocks, and spoke English with a slight Haitian accent. We began to talk, and I learned that he had lived in Brooklyn for ten years and that we had attended the same high school. I told him that I had visited Haiti a few times and spoke some Haitian Kreyòl. Gérard peered at me, switched to Kreyòl, and asked me where my family was from. Sensing that this was a race question dressed in ethnic clothing, I explained, *"Papa m se yon nèg nwè,"* meaning that my father was black.

Gérard had been born in Port-au-Prince and, at the age of eleven, had migrated to the United States with his mother and younger brother. During his junior year at Erasmus Hall High School, he got into a scrap with a Panamanian student, a recorded rap artist known as "the General," and stabbed him, though not fatally. As a result Gérard was expelled from school and began "hanging out with the wrong crowd," as he put it to me. Increasingly at odds with his mother and stepfather over his illicit activities (drug dealing, he would later confide), he decided to return to Haiti and make a new start. Back in Haiti, then under the presidency of Jean Bertrand Aristide, Gérard became involved in antigovernment activities. He would later tell me that his family had close ties to the ousted regime of Jean Claude Duvalier and that his uncle was Colonel William Regala, a powerful and notorious figure in the Haitian military.[1]

Aristide had betrayed the Haitian people, Gérard explained, and was a hypocrite and a drug trafficker. As he spoke, his expression alternated between an ironic grin and a ferocious glare that was unsettling. Gérard also had the disconcerting habit of punctuating each point expressed with emotion with a forceful, "Do you under*stand* me?" a literal translation of the less abrasive Kreyòl, *"Ou konprann?"* It was for these reasons, he said, that he had taken part in a failed plot to assassinate President Aristide. After spending three months at the notorious Fort Dimanche prison in Port-au-Prince, Gérard was released, thanks to the intervention of relatives in the Haitian army. Unable to remain in Haiti or return to the United States, where his residency had been revoked, Gérard fled to the Dominican Republic in 1991.

At this point in our conversation, I was having doubts about the veracity of Gérard's narrative, and it occurred to me that his Aristide story, in particular, might have been one that he would have imagined a U.S. citizen would want to hear. As I would learn, Gérard was a masterful raconteur and used his narratives to craft relationships with potential clients for his guided tour business. Whatever the case, I told Gérard about my project and said that I was looking for an apartment. Happily, he replied, there was a vacancy in his building—an eight-unit apartment complex in Bella Vista, just north of the highway. Gérard took me on the back of his motorcycle to meet the building's manager, a Dominican man named Chamón, who captained a sportfishing boat for the Hotel Don Juan. The one-bedroom apartment was perfect, situated in a tightly knit barrio where "everybody is family," as Chamón put it. Next door to the complex was a bustling, informal car repair shop. Down the street was a family-operated *colmado* and a small church where the *junta de vecinos* held their weekly meetings. The remaining buildings on the block were homes of working-class people—cab drivers and hotel and airport employees, as well as the president of the *junta.* I left a deposit on the apartment and returned to New York.

I want to write about my relationship with Gérard not only to reflect on how ethnographic knowledge is enabled, shaped, and coproduced by others in the field but also to foreground Gérard's understanding of the cultural politics of Haitian identity in Boca Chica. On the one hand, our relationship strongly influenced the directions of my research and the contours of my social networks and also how I was positioned as a researcher in a dauntingly complex sociocultural landscape. Moreover, our relationship was shot through with ambiguities, ambivalences, and misapprehensions that, though common in ethnographic encounters where wealth and power differentials are sizable, are often elided in the process of text making. Attending to this ethnographic dissonance provides occasion to reflect on how these asymmetries influence the research process—the methodological decisions made and the practices adopted—and configure the production of ethnographic knowledge.

On the other hand, as a smart and multilingual cosmopolitan, Gérard was an astute observer and critic of life in Boca Chica. From this perspective, our projects were not unrelated. As someone who made his living on the illicit fringes of the tourism industry, questions of power, difference, and global economic change were of as much interest to Gérard as they were to me, and certainly more pressing. On this score, I want to disorder and problematize the epistemological distinction that is too easily drawn between anthropological subjects who "interpret" the world and anthropologists who "theorize" it by taking seriously Gérard's analysis of the way things were.

This chapter is also a meditation on the relationship of the racialized subject to power, on the slippery dialectic between subjection and agency, and on the discourses, practices, and bodies through which subjection is channeled and mediated. Gérard referred to this problem as his "struggle" to be something other than what he was or, better, had been made to be. In large part, this struggle was economic: the ever pressing problem of making a living under circumstances that were anything but favorable. But this endeavor was also aggravated by a weightier, ontological problem of "crafting a self" (Kondo 1989) across a sociopolitical field where the fact of being Haitian overdetermined not only one's location within the division of labor but also the nature of one's being—one's "corporeal schema," as Fanon (1967: 112) put it. For from the vantage point of Dominican political and economic elites, the Haitian, as a master trope of blackness, "has no ontological resistance" (Fanon 1967: 110), and it was this historically forged "fact" that rested at the core of Gérard's life and death.

POWER, KNOWLEDGE, AND THE CRAFTING OF SUBJECTIVITY

When I returned to Boca Chica in December 2000, I ran into Gérard as he was entering his apartment. "You're just the person I want to see," he said cheerfully, before inviting me in for coffee. Gérard told me that he needed my help to translate his Haitian birth certificate into English. He explained that he needed to fax the document and its translation to his British fiancée in London, who would be sponsoring him for a three-month marriage visa. Gérard showed me a photograph of Margaret, taken on the night they had met in Puerto Plata. Margaret was fifteen years his senior, he said, but she loved him. "Boca Chica is my prison," he continued, "and Margaret is my way out. If I don't marry her, I'll be stuck here for the rest of my life."

We translated the document. Gérard was born at 10:00 P.M. on July 28, 1969, at Hôpital Français in Port-au-Prince. His mother was Virginie Pierre, a seamstress, and his father, Ernest Avin, a mechanic living in Delmas. Gérard told me that his parents had divorced long before the family left for New York, where his mother found work in a garment factory. Although his mother remarried, Gérard came to despise his abusive stepfather, and this soured his relationship with his mother. Though he had once hoped to petition for the reinstatement of his U.S. residency, Gérard believed that the prospect was slim without his mother's cooperation.

We finished our coffee and headed downtown to fax the documents to Margaret from the Western Union office on Calle Duarte. Along the way, Gérard stopped to speak with nearly everyone we encountered along the way—*motoconchos,* vendors, shopkeepers, and others—and the breadth of his social networks impressed me. Near the Coral Hamaca Beach Hotel a man on a motorcycle approached us. The man eyed me, guardedly, and Gérard asked me to let them speak in private. When the man left, Gérard told me that he was a friend, a former soldier in the Haitian army, who was looking to buy a European passport for

US $5,000. Gérard explained that there was a lively black market in authentic and forged documents in Boca Chica, ranging from foreign passports to Dominican birth certificates and *cédulas*. I would later learn that Gérard had contacts at one of the Civil Registry offices in the capital and could arrange identification papers for a price.

Gérard reached for his wallet and pulled out a Dominican *cédula*. "This is the Dominican me," he said, grinning roguishly. The *cédula* bore the name Máximo Gómez, which Gérard had borrowed from the Dominican-born general Máximo Gómez y Báez, who fought in Cuba's nineteenth-century wars for independence. Gérard explained that he had fashioned this alter ego after his son, Hassim, was born.

Not long after arriving in the Dominican Republic, Gérard married a Haitian woman whom he had known in Port-au-Prince. They rented an apartment in the capital, and soon afterward his wife gave birth to a son. Since Dominican authorities did not issue birth certificates to children born of Haitian parents, Hassim was born stateless. To resolve this problem, Gérard paid a Civil Registry official US $500 for a false birth certificate for himself, which he then used to obtain a *cédula,* a driver's license, and other documents in support of his identity as Máximo Gómez. On the basis of this Dominican identity, Gérard petitioned for the issuance of a late birth certificate for Hassim, which made it possible for him to attend public school and qualify for other public services.

When Hassim was four years old, Gérard's wife was killed in political violence while visiting relatives in Haiti, leaving him a single parent. As was the case with much of what I knew about Gérard, there were alternative versions of this story. A Dominican woman and mutual friend told me that Gérard had spent his early years in the Dominican Republic trafficking drugs and other contraband across the Haitian border. In her version of the story, Gérard's wife was murdered in a drug-related robbery.[2] The two versions of this story, not unlike much of what was publicly believed about Gérard, represented two discursive poles in a politics of rumor and gossip about Haitians in general and Gérard in particular that revealed more about the speaker's social relations and politics than the "truth." Because Gérard was viewed by Haitians and Dominicans alike as an astute and relatively successful man of ambiguous origins, he was a lightning rod for gossip.

When we left the Western Union office, I stopped to buy sunglasses from a sidewalk vendor. Gérard interceded and greeted the man in Kreyòl. "Give him a good price, he's Haitian." The vendor looked at me quizzically. "His father's Haitian," Gérard explained. "He's from New

York." At the time I thought that Gérard had said this to get me an insider's price. I later realized that in the months since I had last seen him Gérard had brought himself to believe that I was Haitian, or half Haitian. I later surmised that it had been my use of the Kreyòl term *nèg nwè* (black man) to describe my father. Or it could simply have been that Gérard had misremembered me, whether willfully or not.

It was not uncommon for persons' identities to be publicly in dispute, ambiguous, and shot through with contradictions. In a sociopolitical milieu where full citizenship rights were difficult to achieve, subject to recurrent verification, and at risk of being diminished and even negated, much was at stake in whom people were believed to be. Rumor and gossip concerning one's identity, as well as one's appearance, could be as significant in influencing the actions of the police and other authorities as the papers in one's possession. It was not uncommon for those perceived to be Haitian—typically, on the basis of skin color—to be detained by the police or army and deported to Haiti, irrespective of the papers in their possession. For example, after the signing of an expulsion decree by President Balaguer in 1991, six thousand children and elderly persons were deported to Haiti, many of whom were Dominican born (Corten and Duarte 1995).

In Gérard's case, his "flexible citizenship" was the subject of much speculation and debate (Ong 1999). Some Dominicans believed that at least one of Gérard's parents had to be Dominican. As a *motoconcho* put it to me, "No Haitian can speak Spanish like a Dominican, not even one born in this country."[3] Gérard was fascinated by languages and worked assiduously to improve his mastery of them. Moreover, he selectively stressed and even fabricated elements of his past in order to appeal to the interests, desires, and fantasies of his clients and others whom he encountered. For example, Gérard identified strongly with Rastafarian culture and philosophy and, in his English-language dealings with people, would often simulate a Jamaican accent and pepper his speech with phrases from the Old Testament and Rastafarian *livalect* (dialect).[4] These practices of cultural sampling had led to speculation that Gérard's father was Jamaican or Jamaican American.

For Gérard and others, this simulation—and dissimulation—of identity was not only a strategy for establishing and negotiating citizenship rights but also a modality of practice through which they claimed disparate forms of social and cultural capital and attachments to the global order. As identity (racial, ethnic, and linguistic) was linked to social mobility, both real and imagined, its crafting was a status-bearing claim to prestige and prerogatives across the hierarchical landscape of the *zona turística* and the world beyond.[5]

Many people—typically, those with weak claims to citizenship—fabricated transnational pasts patterned after the migration experiences and transnational networks of others. Richard, whose parents were Haitian immigrants, told me and others he met along the beach that he had been raised by an African American grandmother in Harlem before returning to Boca Chica to help his parents. (He would later tell me that he had been raised by a grandmother in Haiti, where he had been sent to attend school and learn English.) This fictive, or, better, "imagined transnationalism," made plausible by Richard's command of English and immersion in hip hop cultural aesthetics, facilitated his interactions with the growing number of African American tourists who visited Boca Chica. Using low-cost Internet cafés, Richard maintained email contact with networks of African American men in Miami, Chicago, and New York City who regularly visited the Dominican Republic and employed his services as a guide.

Moreover, Richard's claim to an African American past was an appropriation of diasporic, cultural, and political resources in a sociopolitical milieu where African heritage was both devalued and, as Silvio Torres-Saillant (1998) put it, "deracialized." This exercise of the imagination, to paraphrase Appadurai (1996), enabled by the circulation of mass-mediated black cultural forms and by the growing commerce in tourists of African descent, disrupted and challenged the elite-driven conflation of blackness with Haitian identity, constructed both as external to the nation and as pathologically Other. This is not to suggest that this crafting of identity was merely an instrumental "rational choice"; rather, acts of self-representation had important economic and political consequences within the tourism economy and the nation as a whole.

My own mistaken identity had far-reaching consequences for my research. Most Haitians in Boca Chica refused to speak to me in Spanish, choosing instead to converse in Kreyòl, despite my very limited abilities. Typically, Gérard would code-switch to Kreyòl from English whenever he spoke to me about sensitive topics that presupposed intimacy or complicity, such as shady business deals, racism, or when he wanted to borrow money.

In any case, like Gérard, many Haitians and Dominicans came to believe that I was at least part Haitian. My first impulse was to correct the misunderstanding. However, in the context of Dominican racial and ethnic politics, recasting my identity would not have been so straightforward. Haitian migrants often accused Dominicans of Haitian descent of refuting their Haitian origins, for example, by refusing to speak Kreyòl in public or by adopting Spanish names. My attempt to edit my identity would readily have been viewed as a disavowal that was all too familiar.

Moreover, in the weeks that followed, I came to realize that Gérard had actively contributed to the fiction. Through rumor and gossip, Haitians in Boca Chica had come to believe that my family was from Petionville, that Gérard was a distant cousin, and that we had known each other in New York. Since the idioms of kinship and coethnicity were frequently used by both Haitians and Dominicans to conceptualize, express, and congeal relationships that implied mutually recognized rights and obligations, my mistaken identity was not at all extraordinary.

His documents faxed, Gérard bought two beers and we took seats in front of a *colmado* next to the town plaza. Gérard had arranged for his son to meet him there after school, where they would catch the bus to *la pulga* (from the Spanish word for "flea"), the secondhand clothing market in Andrés. *La pulga* was organized by Haitian women who rented stalls in the central market in Andrés and processed bales of used clothing shipped by truck from Haiti. Moments later, a man came rushing toward us, distraught and with a woman's purse dangling from his hand. It was Jean Paul, a Haitian man of about thirty whom I had met the summer before.

In a fury, Jean Paul recounted how a mutual acquaintance, a Haitian woman, had stolen 1,200 pesos from him. In his account the woman had offered to rent him a room in the building where she was living but then absconded with his money. Only moments earlier Jean Paul had confronted Marlene in a restaurant on Calle Duarte. When Marlene refused to return his money, Jean Paul snatched the purse containing her passport. In the ensuing melee, Marlene was detained by the police and Jean Paul slipped away.

Jean Paul wanted Gérard to go with him to the police station to file a complaint against Marlene, arguing that the latter's command of Spanish and ambiguous identity would work in his favor. Gérard agreed, and, once his son had arrived, we headed for the police station across the plaza. Midway there Gérard stopped and told Jean Paul that filing a complaint would be a bad idea because the police treated Haitians badly. *"Ravet pa janm gen rezon devan poul"* (Roaches are never right when facing chickens), he told us. The legal procedure would only raise suspicions about both parties. Instead Gérard left his son with Jean Paul and asked me to go with him to the station.

We approached the side entrance to the squat lime green building, which opened onto an interior courtyard that also served as a holding pen. On weekends the courtyard would often be filled to capacity with sex workers, *motoconchos,* and others detained during the course of identity checks. It was now empty, and Gérard spotted a sergeant he recognized crossing the courtyard with a stack of papers tucked under his arm.

"*Primo*" (Cousin, a familiar term of address), Gérard called to the sergeant. The officer approached and looked us over. Gérard told him that there was a little problem that he needed help resolving.

"Two Haitians that I know," he explained, "are having a small conflict that I would like to settle without bothering the police. Something minor and not worth much trouble." Máximo Gómez was now speaking.

"OK, tell me," the sergeant replied, seeming impatient.

"Is there a *negrita* [black woman], a Haitian, in the station named Marlene?"

"No, there are no Haitians here," the sergeant replied and walked away.

Gérard, it seemed, wanted to know whether Marlene had been arrested or had filed a complaint of her own. By marking Marlene as a *negrita* and a Haitian, Gérard had positioned himself as a Dominican on the side of the law, demonstrating his skill at manipulating the linguistic and visual cues by which people recognized ethnic identities.

As we returned to the plaza, Gérard explained to me that Marlene had only arrived from Haiti the month before and was working as a hostess at a discotheque. Marlene, he said, had probably used the money to pay her own rent since she had approached him the week before to borrow money. "She robbed Jean Paul to pay Peter," he quipped, pleased with his twist of the phrase.

With his son in tow, we headed for a small side street where a group of Haitian painters displayed their work. Gérard wanted to find out where Marlene was now living. Dozens of paintings were fastened to a cinder-block wall. Three painters were working on canvases propped up on improvised easels. Others were having their midday meal, which had been prepared over an open fire.

These painters worked independently and were not affiliated with the tourist galleries on Calle Duarte. The gallery painters received 40 to 50 percent of the sale price of their paintings, depending on their skill and on the volume of sales. The balance was paid as a commission to the

27. Toto, a Haitian painter, working at a gallery on Calle Duarte. Photo by the author.

Dominican gallery owners. The independent painters were spared the commission fees but had to collectively (and unofficially) pay the police 5,000 pesos per month for the use of the public space. Whereas gallery affiliation provided some protection from police identity checks and deportation, the independents were vulnerable to the caprice of the authorities.

Gérard asked the painters about Marlene. One pointed to a low-budget hostel up the road where many transient Haitian workers stayed. Gérard then began telling the story of Marlene's theft to the dozen or so painters who had gathered around us.

"This was not money that he was going to use to buy fancy clothes," Gérard said, "or to go out and party, or buy rum. Do you understand? This was money for a place to live, money to buy food." The painters nodded in agreement and glanced at Jean Paul who was standing with his arms crossed, looking angry and injured.

"I know that Marlene has problems," Gérard continued. "All Haitians in this country have problems. But she was wrong to rob from a Haitian." "This man," he said, pointing to Jean Paul, "has come to this country to work just like her, to feed his family. What is he going to do now? Do you under*stand?* He has no place to live."

The painters discussed the problem among themselves as Gérard inspected the contents of the purse. He then turned to me. "Steven," he said casually in Kreyòl, "give him the money." Taken aback, I hesitated before handing 1,200 pesos to Jean Paul. The matter settled, Gérard left with his son for Andrés and I went home.

Later that evening I stopped at Gérard's apartment. He had invited me for dinner and had prepared *lambi criolla,* conch stewed in a tomato-based sauce. Hassim, who had just turned eight, was busy setting the table.

"Hassim," Gérard said in English, "you always put the fork on the left side of the plate and the knife and the spoon on the right."

"Cómo?" Hassim replied.

"Oh! What's the matter? You speak English. Don't be shy. He's from New York like me. *Fouchèt la,*" Gérard added, supplying the Kreyól word for "fork."

While we were eating, Gérard explained that he never spoke Spanish with Hassim, only Kreyòl and English. "This way, if we go to England or to Haiti, he won't have problems in school, adapting to the way things are over there."

"But I like to speak Spanish," Hassim protested in English.

"But you're Haitian too," Gérard replied in Kreyòl. "Your mother was Haitian, your father is Haitian. Even though you live in this country, your roots are in Haiti."

After dinner I asked Gérard why he had decided against going to Marlene's house to collect the money. Questions seemed to irritate him, as if they were disturbing intrusions into the smooth transactions of everyday life. Gérard preferred to leave things unsaid, communicating with actions and through the manipulation of context rather than with words.

"There was no point," Gérard replied, "Marlene doesn't have it. But now everyone in Boca Chica knows what she did." He switched to Krèyol to express an annoying thought. "Brother, that's what happens here. Haitians come to this country and they forget where they've come from. She'll pay back the money—this month, next month, whatever. And then I'll give her back the passport."

Gérard reached into his pocket and handed me the 1,200 pesos that I had earlier given to Jean Paul.

"But why did you ask me to give him the money?" I asked.

He paused as if he had given it no thought. "See, I wanted those Haitians to see *you* give him the money. Do you understand me? This way, when they see you walking down the street, they'll know who you are because, in this place, you've got to have people watching your back. Believe me I know."

Gérard's mise-en-scène was an object lesson in the ethics of solidarity and reciprocity that informed the social relations and exchanges among Haitians in Boca Chica. Though not peculiar to the Haitian community, this sense of communal, ethical obligation took on urgency in a context in which Haitians lacked citizenship rights and access to state institutions. Rather than pursue legal action or confront Marlene directly, Gérard appealed to a sense of justice that, rooted in ethnic solidarity and enforced through gossip, would shame Marlene into making things right. By prompting me in public to compensate Jean Paul, Gérard had injected me, however tenuously, into the web of reciprocally reckoned rights, obligations, and exchanges that shaped social relations among Haitians in particular and the laboring poor in general.

In the months that followed, I learned that Gérard was recognized as an honest broker in the settling of disputes in the Haitian community and between Haitians and Dominicans. Once, for example, the Dominican owner of a gift shop called out to Gérard as we were walking down the street and asked him to intervene in a dispute that he was having with a Haitian employee. The employee believed that he should have received the mandatory Christmas bonus of one month's salary that was paid to permanent employees under Dominican labor regulations. The shop's owner argued that the Haitian was not entitled to the bonus because, at the time, he had not completed the three-month probationary period. Gérard supported the employer's position but added that he should have given the Haitian worker "a little something to sweeten things."

Gérard had also helped new arrivals from Haiti to find jobs and housing and loaned money for rent and other expenses; he had the reputation of a *gwo nèg,* or big man. When he had money Gérard spent it freely and ostentatiously in Boca Chica's restaurants, bars, and nightclubs, often treating groups of friends to a night on the town. For many, Haitians and Dominicans alike, Gérard's lifestyle was emblematic of success in the fast-paced, multilingual tourism economy, where image, acumen, and, above all, interpersonal finesse were prized possessions.

RACE, LABOR, AND THE CULTURAL POLITICS OF HAITIAN IDENTITY

Though there were no estimates of the size of the Haitian population in Andrés–Boca Chica, most agreed that it was significant in comparison to surrounding areas because of the relatively large number of Haitians working in the construction, tourism, and (declining) sugar industries. The older and more settled population—first-, second-, and third-generation—associated with Ingenio Boca Chica and its cane fields was dispersed throughout Andrés, Boca Chica, and squatter settlements north of the highway. Most had entered the country as seasonal cane cutters. Transient workers, in contrast, tended to live in predominantly Haitian hostels. Haitian-Dominican intermarriage was not unheard of, especially among Dominicans and Dominican-born Haitians.

For example, Claude Delalou, the son of a cane cutter, had been born in Batey Esperanza in the sugar-producing province of La Vega Real. In the mid-1980s, at the age of nineteen, Claude left the *batey* and migrated to Boca Chica, where he had heard that there was construction work for people who were *sin papeles.* The late 1980s and the 1990s were a boom period for Boca Chica's construction industry, and many small and mid-sized hotels and housing complexes were constructed, along with the Boca Chica and Don Juan resorts. Claude married a Dominican woman who worked as a housekeeper for a small hotel, and the couple rented a wood-frame house in Andrés. The household was soon joined by his wife's mother and younger brother, and the couple had two children. In 2001, at the age of thirty-four, Claude was still working as a day laborer, but the couple owned two motorcycles that they rented out for 200 pesos per day to *motoconchos.* To ensure that both children received birth certificates, Claude's wife had returned to her natal town in the Cibao to give birth.

There was also a sizable more transient population of Haitians migrants who worked as day laborers in the construction industry, tourism-related occupations, and as traders and domestics. Among them were Haitians who had entered the country legally on renewable work visas and undocumented workers who had arrived *anba fil,* or illegally, "under the wire." Many of these workers were circular migrants, traveling back and forth between Boca Chica and Haiti in response to job opportunities, living costs, and political conditions on both sides of the border (Martínez 1995). Marlene, for example, had quit her job at the Megatex garment factory in Port-au-Prince before arriving in Boca Chica on a three-month work visa in search of a better-paying job. At Megatex, a contractor for the Walt Disney Company, Marlene had earned 36 gourdes (about US $2.20) for an eight-hour day. Marlene's sister, a bartender at the Laser Discotheque, had emigrated to Boca Chica the year before and secured Marlene a job as a hostess at the same club.

Much has been written about the status of Haitian migrant workers and, more generally, people of Haitian descent in the Dominican Republic, and their condition has attracted the attention of human rights advocates and organizations. Dominican attitudes about Haitians (and, inseparably, racial identity) are diverse, rooted in the Republic's history and integration into the international capitalist economy and shaped by class-*cum*-culture evaluations. The Ur moment in the elite construction of *anti-haitianismo* (anti-Haitianism) was the 1822 invasion of the Spanish colony of Santo Domingo by Haiti under President Jean-Pierre Boyer. Anxious over reports of an impending French invasion (the third since independence), the Haitians reasoned that France would use Santo Domingo as a base of operations, and they were wary that Spain would remain neutral in the ensuing conflict (Moya Pons 1995). With Haitian encouragement and support, pro-Haitian elements in the Dominican border towns of Dajabón and Montecristi declared their independence from Spain on November 15, 1821, and appealed to the Haitian government for arms and protection.

In Santo Domingo a group of conspirators led by Licenciado José Núñez de Cáceres, lieutenant governor of Santo Domingo, had been planning the overthrow of Spanish rule on their own with the intention of allying with Simón Bolívar's La Gran Colombia. Alarmed by the pro-Haitian rebellion in the west, the plotters took action, and on November 30, 1821, troops loyal to Cáceres captured the fortress of Santo Domingo, imprisoned the Spanish governor, and declared their independence from Spain.

Although Cáceres had expected Haiti to recognize the new government in Santo Domingo, Boyer argued the impossibility of maintaining two independent governments on the island and, consequently, informed Cáceres of Haiti's intention to unify the island to safeguard its independence. Lacking the political and military resources to oppose the Haitians, Cáceres accepted the protection of the Republic of Haiti. On February 9, 1822, a Haitian army arrived in Santo Domingo, and Jean-Pierre Boyer assumed the presidency of the unified island.

After defeating an ill-equipped French invasion force in Samaná, Boyer implemented agrarian reform policies that sought to redistribute *terrenos comuneros* (much of which were under the titular control of émigrés and the Catholic Church) and to stimulate commercial agricultural production among the peasantry (Moya Pons 1995). These reforms were resisted by both peasants and landholders on both sides of the island, and, on March 13, 1843, Boyer was overthrown by a coalition headed by General

Charles Hérard and based in Ley Cayes, Haiti. In Santo Domingo opposition to Haitian rule gathered steam among La Trinitaria, a secret pro-independence society headed by Juan Pablo Duarte. After suffering some setbacks, on February 28, 1844, the Trinitarios staged a successful insurrection and proclaimed the birth of the Dominican Republic.

After independence, Dominican nationalists aimed to fashion a national identity against the persisting Haitian threat—one that emphasized the new republic's Hispanic, rather than African, origins and its racial distinctiveness from black Haiti. Immigration policies in the new republic applied stringent controls on nonwhite entrants as part of a broader scheme to whiten and "improve" the Dominican gene pool (Gavigan 1995; Sagás 2002). Importantly, as Torres-Saillant (1998) has noted, Dominican racial identities and ideologies were structured as the newly independent nation was being integrated into an economic system dominated by the United States and Europe, where "white supremacy" was long-standing and firmly entrenched (see also Derby 1994).

U.S. Secretary of State John C. Calhoun, for example, argued for the recognition of the new republic in 1844 as a means to thwart "the further spread of negro influence in the West Indies," and Torres-Saillant (1998: 127) has noted that throughout the nineteenth century U.S. officials and commentators conceived of the Dominican population as "other than black." "It is not inconceivable," Torres-Saillant observed, "that the texture of negrophobic and anti-Haitian, nationalist discourse sponsored by official spokespersons in the Dominican state drew significantly on North American sources dating back to the first years of the republic" (129).

Anti-Haitianism both informed and was embodied in the structuring of the division of labor in the Dominican sugar economy, which reached an industrial scale of production during the 1870s. By 1900 the sugar industry was reliant on seasonal migrant labor, brought in first from the Lesser Antilles and later from the Republic of Haiti (Martínez 1995). Ernesto Sagás (2002) has pointed out that the introduction of Haitian migrant labor was advocated by the United States to satisfy labor shortages on the largely U.S.-owned sugar estates, against the wishes of many Dominican Nationalists (see also Martínez 1995). However, it was not until 1920 that the number of Haitian sugar estate workers equaled that of West Indians.

U.S. influence in the Dominican Republic, culminating with the military intervention in 1916, shaped the process of Dominican state formation. Lauren Derby (1994) has pointed out that the Dominican-American Convention of 1907, which gave the United States receivership over

Dominican customs duties, prompted the demarcation of the hitherto porous frontier as U.S. authorities clamped down on transborder contraband. This "Americanization" of the border, supported by a host of border control legislation, incited a differentiation of the heterogeneous frontier population with respect to formal citizenship, language, and "invisible codes of difference," which could be opportunistically invoked in anti-Haitian discourses (Derby 1994: 502). "As the border was brought into the gaze of the state," Derby has observed, "the border began to be seen as the skin of the body politic but one all too frequently seen by capitalist elites as bleeding into Haiti" (500). That the borderlands economy was oriented toward Haiti and dominated by Haitian merchants, many of whom were women, gave rise to a gendered valuation of the Haitian threat according to which Haitians were seen "as the very embodiment of money magic" and as "social filth"—a threat to both the integrity of the economy and the body politic (489). This unstable, polysemic construction of Haitians as possessing a mystical, hence illegitimate, economic agency—one coded as aggressively female—informed elite interpretations of the Haitian presence in Andrés–Boca Chica as well.

When General Trujillo took power as dictator in 1930, tens of thousands of Haitians were living as peasants and traders along the vague border with Haiti—a border that had been resolved only in 1929—and working on the sugar estates in the interior of the Republic. In the Trujillo-era nationalist imaginary, the Haitian threat was transposed from that of a military invasion to that of an *invasión pacífica* (peaceful invasion), and a host of legislative attempts were made to suppress Haitian migration and evict migrants (Martínez 1995: 44). In October 1937 Trujillo proclaimed that the presence of Haitians in the border provinces would no longer be tolerated and decreed further that all those who remained would be exterminated. In the days that followed, Trujillo let loose the *corte* (mowing down) of Haitians in the border regions and the northern Cibao Valley, which resulted in the massacre of as many as twenty-five thousand men, women, and children by the Dominican army and paramilitary forces (Martínez 1995).

In the wake of the massacre, the Trujillo dictatorship embarked on a renewed negrophobic, anti-Haitian campaign that infiltrated public education and other Dominican institutions. Haitian labor contracting continued, though not without interruption, after the assassination of Trujillo in 1961, ending only with the overthrow of the regime of Jean Paul Duvalier in 1986. In its final years, contract migration brought about twenty thousand seasonal workers a year to the Dominican Republic for the sugar harvest (Martínez 1995).

Official anxieties and discourses concerning an *invasión pacífica* persisted throughout the post-Trujillo era. In June 1991 President Balaguer oversaw the expulsion of six thousand Haitian migrants and persons of Haitian descent, and the resulting "pogrom-type atmosphere" provoked the departure of another twenty-five thousand (Corten and Duarte 1995: 97). Further waves of expulsions occurred in 1996, 1997, and 1999. During the period of my fieldwork, "the Haitian question" was continually in the news. For example, in a 1999 article Máximo Díaz, director general of migration, recognized the nation's dependence on Haitian labor but assured readers that the government would never permit the presence of Haitian workers in tourism and in the free trade zones, the growth areas of the Dominican economy (*Listín Diario,* August 18, 1999, 20A).

"AN AFRICAN THING": HAITIANS AND THE SOCIAL DIVISION OF LABOR

Although Haitian migration over the past century and a half had been driven by the labor needs of the sugar industry, Haitian migrants increasingly found work in construction *and* tourism-related services. In Boca Chica Haitian workers were clustered in gendered occupational niches, which, paradoxically, instantiated elite views concerning the quality and value of Haitian labor—assessments that had been shaped by their exploitation as cane cutters and elite attitudes toward race. For example, most, if not all, of the women who braided hair on the beach were of Haitian descent. They marketed their services primarily to foreign tourists (the Bo Derek beach look), charging from 500 to 1,000 pesos to braid an entire head and often working cooperatively as a means to distribute income. One of the hair braiders, Solange Saint Paul, worked in concert with two other women with whom she shared a room. If any of the three women found a customer, the others would assist her in the time-consuming task, each receiving 25 percent of the fee. All three women had been born in the *bateyes* and were without papers.

Dominicans with whom I spoke shared the view that hair braiding was a skill and style peculiar to Haitians, one linked to their ethnic/racial identity. Danilda, a Dominican woman who cut my hair, explained to me, "Dominican women don't wear their hair like that. It's a style that is Haitian. It's not Dominican. It's, I don't know, an African thing. For a Dominican woman, it would be difficult to do." Danilda's remarks sug-

28. Anti-Haitian graffiti in Boca Chica ("Haitians Get Out with [President] Hipólito"). Photo by the author.

gest that hair braiding expresses an aesthetic that is African in origin and, therefore, external to Dominican society. The statement "It's, I don't know, an African thing" situated style and skill in ancestral origins and in an essentialized reading of Haitian identity—a transposition from cultural to racial identity that was marked by the disavowal, "I don't know."

Haitian women also maintained that hair braiding was a technique best performed by Haitians but attributed this to cultural and aesthetic, rather than racial, distinctiveness. Few hair braiders straightened or "relaxed" their hair, and Haitian women often criticized what they perceived as the Dominican obsession with *pelo fino* (fine, i.e., straight, hair). "I am content with who I am," one braider told me. "I don't want to change my hair with chemicals to look like somebody else." Most Haitian women wore their hair "natural," whether braided, tied into a variety of buns, or woven into extension braids—a practice that also gestured to African-influenced, African American hairstyles. However, Dominican attitudes regarding hairstyles were not monolithic. As noted in chapter 4, women of Dominican descent often adopted hairstyles associated with black women in the African Diaspora, gesturing both to a transnational sense of style and to an unconventional, if not stigmatized, racial and cultural identity.

The increasing numbers of visitors and tourists of Dominican descent

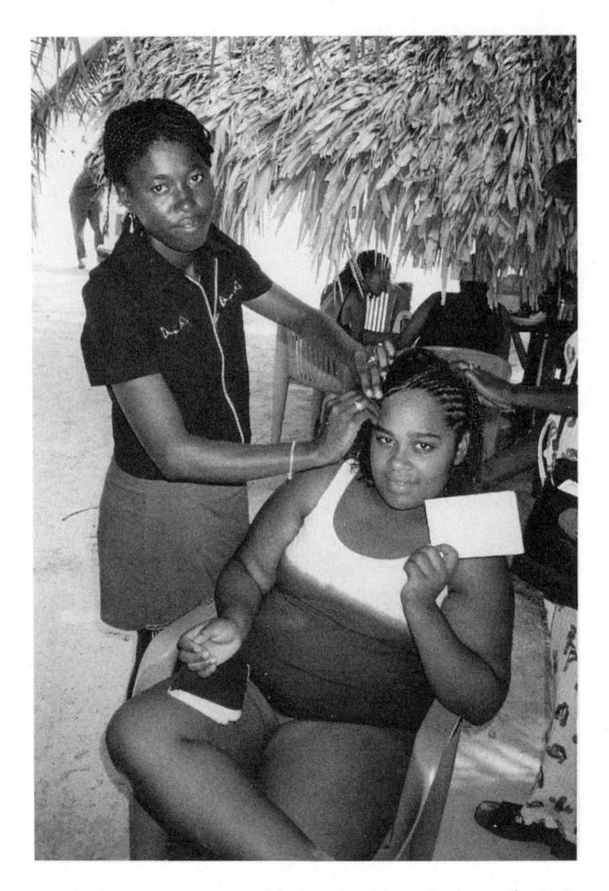

29. A Haitian woman and helper braiding the hair of a U.S. citizen of Dominican descent on the western, "Dominican end" of the beach. Photo by the author.

to the Republic has also had an important influence on how Dominicans think about racial identity in general and style in particular (see Torres-Saillant 1998). A seventeen-year-old, New York–born tourist of Dominican descent told me, "Me, I don't see myself as being, I don't know, an *india* [Indian, but in this context copper-toned], or whatever. I see myself as black. People over there [i.e., New York] think different than they do here. For example, I like merengue and bachata but not all the time. Not every day. I also listen to rap 'cause I like that style."

Similarly, Haitian painters were often described to me as possessing a style that was uniquely Haitian, and few, if any, painters in Boca Chica were not of Haitian descent. A Dominican salesman who worked at the largest gallery in town once assured me that the Haitian painters had all attended the same "art academy" in Port-au-Prince, which accounted for their trademark motifs and technical skills. This belief, shared by many, was unfounded. In fact, most Haitian painters learned their trade in the Dominican Republic. Once again, it was racial identity—the association with a black, African past—that gave rise to the notion of a "natural" Haitian aesthetic and technical skill and, as a result, yielded a racialized labor niche within the tourism economy.

A Dominican gallery owner told me that the motifs foreign tourists desired tended to be scenes that, paradoxically, were not characteristic of the Dominican Republic. When I asked him to explain, he pointed to an example of one of the most popular motifs: a highly stylized market scene depicting a dozen or so market women, rendered black in silhouette, squatting among their baskets (see figure 27).

"But there are markets in this country, aren't there?" I asked.

"Of course, but they are not like this one. This type of market you would only see in Haiti or in Africa—black women *(morenas)* with their baskets, and the style of dress, sitting on the ground.[6] But the tourists like this style."

"But what about this one?" I asked, pointing to an unpopulated sunset, with palm trees and a boat in silhouette.

"No, that's different. But, you understand, the Haitians have a vision, a perspective that is unique." He drew his finger along the trunk of a palm tree. "That's why there are few Dominicans who paint like this—only Haitians and *rayanos* [pejorative term for Dominicans of Haitian ancestry]. Of course, Dominican painters exist in the country, but they do not work like this, in this style."

The notion that there was a marketable and essentially Haitian style that only Haitians could execute was so pervasive that Haitian men, hoping to cross the border, sometimes carried paints, brushes, and canvases in order to improve their prospects with border officials.

There were also Haitian niches within the social division of labor that were not directly figured by elite constructions of Haitian identity or the desire of foreign tourists. Many tourism-related businesses in Boca Chica employed Haitians in positions where multilingualism was necessary for interacting profitably with tourists, for example, as touts for restaurants and tour companies, as salespersons in gift shops, and as hostesses in bars and nightclubs. Haitians employed in these jobs were typically

Haitian born and high school graduates competent in Spanish, French, and English and therefore able to communicate with a wider public—and at lower wages than their Dominican counterparts.[7]

For example, Eddie Dorsainville worked in 1999–2000 for the Coral Hamaca Beach Hotel and Casino, soliciting tourists to attend sales presentations for time-shares. Equipped with a photo album of the hotel's facilities, Eddie would sway tourists to visit the Hamaca and meet with a time-share salesperson. If the tourist remained at the aggressive sales pitch for at least one hour, Eddie was paid 200 pesos. On a good day Eddie could earn from 400 to 600 pesos. The Hamaca sales positions were considered by Haitians the best legal jobs available to them, in terms of both compensation and the respect workers received from employers and the authorities.

Eddie's tortuous migration experience illuminates the multifaceted "push-pull" factors shaping Haitian migration to the Dominican Republic. He had been born in Port-au-Prince, and he and his two sisters were raised by his widowed mother, who was employed at an FTZ garment factory in Delmas. When his mother could no longer afford his school fees, Eddie dropped out of high school and joined the Haitian army in the midst of the popular revolt that ultimately toppled the regime of Jean Claude Duvalier in 1986. Disaffected by his low wages and by the army's increasing role in the repression of protests, Eddie deserted in 1985. Soon afterward, a friend told him that there was better-paying work in the Dominican Republic, and Eddie decided to go.

"But my problem was money," he explained as we sat at a table at Hostal Zapata. "I only had 25 gourdes. But then my friend told me, 'Hey Eddie, I just had a dream. And in my dream a stranger came to me and gave me 50 centimes.' My friend told me that whenever he had this dream someone he knew won the lottery. So I played the lottery for 10 gourdes and won 50. I played again, and I won 50 Haitian dollars. I gave 10 dollars to my friend as a commission and kept 40. Then I knew that my future was in the Dominican Republic."

At this point in the interview, a waiter at the hotel approached us and asked Eddie to leave. Although I was staying at Zapata's hotel and had bought beers for the two of us, he insisted that Eddie leave. Zapata intervened and told the waiter to leave us alone.

"You see," Eddie said to me. "It is because I am black, and Haitian. They don't want me here because they think that it looks bad to the guests."

Though we were nonplussed by the rude interruption, we continued the interview.

"I didn't have the intention to paint. But my friend told me that I needed something in my hand, a business. So I bought five cans of paint, I bought wood and canvas, and then I called another friend who used to paint and told him, 'Hey, man, I want you to show me how to do this. I want to be a painter. I need something in my hand so they will let me pass at the border.'

"My friend made one painting for me and told me to do it the same way. He showed me how to make palm trees, and the sky—how to use the brush. I made one painting, it wasn't bad. I made another, it wasn't good. But I tried. I made four paintings and then packed my tools in a bag and went to the border."

Eddie reached Anse-à-Pitres, a Haitian border town on the south coast of the island, which was reputed to be a "soft border," without a formal immigration post. However, lacking a Haitian passport or 500 pesos to bribe the Dominican guards, Eddie was stopped at the border. After two months in Anse-à-Pitres, his savings exhausted, Eddie joined a convoy of Haitian cane cutters being formed by labor contractors (more than likely, one of the last) in Anse-à-Pitres and crossed with them to Pedernales on the Dominican side of the border.

"I spent the night in Pedernales. But in the morning they made us form a line so that the police could check everybody's hands to see if they had cut cane before. When they got to me, they said that my hands were soft and had never done hard work. I had Adidas [sneakers] on my feet and Levis jeans. So they didn't believe that I knew how to cut sugar. They said to me, 'Hey, you haven't come here to cut sugar. What kind of job did you do in Haiti.' I told them that I was a painter and showed them the paintings.

"They said that they didn't care about painting and that if I wanted to stay in the Dominican Republic I would have to cut sugar. So, I said 'OK, I will cut sugar.' They took me to Sabana Grande [in La Vega Real]. When I got there, I looked around me and there was sugar everywhere—only sugar. I had no money left, just 10 pesos. They gave me a machete and some food. And they gave me a stone to make the machete sharp.

"I knew that I wasn't going to stay there. But my friend told me, 'If you try to get away and they catch you, you will have trouble. They will put you in jail and beat you.' And then my friend showed me how to cut sugar. How to cut the head first and then cut the rest of the cane. He said

30. Eddie Dorsainville at work in front of the Coral Hamaca Beach Hotel and Casino. Photo by the author.

to me, 'First you work slow, and then, when you have the skill, you can cut faster and make more money.' But I needed money. So I started to cut the sugar fast and, on the first day, I cut my leg. I stayed there five days, maybe six.

"Then I met a Haitian who lived in San Francisco de Macorís. He said to me, 'Eddie, if you speak English and French, you can go to Puerto Plata or Sosúa where the tourists come, and you can make money. Don't stay here, because you can't do this job.' So I sold my paintings to this man for 300 pesos and went to Puerto Plata."

Desperate for money, Eddie found work in Puerto Plata as a cement mixer for a construction company. Working twelve hours a day, seven days a week, Eddie earned 900 pesos (US $56) a week. After saving for six months, Eddie quit the job, bought new clothes, and went to Susúa, a popular tourist destination not far from Puerto Plata.

"In Sosúa I met a Dominican who owned a gift shop, and he needed someone to work with him who could speak English. The man wanted to test me, but he didn't speak English. So he told another Haitian guy who was there to speak English to me.

'OK,' he said to the Haitian guy, 'talk to this man in English. I want to see how well he speaks.' But the Haitian guy started talking to me in Kreyòl, not in English. He mixed it with English words like, 'My friend, I want to talk to you.' That was all he knew! But the Dominican guy gave me the job."

Eddie worked at the gift shop for two years and then found a job soliciting tourists for tours offered by a French-owned hotel in Sosúa. Eddie married a Haitian woman who sold used clothing at a market in Puerto Plata. However, in 1991 Eddie was arrested by the police in a migration sweep and deported to Haiti. Back in Haiti, Eddie's sister, by then a schoolteacher, gave him US $100 to buy new clothes, obtain a passport, and pay the US $40 fee required for a Dominican visa. In 1992 Eddie returned to Puerta Plata, once again by way of Pedernales but this time with documents. Despite his legal status, Eddie and other Haitians in Sosúa were routinely jailed by the police and required to pay bribes for their release. In 1997 Eddie and his family moved to Boca Chica, where, as he put it, "the police were quieter."

Despite his troubles, Eddie counted among the elite of Haitian workers who were able to use their linguistic skills and education in relatively stable jobs. However, in general, Haitians were systematically excluded from occupations in which multilingualism might also have been viewed as an advantage, such as in restaurants and hotel service jobs.[8] What the service jobs held by Haitians had in common was that they located the worker at the spatial and symbolic fringe of commerce and its core transactions. Touts, for example, worked in the public streets and were rarely given responsibilities that brought them into the interior of businesses. Jean Paul worked as a tout for a French-owned restaurant that was popular among French-speaking tourists. When the restaurant's owner decided to open a bar in the courtyard, Jean Paul asked for the bartender job and was rejected. Instead the owner hired a Dominican who spoke neither French nor English. Infuriated, Jean Paul told me, "It's because I'm black, because I'm Haitian that they don't want me in their restaurant." As salespersons, Haitians typically negotiated the sale but were not permitted to execute the transaction; instead they had to bring the customer to the Dominican owner or employee, who completed the transaction.

The exclusion of Haitians from the interior of commerce was, as Jean Paul noted, firmly rooted in racial and ethnic prejudices. In fact, when I asked the restaurant's owner why Jean Paul would not have been suitable for the bartender's job, he replied, "It would be bad for business to have a Haitian working inside." This exclusion iterated hegemonic notions about the character of Haitian labor that, shaped by historic patterns of Haitian labor exploitation, were shared by Dominican elites and expatriates alike.

Many people viewed Haitians as crafty, aggressive, and ruthless in their economic pursuits—assessments that resonated with earlier constructions of Haitian agency in the borderlands studied by Derby (1994). The observation that Haitians would work "like slaves" in the cane fields and in the construction industry was often cited as evidence to support the claim that, as a policeman told me, "Haitians would do anything for money, even sell their own children." This evaluation fed the claim, often voiced by elites and police, that the scores of Haitian children who worked as beggars and shoeshine boys in Boca Chica (the so-called *palomos,* or pigeons) had been dispatched from the *bateyes* by their unscrupulous parents to earn money. From this perspective, Haitians were well suited for the multilingual and cross-cultural negotiations required to inveigle foreign tourists—a no-man's-land of alterity and cunning—but not appropriate for *interior* commercial functions that required *confianza* (trust) and were constitutive of tourism's "atmosphere."

In this way historically forged constructions of Haitian racial identity and labor power conditioned their modes of entry and locations within Boca Chica's social division of labor, marginalizing most to the informal economy but permitting the crystallization of racialized, occupational niches within the tourism economy—locations where exotic constructions of blackness could turn a profit. In fact, it was the desire of foreign tourists for "authentic" and racialized tokens of the Caribbean experience that generated the demand for braided hair and the Haitian painterly aesthetic.

Haitian workers were not unaware of this paradox: the copresence of a tourism industry that thrived on racialized constructions of the exotic and an elite ideology that coded blackness and Haitian identity as radically Other and external to the nation. In fact, some Haitians mined this "imagined geography," as Edward Said (1978) called it, to accentuate their differences vis-à-vis Dominican society. Haitian painters, for example, often spoke of their skills as deriving from their *konesans,* which, in Kreyòl, conveyed a sense of secular *and* spiritual knowledge or force. I once overheard a Haitian painter pitch his work to a group of foreign tourists by claiming that he had descended from a long line of *houngan* (vodún priests) and that this accounted for his artistic inspiration and unique style. Although Haitians never painted vodún-related motifs, many people—gallery owners included—believed that their skills were, in part, mystically inspired.

Moreover, many Haitians, especially young workers in the informal economy, inhabited styles of blackness that stretched beyond and challenged elite constructions of Haitian cultural and racial identity. Like their black-identified, Dominican counterparts, Haitians practiced styles of dress, language usage, and musical taste that were influenced by globally mediated hip hop cultures as well as by Jamaican Rastafarian cultural practices. Like Gérard, Haitian workers frequently sampled the lyrics of rap and reggae songs to articulate their views concerning racism and other injustices and to inhabit a wider, diasporic identity and political culture.

For example, on the night that Jean Paul argued with his French boss over the bartending job, I encountered him in front of the restaurant, incensed and recounting his predicament in Spanish to a group of *motoconchos*. At the end of the story, he code-switched to English and recited lyrics from Bob Marley's "Redemption Song." "Emancipate yourselves from mental slavery," he told them, pointing to his head, "none but ourselves can free our minds." Then, continuing in Spanish, Jean Paul explained. "That man can't keep me down, because my mind is free. No one has the power to take my mind." Arms crossed, the *motoconchos* nodded their heads in solemn agreement.

If, as Torres-Saillant (1998: 140) has argued, blackness in the Dominican Republic historically has been "relegated to the realm of the foreign," and this has served to deracialize the consciousness of Dominicans of African descent, then the cultural practices of some Haitians and black Dominicans, insinuated with the mass-mediated cultural forms of the African Diaspora, contested the externality of blackness to the Dominican Republic and its conflation with stigmatized constructions of Haitian cultural identity. In this respect, informality constituted a cultural space of rebellion within the social division of labor—a sociospatial field within which workers eluded, critiqued, and resisted modes of discipline and governance directed at their labor power and their subjectivity.

Appadurai (1996: 199) has called attention to the cultural dynamics of deterritorialization—to the loosening of attachments between locality and the process of cultural reproduction that has accompanied transnational and often mass-mediated flows of "images, ideas and opportunities that come from elsewhere." For people of Haitian descent, the sampling of African American, Rastafarian, and other cultural practices and identities was both an exercise of a black diasporic imaginary and a modality of practice through which they subverted, complicated, and contested the conflation of Haitian identity with stigmatized blackness. It would be this *politics* of the imagination that would become the focal point of Gérard's life in the months to come.

THE BODY IN DISPUTE

> Illness is the night-side of life, a more onerous citizenship. Everyone who is born holds dual citizenship, in the kingdom of the well and in the kingdom of the sick.
>
> Susan Sontag

> *Pueblo pequeño, infierno grande.* (Small town, a hell of gossip.)
>
> Dominican proverb

During my first two months in Boca Chica, I spent a great deal of time with Gérard and would often accompany him on the loosely structured tours that he arranged for tourists. My cachet as an anthropologist enhanced the marketability of his excursions, and he would often have me explain aspects of Dominican culture that he knew much better than I. Gérard maintained an international network of clients—from the United States, France, Canada, and elsewhere—who were frequent visitors to the Dominican Republic and who recommended his services to others. Typically, Gérard met his clients at the airport, arranged car rental and hotel, and served as driver and guide during their visits.

Beyond expenses, Gérard charged a per diem fee ranging between 1,000 and 1,500 pesos (about US $60–$95) and collected 5 percent commissions from hotels, gift shops, and other businesses where he brokered transactions. Gérard's business networks in the capital were extensive, as were his contacts with tourism-related concerns in Puerto Plata, Juan Dolio, La Romana, and other tourist destinations.

Once I accompanied him on a trip to the capital with three African

American men from Miami, a music producer and two entertainment-industry lawyers. The men were representative of a growing number of predominantly male, African American tourists who visited Boca Chica in 2001, a result, in part, of the network-building work of Gérard and others in the informal economy. We spent the day in the Zona Colonial, where the men went on a shopping spree along El Conde, stopping in cigar stores and shops that specialized in amber jewelry. Gérard served as translator and negotiated prices with merchants. At one point, growing impatient with their protracted shopping, Gérard said to me, "These guys have so much money they don't know what they want to do."

Over time, my relationship with Gérard began to cool. For his part, I suspect that the novelty of our relationship had begun to wear off and that my constant queries had become distracting, if not irritating. Gérard also owed me a sizable sum of money, and it seemed that he was avoiding me. Money had become an issue in our relationship. One day, for example, Gérard borrowed 3,000 pesos from me to renew his Haitian passport and fix his car. However, when he returned from the capital, he told me that the Haitian consulate was closed; instead he bought a pool cue.

I was less concerned with the money than with the ambiguity of our relationship and, more to the point, the nagging feeling that he was treating me more as a client than as a friend. It was common among the working poor to loan, borrow, and make gifts of money, services, and goods to address needs and cultivate exchange-based relationships with others. In the context of the informal economy, these exchanges constituted transactional networks and bonds of trust among people whose livelihoods required the maintenance of an extensive web of economically significant relationships.

Once, for example, I ate dinner with Gérard at Cheche's *comedor,* a family-owned restaurant around the corner from where we lived. When I went to pay the bill, Gérard stopped me and explained that the food was a commission, paid to him by Cheche for bringing foreign tourists to the restaurant. "When you are with me, you don't have to pay," he said. Gérard maintained similar commission-based relationships with merchants, vendors, bar and restaurant owners, and sex workers to whom he brought clients. "When I have tourists here," Gérard explained, "I take them around town, to a gift shop here, or to a restaurant there, or maybe for a massage so that everybody gets a piece of the action. And then, when I need business, they bring things my way. What goes around comes around."

Within these exchange networks, the granting of a loan or a gift to someone in need was considered a moral obligation. In the case of Marlene's theft, Gérard told me that he felt obligated to restore Jean Paul's money, "because he's Haitian, and we do business together." Gérard often brought tourists to the restaurant where Jean Paul worked, and in return the latter referred clients to Gérard's tour business.

My relationship with Gérard was more ambiguous and asymmetrical because the source of my livelihood, like that of the clients for whom he worked, lay elsewhere and was not integrated into his exchange networks. Consequently, although I had the financial resources to address the needs experienced by some, there were few ways that Gérard and others could reciprocate. And I believe that this haunted him as much as it did me, undermining the possibility of deepening our friendship.

For my part, I was also attempting to project my relationships beyond Gérard's social networks and the *zona turística*. For example, I had been spending more time in Andrés with Minaya, the vendor, and with my research assistant who lived there as well. With Milquella's help, I had begun my collaboration with Turivisión. More worrisome, I had heard rumors from a number of sources that Gérard was dealing cocaine. Although skeptical of the rumor, I was concerned that too close an association with Gérard and the racier elements of the informal economy would compromise my research and reputation in other contexts—most notably, among public officials and the police.

Following a two-week trip to New York, I returned to Boca Chica to find Gérard seriously ill. He had lost weight and had what seemed to be a lung infection. In addition, the lymph node on the right side of his neck was dreadfully swollen, which, he told me, made it difficult for him to eat and speak.

During my absence, rumors had begun to circulate that Gérard was suffering from illnesses related to HIV/AIDS. Initially, I took the rumors with a grain of salt as they were often used, along with accusations of drug selling, to stigmatize Haitians and Dominicans who, for whatever reasons, were perceived as *delincuentes* and threats to the tourism economy. Many people, myself included, had suffered through an especially virulent strain of the flu that season, which sometimes produced lung complications. People had named this flu strain *el paquetazo* (the big package) because of its varied symptoms. Like other popularly coined names for earlier flu outbreaks (e.g., the Kosovo flu), the "big package" gestured to current events, in this case, the Mejía administration's stalled effort to overhaul the social security system, labeled *el paquetazo* by the press.

Gérard was aware of the AIDS rumor and complained bitterly about it. "Any time Haitians lose weight in this place," he told me, "people say that they have AIDS. It just shows you how racist they are here." Gérard was also aware that the rumor would make it difficult, if not impossible, for him to work because of the stigma attached to HIV/AIDS and the misinformation concerning its transmission. Finally, he was worried that his health problems would undermine, if not eliminate, his prospect of receiving a British visa; he had not yet taken the required physical examination. It was for these and, perhaps, other reasons that Gérard had chosen not to see a doctor. I learned that he had been medicating himself with a variety over-the-counter antibiotics, based on the assumption that he had pneumonia or, as he later surmised, a kidney infection.

Although there was considerable awareness of the effectiveness of condoms in protecting against sexually transmitted illnesses, especially among sex workers, few people whom I encountered understood the etiology of HIV/AIDS, and that unawareness influenced how people thought about prevention and treatment. Though most people were aware of the sexual behaviors that put one at risk of HIV infection, they often held culturally constructed notions of *who* was at risk.[9] For example, as I was leaving my building one day, Paredes called me over to the repair shop next door to inquire about Gérard's condition. Paredes, about thirty-five years old, worked as a welder at the shop and was an Evangelical Christian and former schoolteacher. Two weeks earlier he had tried to leave the island for Puerto Rico in a *yola,* a small fishing boat. I replied that Gérard seemed about the same—no better and no worse.

"Do you know that five out of every twenty women in Boca Chica have AIDS?" Paredes asked the man whose scooter he was repairing.

"*Diablo!*" the man blurted. "Life is like a lottery."

Paredes appeared shocked by the man's comment and told us that he had just read a 167-page book about HIV/AIDS. He explained to us that the HIV virus weakened the body's immune system by reducing the number of antibodies. He likened antibodies to the police responding to a crime. But, Paredes continued, the virus played a trick on the mind: it fooled the mind into thinking that the antibodies were the criminals.

"How is that possible?" the customer asked, incredulous.

Paredes thought for a moment. "It's like when the [police] anticorruption squad gets out of control and arrests officers who are really honest." "You have to have a strong mind to be safe from the virus," he concluded. "You must discipline your mind."

31. Paredes (left), Héctor, and the latter's son at Tapa's curbside repair shop. Héctor was training his son as a mechanic on the job. Photo by the author.

Paredes's appeal to social metaphors to explain the body's response to the virus underscores the degree to which social processes and relations suffuse the ways in which people experience and conceptualize their bodies and the tendency to regard HIV/AIDS, in particular, as a risk linked to a subjective failing (moral, spiritual, or otherwise) and, therefore, to subject AIDS to the logic of the social rather than to biology. Paredes's appeal to a "strong mind" as a defense against the virus reiterated a view that he had expressed to me after his failed migration attempt. He had survived the maritime odyssey, while some had died of exposure and dehydration, by disciplining his mind through biblical study during the eight-day voyage. Gérard and others, I would learn, held similar notions of the interrelationship of risk, subjectivity, and disease.

I did not know the source of the rumor about Gérard, but I first heard it from Miriam, the caretaker of the building in which we lived. One morning, as she was sweeping the hallway, she approached me and whispered, "They are saying that Gérard has AIDS. Do you see how skinny he is?" She held up her little finger to illustrate.

As word spread that Gérard was ill, the nature of his illness became the subject of heated discussions and debates at a variety of venues. Because I was Gérard's neighbor and we were known to be friends, many people approached me in the street, sometimes strangers, with questions or comments concerning his illness. Gérard's Haitian and Dominican friends vehemently denied the AIDS rumor, opining that he had tuberculosis instead. Milquella, who had known Gérard for years, told me bluntly, "Look, if Gérard had AIDS, he would already be dead. It's all a big lie." Still others disputed the rumors by stressing Gérard's qualities as a person: his intelligence, his generosity, and, in the case of Haitians, his spiritual strength, or *konesans*.

The appeal to Gérard's character, achievements, and *konesans* to dispute the AIDS rumor underscores the degree to which, as Paul Farmer (1992: 242) noted in Haiti, HIV/AIDS was viewed as a "disorder of the poor" and one subject to being interpreted through the logic of sorcery. With regard to the former, Gérard was relatively successful and therefore did not conform to the social etiology according to which many reasoned the HIV virus. For example, HIV/AIDS was often spoken about as a last stage—a coup de grâce, as it were—in a deeper economic, moral, and social decline.

With regard to the latter, Gérard's generosity argued against the possibility that he was the victim of a sorcery attack triggered by envy from within the Haitian community. Accusations of *maji* (sorcery) were often invoked by Haitians to explain illnesses, especially when suffered by someone who was believed to be the target of envy and jealousy. For example, Frito, a Haitian painter whom I met in 2000, was reputed to have been one of the most talented artists in Boca Chica. When I interviewed him, he told me of his plan to leave the gallery where he worked and rent his own space. When I returned to Boca Chica in 2001, his wife informed me that Frito had succumbed to a mysterious illness not long after opening his gallery. She told me that the Haitian painters who worked at Frito's old gallery were envious of his success and had attacked him with *maji*.

Similarly, when Marie became ill and disappeared from her hostess job at the Laser Discotheque, a rumor circulated among Haitians that she had been stricken with AIDS and that her illness had been effected through sorcery. Marie, viewed by Haitians as *moun klè* (light-skinned), was often criticized for denying her origins and refusing to speak Kreyòl and associate with other Haitians. "That one," a Haitian candy vendor once said, pointing to Marie, "thinks she's better than us. She's racist."

Gérard's illness became a lightning rod for discussion and dispute concerning not only the nature of HIV/AIDS but also its moral and sociopolitical epidemiology. For at stake in this dispute was a suturing of relations between what Nancy Scheper-Hughes and Margaret Lock (1987: 7) identified as the three "realms of the body": the individual body as lived experience, the social body of symbolic representation, and the body politic of power. These three registers of bodily representation became progressively conflated or, better, cross-indexed as Gérard's condition worsened and became public. In short, Gérard's body, illness, and personal history increasingly "said" things to people about him, the Haitian community, and the latter's relationship to Dominican society.

Among Haitians, the AIDS rumor took on conspiratorial overtones. Jean Paul, who had known Gérard in Haiti, assured me that the rumor was being spread by members of the National Police, who were envious of Gérard's success and resentful of the fact that it had been achieved by a Haitian. "They want to bring Gérard down," Jean Paul told me, "because he's Haitian. They want to bring all Haitians down. That's why they are saying these bad things." Others echoed this view, subjecting the AIDS accusation to the logic of sorcery and reading onto both the economic elites and the National Police envy and a desire for retribution. A *motoconcho* of Haitian descent assured me that tour operators in Boca Chica were behind the accusation; that they were using it as a weapon to destroy Gérard's relatively successful informal tour business.

There was some evidence to support this view. I learned from Milquella that Gérard had once worked as a guide for Ravi Tours, the largest tour operator in the area. While at Ravi, Gérard had become romantically involved with a Dominican employee, and the two decided to go into business for themselves. With financing provided by a British expatriate, the couple bought two used pickups, which they converted into "safari" vehicles. Although they were operating without a license, Gérard's British investor provided some protection from the police, and the tour business prospered. In response, Ravi Tours pressured the police to shut down the unlicensed operation.

In Milquella's version of the story, a lieutenant in the National Police took a liking to Gérard's wife and business partner and, to remove Gérard from the scene, planted two ounces of cocaine in one of their safari vehicles. Gérard was arrested for drug possession and sentenced to a five-year term at La Victoria, a notorious prison in Santo Domingo. Although Gérard was released after serving only one year, his wife left him, and his British investor sold the safari vehicles.

The AIDS accusation was interpreted by Milquella and by others in Gérard's social networks as a continuation of a pattern of persecution directed at a Haitian who, having risen above his imagined station, violated dominant, racialized norms regarding Haitian identity and the value of Haitian labor. Gérard's condition became a metaphor for the exclusion of Haitians from the Dominican economy and body politic.

Conversely, there were others who claimed that Gérard did in fact have AIDS and viewed his illness as confirmation of his illicit activities and Haitianness. To shore up their case, they would point to his alleged activities as a drug trafficker and Sanky Panky. Others opined that he had contracted AIDS while imprisoned at La Victoria, implying involvement in homosexual relations. A police sergeant told me that Gérard had contracted AIDS through drug use and consorting with Haitian prostitutes. "Everyone knows," he told me, "that AIDS was brought here by the prostitutes from Haiti. Before then, AIDS did not exist in Boca Chica." From this vantage point, Gérard's illness became a target for metaphor, rendering transparent and concrete the chain of equivalences that underpinned elite-driven constructions of Haitian bodies as radically external to the Dominican social body.

The dispute over Gérard's illness did not break down neatly along ethnic or class lines. Although Haitians tended to uniformly deny the AIDS accusation (at least in public), Dominicans who knew Gérard and were integrated into his social and exchange networks challenged it as well. Because the accusation conflated the social transmission of a disease with Haitian racial identity, drug use, deviant sexuality, and, more broadly, illicit uses of the body, the rumor also functioned as a broader attack on Gérard's social networks. In this sense, one was either with Gérard or against him.

Gérard had also begun to develop his own theories about his illness. One day when I was at his apartment, I noticed a human anatomy book on the kitchen table. Noting my curiosity, Gérard opened the book to a diagram of the body and explained to me how the infection had begun in his lungs, spread to his kidneys, and then, because of his nagging cough, had "traveled" to his neck. I was alarmed because I believed that it was possible he was suffering from AIDS-related illnesses, and, in that case, to delay diagnosis and treatment would be fatal.

But because he had denied this possibility, I felt that for me to suggest it would have been a betrayal—an affirmation of the rumor and its underlying stereotypes. Faced with this dilemma, I searched for a way to speak to Gérard about his health that would raise the possibility that he was suffering from AIDS-related illnesses but that would not name them as such. I settled on a compromise. Whenever Gérard offered a new theory of his illness (variously pneumonia, a kidney infection, and tuberculosis), I would respond, "Look Gérard, *whatever* you have, you need to see a doctor. They can do something for you. They even have drugs that can treat AIDS."

During his illness, Gérard received considerable support from his extensive social networks based largely, although not exclusively, in the Haitian community. People whom I had never seen before appeared at his apartment with food and other necessities. Others cleaned his apartment and helped to take care of his son. As his condition worsened and he became bedridden, his relationship with his British fiancée became strained, as he was now regularly asking for money to support himself and his son.

One Friday, Chamón and I were able to convince Gérard to go to the hospital. We took a cab to the Padre Bellini hospital, a respected medical center in Santo Domingo. Once there, Chamón took Gérard into the admitting room and I waited in the reception area with our cabdriver, a neighbor. An hour later Chamón reappeared and walked briskly across the lobby, leaving us behind. He was upset, and when I asked him what had happened he stated brusquely, "It's over. He's gone. We've lost a friend." During the ride back, Chamón told us that the doctor had taken him aside and told him that Gérard would not survive the weekend. She had drawn her index finger across her throat.

By that night word had been spread—no doubt, by *motoconchos*—that Gérard was in the hospital. Downtown, an assortment of people stopped me to ask about Gérard. Believing what the doctor had told Chamón, I wanted to emphasize the gravity of his condition, thinking that this would encourage people to visit him before it was too late. When I told people what I thought I knew, I was careful to use the impersonal construction, "*Se dice que . . . ,*" or, in Kreyòl, "*Yo di . . .*" "*They say* that he is dying. They say that he has AIDS." The next day I left for a three-day trip to San Pedro de Macorís. When I returned, word on the street was that Gérard had been moved to an AIDS isolation ward in another hospital, but no one knew its whereabouts. Some people were speculating that Gérard had already died.

THE RETURN OF THE PRODIGAL SON

SG: Jean Paul, what's up?

JP: My nigga! What's up, son? *Anfòm?*

SG: M ap boule. Sa ou ap fè la a?

JP: Chillin', just chillin'. Man, you're serious. You said you would call me.

SG: That's right. What about the interview?

JP: M ap vini. You'll be there?
SG: I've been here all day waiting for you. Don't bullshit me.
JP: No bullshit, son. Jah love.

This was my third attempt to interview Jean Paul. Twice he had stood me up, and he was now more than four hours late. Jean Paul had been raised in Port-au-Prince and had been in the Dominican Republic for two years on renewable work visas. He had first tried his hand at painting but, as he told me, did not have *lafòs* (inspiration) to do it profitably. For a time, he had worked in the capital touting cell phone promotions. He was now working at a restaurant, saving money to return to Haiti for his sister's wedding.

Within my Haitian networks, Jean Paul was the most virulent critic of anti-Haitianism in particular and racism in general and was quick to confront anyone when he felt slighted. He once told me that Bob Marley was the black Messiah and that from his lyrics could be gleaned the road to black emancipation. Jean Paul was also a fastidious dresser, attuned to the latest trends in hip hop style, and his everyday speech was, at times, a disconcerting mix of Krèyol, Ebonic slang, and Rastafarian livalect. In a manner that would have made Bakhtin proud, Jean Paul used this heteroglossia to confound and disrupt stereotyped constructions of Haitian culture and subjectivity. To borrow a term coined by Manthia Diawara (1998), Jean Paul was a "homeboy cosmopolitan," who relentlessly fashioned and performed his attachments to the African Diaspora. Jean Paul also aspired to be a spoken word performer and, along with Bob Marley, revered the Jamaican dub poet Mutubaraka and the Nigerian band leader and activist Fela Kuti. He kept a tattered notebook folded in his back pocket in which he scribed lyrics and rhymes when business was slow.

I asked Jean Paul in English about his migration experience, intending to lead him eventually to the topic of race. "When I came to Santo Domingo, I thought I could make money to improve myself and to help my family. You know, push them up, pay for their school. Because in Haiti, when you don't have no job, you don't have no family."

"But you have a child?" I asked.

"I have a baby girl. But I left that baby girl, because I didn't have no money to help her, or her mother. I don't let them see me like this. I'm always away, looking for something to send to them. Because money talks and bullshit walks. If you have money, you can do anything. Without money you can't do nothing. And I want to be something. I want to move—to go to school and make something. You know what I'm sayin'?"

I asked him how he had found the job at the restaurant, and he replied that it had been through a Haitian friend who knew the restaurant's French owner. "They gave me that job, but I could see that they wanted to take everything that I had in my mind. They wanted to use me to get their customers, because they can't speak English or Spanish. They play Haitians like a game, because they know that we can't go back to our country."

"But what about Dominicans?" I asked. "Is it the same with them?"

"Here, they don't have respect for poor people. I see that all the time. They don't have respect for Haitians. They think the Haitian is a dog. Not all Dominicans, because there are Dominicans like me who are trying to push themselves up, and they help me. We make business together."

"Why is that?" I asked. "Why do they think like that?"

"Because they don't want blacks in their country. They are black. Every Dominican is black, but they don't think like that. You know what I'm sayin'? And I say to people all the time, 'Yo, don't you know that your ancestors came here from Africa? That you are black just like me?' If you are black, you are supposed to have respect for every black person. It's not just for blacks only, it's for everybody. Because, like Michael Jackson—he makes music for black and white."

Near the end of the interview the conversation turned to Gérard. Jean Paul told me that he had known Gérard in Port-au-Prince and that Gérard had loaned him money for room and board when he first came to Boca Chica in 1999.

"They say that he is in the capital, in a hospital. Maybe that's true. I don't know. But Gérard doesn't have AIDS. They just want to push him down." Jean Paul switched to Kreyòl. *"Ou konprann? Lè yo vle touye chen yo di l fou."* (Do you under*stand?* When they want to kill a dog, they say it's crazy.)

A few days after the interview I was making my rounds on Calle Duarte when Jean Paul called me over to the restaurant where he worked. "Did you see Gérard?" he asked, animated. I was stunned and told him no. Jean Paul said that he had seen Gérard earlier that afternoon, visiting his old haunts on Calle Duarte.

"You see," Jean Paul continued, "Gérard doesn't have AIDS. It's a big lie. His spirit is too strong." He pointed to his head for emphasis.

I did not see Gérard that day, but the next morning I found him working on his car in front of our building. He looked emaciated but otherwise well. We exchanged pleasantries, and he explained that the doctors had lanced the cyst on his neck and prescribed a costly regimen of drugs for his lung infection. He put his wrench down and peered at me.

"Steven," he began, "you know that everybody in Boca Chica thought that I was dead." I agreed that this was the impression. He grinned and switched to Kreyòl. "People say that it was you who told them that I was dead—that I have AIDS."

Taken aback, I replied that they were lying. I explained to him why I had said what I said and added that I had never told anyone that *I* thought he had AIDS. It was a subtle distinction, but Gérard seemed to accept it. He reverted to English and explained why the engine kept stalling; it had something to do with the turbo-charger.

Things returned to a kind of normalcy, and we resumed our work on his British visa. I typed a letter of recommendation certifying that Gérard had assisted me in my anthropological research, which served as an employer reference. Margaret had sent the visa application by FedEx, and Gérard intended to submit the application to the British embassy in Haiti. He had decided to renew his Haitian passport rather than run the risk of applying for a Dominican one on the basis of his fabricated identity. But this would require leaving his son, Hassim *Gómez,* behind because Hassim's Dominican citizenship undermined his claim to paternity. Gérard told me that he would send Hassim to live with his aunt in Haiti while he and Margaret worked from London to "adopt" him.

It was only then that I realized that Gérard was caught in a catch-22 and that this had accounted for his procrastination in completing the visa application. Save for his expired Haitian passport and birth certificate, all of Gérard's papers were in the name of Máximo Gómez—bank statements, driver's license, and the other documents needed to support his visa application. But because of his drug arrest (in the persona of Máximo Gómez), Gérard was not eligible for a Certificate of Good Conduct, which was required for both his passport and his visa application. (I later learned that he had tried, unsuccessfully, to bribe a police official in the capital to issue one anyway.)

Alternatively, emigrating on his Haitian passport would require not only leaving Hassim behind but also filing his visa application from Haiti, where he would have to gather other supporting documents. This he could not do because, with Aristide's return to power in 1994, Gérard was once more persona non grata. Moreover, in either case, he would clearly not pass the medical exam.

Although Gérard's health had improved, he was often too weak to work. In addition, it was midsummer and the low season for a tourism industry already suffering from the global recession. Gérard was three months behind on his rent and was increasingly borrowing money from me and others to pay for his medicines and living expenses. To make matters worse, his relationship with Margaret was collapsing because of his unremitting appeals for money and his delay in applying for the visa.

"Margaret thinks that I'm playing her for money," he told me, "and that I'm not serious about getting married." That same day Gérard asked me to photograph him in bed with an IV tube in his arm to convince Margaret that he was really ill.

A few days later Gérard stopped by my apartment to inform me of his change in plans. He told me that he did not think that he would pass the medical exam. Consequently, he had decided to move to Sosúa where he would be able to work beyond the reach of the AIDS accusation. Margaret, he explained, had agreed to invest in a new licensed tour business, and she would join him in Sosúa as his partner. He asked me to lend him 2,000 pesos to prepare his car for the trip north.

Later that day I ran into Chamón as I was leaving the building. "Did you hear?" he began. "Cheche is going to adopt Hassim." I was dumbfounded. Chamón explained to me that Cheche, the father of three daughters, had always wanted a son and that he liked Hassim. Because Gérard was no longer able to care for the boy, Cheche had approached him with the adoption proposal, and Gérard had consented. The next day one of Cheche's daughters came to our building, helped Hassim to pack his belongings, and left with him for Cheche's house around the corner.

For a time, the arrangement seemed to be working. I ate most of my meals at Cheche's restaurant, so I would often see Hassim returning there from school or helping Cheche's daughters in the kitchen. He was distant and cold with me, as if he were trying to disentangle himself from his past or, perhaps better, attach himself to a new future. On occasion I would also see Hassim visiting his father. However, about two weeks later, Cheche confided to me that the family was having problems with Hassim: he was acting out at home and often truant from school. If Hassim continued in this vein, Cheche told me, he would be returned to his father.

A few days later I left my apartment and found Gérard and his son in the garden. Hassim's clothes were strewn about the yard. Gérard was shouting at the top of his lungs in English, "You are not my son anymore. You are ungrateful. Go away! You don't live here anymore." Gèrard told me that Hassim had left Cheche's house in the middle of the night and returned to the apartment. Hassim leaned stoically against the building, eyes lowered and expressionless.

"After all I've done for him," Gérard said to me, "this is how he repays me! Do you under*stand?* He's not my son." I had never seen Gérard so angry, his eyes so fierce. It was terrifying. For fifteen minutes, Gérard raved about Hassim's disrespectfulness toward Cheche and about the fact that Hassim had been seen wandering through town during school hours. One night, Gérard said, the eight-year-old had returned to Cheche's house after midnight, disheveled and defiant.

"And now, if Cheche doesn't take him back, what am I going to do? I can't take care of him. I am too sick. Do you under*stand?* He will have to live in the streets. He has thrown away his opportunity." "Pick up your clothes and go," he told Hassim.

Gérard was talking to me but reasoning with Hassim. Clearly, through his anger, he was trying to push Hassim away, back to Cheche, while explaining that he had no alternative. Hassim remained steadfast, staring blankly at the garden. Gérard was fixated on Hassim's acts of defiance and disrespect, which were so out of character. Hassim was one of the most polite, well-mannered, and mature children I had ever encountered, and Gérard took great pride in his parenting skills. To be sure, Hassim had been taking care of his father for months, cooking, cleaning, and doing other household chores.

When Gérard had exhausted himself, I told him what I thought. I told him that children often acted out when they had no other means of expressing their emotions, or of changing the situations in which they found themselves. Hassim's defiance, I reasoned, was not directed at Cheche but against his father's illness and their separation. Gérard, no doubt, understood his child's psychology better than I did. Like Hassim, Gérard had been raging against the inevitable. After listening patiently to my observations, Gérard locked the door to his apartment and stormed off. I gave Hassim 100 pesos to buy food and left for an appointment in Andrés.

For five days, Hassim lived on the street, spending his nights on a neighbor's porch across the street. Cheche had declined to take him back and Gérard had vanished. People offered to shelter Hassim, but he refused, as if, somehow, it would have been a betrayal of his father. Hassim's predicament dominated conversation at Colmado San Francisco and was discussed at the next meeting of the *junta de vecinos.*

Neighbors fed Hassim, washed his clothing, and invited him to use their bathrooms. On the sixth day Gérard reappeared and, to everyone's relief, allowed Hassim to return home.

While he was gone Gérard had decided to move into a cheaper apartment a few kilometers away in La Caleta. He told me that the new apartment had better ventilation, which would improve the condition of his lungs. As I helped him to move his belongings, Gérard told me that he had given up on his plans to move to Sosúa or emigrate until his health improved. "*Piti, piti, zwazo fè nich li*" (Little by little the bird builds its nest), he told me, pleased with his new apartment. Hassim was already busy cleaning.

No longer neighbors, Gérard and I lost contact with each other, though I would run across him on occasion in town working with tourists. I was preoccupied with my collaboration with Turivisión and had begun to follow a controversy that had developed in Andrés and Boca Chica surrounding the construction of a deepwater port at Punta Caucedo (see chapter 6). About six weeks after Gérard moved, I ran into a Haitian musician on Calle Duarte. Félix told me that Gérard was in a coma at the maternity hospital in Andrés. Félix wanted me to meet him later that night to discuss the situation. I was not friendly with Félix, in part, because he was a former member of the *tonton makout,* Haiti's notorious security police under the Duvalier regimes, and he had collaborated with FRAPH, a paramilitary terrorist group that had worked to subvert the Aristide government.[10] I could not get my relativism around that. Moreover, Félix had tried to hustle me for money in the past, so I received his news with suspicion. I told him that I was busy that evening.

The next morning a *motoconcho* stopped me in front of my building and told me that Gérard was dead. In fact, he had died two days earlier. Rumors had also begun to circulate among Haitians that his body had been taken to a morgue in Santo Domingo and had disappeared. The implication was that foul play had been involved, either in Gérard's death or in the treatment of his body, and the rumors related this to the AIDS accusation. A Haitian painter opined that the police had stolen the body so that an autopsy would not be performed—one that would have disproved the AIDS claim.

A few days later I learned that Gérard's mother and stepfather were in Boca Chica. This news surprised me. Gérard and his mother had been estranged, and he had refused my offers to contact her on his behalf. In the end, I think, Gérard must have come to believe that his mother was the only hope for Hassim. That same day I learned from Jean Paul that

Gérard's body had not really disappeared. It turned out that when Gérard's mother went to Santo Domingo to claim the body, she had asked for Gérard Avin. But Gérard had died as Máximo Gómez, the "Dominican him."

Gérard was buried in a cemetery just outside Boca Chica on the day before I left the field. This news also surprised me. I had assumed that his mother would take the body back to Haiti. Although I do not know the facts, I imagine that in death, as in life, Gérard could not overcome the barricades that had made him a prisoner in Boca Chica.

It goes without saying that the personal is political, but I would go further and argue that the understanding of either requires an examination of how structural, economic, and political forces are experienced, not by the *individual,* but by the person, an embodied nexus of social relationships, meanings, and intersubjective agency. For it is only by attending to the complex mediations between structural, indeed, global, relations of power and their embodiment in the everyday lives of social actors like Gérard that we can come to terms with the cultural forms and conduits through which these social forces configure subjectivity, frames of decision making, the sense of what is possible and what is not, and the structures of feeling through which people experience their lives and act in the world (Ortner 1995; Farmer 1997).

The rumors that enveloped Gérard's body crystallized hegemonic ideologies concerning the nature and identity of Haitians and their far from transparent relationship to the Dominican body politic. Indeed, his body became a site of "social, cultural and geographical inscription," as Elizabeth Grosz (1994: x–xi) put it. Although deeply rooted in the development of Dominican nationalism and sovereignty, this elite-produced knowledge of Haitian bodies was socially reproduced, enlivened, and embodied through the quotidian exploitation of Haitian labor and through the structuring of the division of labor and its constituent web of distinctions. That Gérard, in particular, and Haitians, generally, labored in occupations that were typically criminalized and often racialized—whether as slavelike cane cutters or mystically inspired artists—rendered their bodies prime targets for metaphoric thinking. It was this metaphoric reading of his body and illness that Gérard and his supporters disputed, advancing alternative, albeit fatally flawed, interpretations of his symptoms and illness. If, to recall Fanon, black people offer no "ontological resistance" to the racist's gaze, then Gérard's resistance to the AIDS accusation and its constituent metaphors must be viewed as precisely that: ontological, an assertion of being within a discourse of nonbeing that rendered his disease "adjectival" (Sontag 1978: 58).

Gérard's response to his illness was complexly motivated and shot through with ambivalence and indecision. I do not pretend to understand why he acted as he did, nor would I reduce his ordeal to an act of resistance. If the AIDS accusation stigmatized his person and community, the facts of his illness, no doubt, provoked feelings of denial and rage and confronted him with the daunting practical problems of caring for his son, making a living, and obtaining his visa. Moreover, given the "systemic failure" of the Dominican health care system, as a group of researchers concluded, it is not at all certain that more effective treatment options would have been available to him as a person of limited economic means (La Forgia et al. 2004: 173).

Rather, it is through the dense fabric of Gérard's social relations with Haitians and Dominicans alike that the question of resistance must be posed. For if his illness was a polysemous metaphor in elite circles, stigmatizing Haitians and the unruly poor, for the latter, it became a cause célèbre, inciting public repudiation of both the AIDS accusation and racism, and a practical affirmation of the reciprocally reckoned rights and obligations upheld by the Haitian community in particular and the laboring poor in general.

POSTSCRIPT, 2002–2003

When I returned to Boca Chica in summer 2002, Jean Paul told me that Gérard's son, Hassim, was living at an orphanage in the capital. He had heard rumors that Gérard's mother had tried to adopt the boy but had been unable to establish her relationship to her grandson. In 2003 I heard more rumors. A waitress of Haitian descent told me that she had seen Hassim in Boca Chica with Gérard's English fiancée, Margaret, and she assured me that the boy was now living in London. Gérard's reputation as a *gwo nèg,* a big man, had grown considerably, and he was remembered by many as a Robin Hood who had hustled the wealthy to uplift the poor.

6

The Politics of Transnational Capital

In February 2001 a multinational consortium announced the completion of planning for a large port facility at Punta Caucedo, just to the west of Andrés and Boca Chica. The plan, officially dubbed the Zona Franca Multi-Modal Caucedo (Caucedo Multimodal Free Trade Zone), called for the construction of a state-of-the-art, deepwater containership port linked to an FTZ industrial park.[1] The Megapuerto (Megaport), as it came to be known, was the result of a $250 million joint venture between U.S.-owned CSX World Terminals and the Caucedo Development Corporation, a partnership of three Dominican businessmen. The project was financed by a consortium of international investors led by the Scotiabank Group. Permission to develop the port and free trade zone had been granted by decree in 1998 by then President Leonel Fernández.

The Megaport project went through a contested public review process that pitted its multinational and Dominican sponsors against Boca Chica's tourism industry and incited public deliberation and debate concerning the region's economic development needs and the future of the global economy. Through an analysis of these tensions and conflicts among capitalists, public authorities, and an assortment of local constituencies, I tease out the complex ways in which local arrangements of power, political struggles, and, indeed, history conditioned the specific manner in which transnational capital was materialized within the space of the nation-state. I stress the composite and sometimes mutually antagonistic composition of transnational capital and the contingent nature of its discourses and practices of accumulation.

On February 2, 2001, a public hearing was held before the *ayuntamiento* in Santo Domingo at which members of the Boca Chica Tourism Development Association expressed opposition to the Megaport. Led by Henry Pimentel, a former government tourism official, the Boca Chica TDA actively lobbied state authorities on behalf of the tourism industry. Alarmed by the project's rapid progress, the TDA called an emergency meeting for March 1 at which "specialists" would make presentations addressing the impact of the Megaport on tourism in Boca Chica. Held in the evening at the Coral Hamaca Beach Hotel and Casino, the meeting drew an audience of about one hundred fifty, largely merchants, bar and restaurant owners, and others involved in tourism-related businesses. Pimentel, executive director of the TDA, sat at a table at the front of the Hamaca's Cayena Salon. Two others took seats next to him: Julio Aybar, vice president of finances for the Coral Hamaca Corporation, and Francisco Geraldes, a marine biologist and director of the Centro de Investigaciones de Biología Marina (Marine Biology Research Center) at the Universidad Autónoma in Santo Domingo. A hotel employee readied a laptop computer and video projection machine that would be used in the PowerPoint presentations to follow.

Pimentel opened the meeting by recounting the development of Boca Chica's tourism industry, following its designation in 1973 as a Polo Turístico, one of four such "poles" earmarked for tourism development by the Dominican government. Pimentel argued that, although the Megaport was being touted as a solution to the region's economic problems, industrial development was not compatible with tourism. "We, the Development Association, are completely in agreement with development, with progress," Pimentel began. "And, hopefully, many Zona Francas will be constructed. Many Dominicans, many people in Boca Chica, will be able to find work. But we also know that an industry that has been here for more than twenty-five years must be preserved—a culture that has been the foundation for all the development that has come [to Boca Chica]. There are many businesses that have developed on this foundation that are not compatible with the industrial activities that will come with the Megaport." Pimental noted the example of Puerta Plata, where tourism had suffered following the construction of a 185-

megawatt power plant on a barge in that city's harbor by the Smith Enron Corporation in 1994.

The claim that industrial development was incompatible with tourism was pursued by Geraldes. He argued that industrial development brought with it intensive use of natural resources and, consequently, produced an immediate and negative impact on the environment. Aided by computer-generated images of the area's ocean currents, Geraldes argued that the construction of the Megaport would impede the flow of water out of the Bay of Andrés. With its exit channel blocked, the water would flow instead over the coral reef and destroy it in the process. With the reef compromised, the beach would erode and, along with it, Boca Chica's tourism economy. Moreover, Geraldes warned, heavy ship traffic through the port would produce oil spills that would harm marine life.

Geraldes then exercised an argument that would often be used by the TDA as it labored to construct a logic of opposition to the Megaport: because Boca Chica was the beach most accessible to capital residents, tourism had an indispensable "cultural value." Therefore, the Megaport posed a threat not only to the environment but also to popular culture and to the *patrimonio nacional* (national heritage). This appeal to the nation and its cultural traditions was intended to offset charges, often made by critics of the TDA, that the group was narrowly concerned with the profits of the resort hotels (and the well-being of their foreign guests) and indifferent to the needs and struggles of the people of Andrés–Boca Chica. In short, the TDA was attempting to reframe the interests of the transnationally oriented tourism industry as those of the nation and locality—the "cultural patrimony" of the nation.

This theme was hammered home by Aybar. Directing his presentation to legal issues, Aybar argued that the construction of the Megaport would violate Dominican law. Specifically, he asserted that the construction of the port would violate Decree 3112, which established Boca Chica and nearby Juan Dolio as a tourism pole, by undermining the secretary of state for tourism's powers of oversight in the area. Moreover, he argued, the Megaport would violate the Dominican Constitution, whose article 47 prohibited the use of public power to compromise legal securities derived from earlier legislation; that is, the building of the Megaport would endanger investments and jobs that had been created as a result of the area's development as a tourism pole. Finally, Aybar contended, the environmental hazards associated with the project would violate the General Law on the Environment and Natural Resources passed in 2000.

Aybar appealed to the audience as business owners whose livelihoods would be affected, if not destroyed, by the Megaport, which he characterized as "caramel candy" that was tempting people to disregard economic realities in the name of progress and modernization. He described the free trade zones as an advantage that had been conferred by the United States on countries in Latin America and the Caribbean during the cold war, with the aim of undermining Cuba's influence in the region and reducing the flow of illegal immigrants to the United States. The FTZs, Aybar contended, were part of a "tributary system" that made it possible for goods to be imported to, and processed within, the Dominican Republic before being reexported to the United States without payment of taxes and duties. However, with the end of the cold war and the expansion of global markets, the conditions that had given rise to the FTZs and their preferential trade agreements had been fundamentally altered. Free trade regulations now hindered, if not disallowed, preferential arrangements with countries such as the Dominican Republic. The North American Free Trade Agreement (NAFTA), Aybar argued, was but one example of the "economic logic" of free trade that was having a negative impact on export processing in the Dominican Republic. Since the future of the FTZs was uncertain, Boca Chica's tourism economy had to be protected.

Having challenged the economic case for the Megaport, Aybar revisited the "nationalist" argument for tourism. "Boca Chica and Andrés," he began, "and the coral reef, are our natural and cultural patrimony and are not subject to negotiation. They are not subject to negotiation because they constitute—they guarantee the viability of the beach. Boca Chica is basically *the* public beach of the city of Santo Domingo. And recreation at the beach is recreation that is extremely cheap, extremely sacred, and extremely favorable for, for conditions of emotional health."

Aybar's presentation underscores the complex and fluid relationship among global capital, the state, and discourses of national interests as they are materialized in practice and within concrete settings. Though few in the audience, let alone the community, believed that the TDA or the *hoteleros* who dominated its leadership were concerned about the tens of thousands of *capitaleños* who used the area's beaches, Aybar constructed an argument that counterpoised U.S.-dominated, free trade interests against an ecologically conscious hotel industry that was defending the nation's cultural heritage. This binary model of debate, pitting national against international and local against global interests, illustrates the plasticity and contingency of capitalist discourse as it grapples with space. For in defense of luxury tourism, the TDA crafted an argument that was not only anti-imperialist but also critical of the Dominican Republic's dependency on U.S. capital—international tourism dressed in the clothing of cultural nationalism. In fact, the meeting succeeded, albeit temporarily, in defining the terms of the ensuing debate, constructing the Megaport as an environmental threat to the Dominican way of life and, indeed, to "emotional health."

Here, I stress the far from transparent character of the relationships among global capital, the political economy of the nation-state, and discourses concerning the nature and trajectory of the global economy. The complex, if not convoluted, arguments mobilized by the TDA highlight the disputed status of the logic of globalization and the fact that the constitution of the global, in relation to national, interests and identities is perhaps better viewed as an *argument* than as a set of intractable, structural relationships between "global" capital and "national" economies (see Tsing 2000). In this key respect the political topography of the Dominican Republic conditioned not only how global processes were materialized in time and space but also how "globalization" was itself ideologically articulated and received.

Word of the debate over the Megaport spread throughout Andrés–Boca Chica, in part, through programming on Turivisión. Only days before the TDA meeting at the Coral Hamaca Hotel, two of the three Dominican partners in the joint venture, Manuel Tavares and Jaak Rannik, had appeared on *Hechos y Noticias* (Facts and News), a news and call-in talk show, to discuss the Megaport and address concerns about its environmental impact. Tavares and Rannik had both stressed the long and rigorous review process through which the project had gone. Both assured viewers that the environmental risks would be carefully studied and that the latest technologies would be used in building the Megaport to ensure that the environment would be safeguarded. Moreover, Tavares informed the audience that, in compliance with the new General Law of the Environment and Natural Resources, the project would be presented to the community for public review and comment. This presentation took place on March 2, the day after the TDA's meeting at the Coral Hamaca Beach Hotel.

Opinions varied concerning the Megaport, complicated by the competing and contradictory claims of the two sides in the debate. Minaya, a friend and vendor who worked on the beach, was concerned that the construction of the Megaport and FTZ would destroy tourism (his livelihood) but told me that in the long run it would bring more jobs to the community: "They say that the Megaport will contaminate the beach, the water, and that tourism will suffer. I don't know, maybe it's true. I am not an expert. But here, in Andrés and Boca Chica, people don't have work. I think that this project will bring progress to the community and to the country."

Minaya's reading of the Megaport was informed by the economy of his extended household. The global recession and decline in foreign tourist arrivals had severely reduced the earnings of his joint family. His own monthly earnings as a vendor had decreased by nearly half, from 5,000 to 6,000 pesos during the previous year to just under 3,000 pesos (US $183). His brother, also a vendor, was earning too little to sustain his stock of cigars and was now working, sporadically, as a day laborer in construction. A brother-in-law and cousin who also contributed to the household's income were idle. To make matters worse, the family's *colmado* had been ransacked and its goods stolen. The looting of the *colmado* was a particularly cruel blow, as the enterprise had enabled the family (seventeen members in all) to buy food and other necessities at wholesale prices. Minaya's wife, Jocelyn, was spending her days trying to collect debts from neighbors for goods bought on credit.

The looting of the *colmado* was part of a wider wave of social violence that swept through the region in 2000–2001 as the economy worsened, the violence and temerity of which stunned residents. In a series of well-publicized incidents, gangs of gunmen broke into homes in La Caleta in broad daylight, raping women and robbing all present. Gérard had been robbed in June by masked gunmen who broke into his apartment in the middle of the night. The worsening economy, coupled with a dramatic increase in social violence, fueled the perception that change was due.

Like Minaya, many who worked in tourism were ambivalent about the Megaport, concerned that their livelihoods, though modest and unstable, would be threatened but reckoning that the Megaport would bring general prosperity to the area. Others, such as the dockworkers at the existing port in Andrés, were skeptical of the promises made by the project's sponsors. "They say that there will be work for us," observed Juan Méndez, a retired dockworker, "but I think that this is a lie. Because I have heard that this project, the Megaport, will be completely automated. They won't need workers, only machines. This is what I have heard."

Rumors abounded, some based in fact and others in the historical imagination. Tapa, who owned an auto repair shop next to where I lived, assured me that the Megaport would really be a U.S. naval base, which he contended the United States had been trying to establish for years. Tapa's judgment read Dominican history through the lens of personal experience. As a mechanic working for the Dominican army in the 1960s, Tapa had witnessed the C-130 troop transports of the 82d Airborne Division land at San Isidro Airbase on the morning of April 30, 1965, initiating the U.S. intervention. Tapa's experience of one intervention informed his memory of an earlier colonial desire: U.S. efforts to secure Samaná Bay as a coaling station for its warships—a desire that was only quenched by the seizure of Puerto Rico and the acquisition of Guantánamo Bay in Cuba. A welder who worked at Tapa's shop told me that he had heard that the United States wanted to use Punta Caucedo as a bombing range to replace Vieques in Puerto Rico.

Gabriel Zapata told me that the Megaport was already a "done deal" and that it did not really matter what the community thought about it. Moreover, he added, the project was beyond the government's powers of oversight and a result of the nation's debt to the United States. "Before," Zapata continued, "when they wanted to get their money, they sent in the marines and took over the customshouse. Now, they don't have to do that. They just come in and say, 'Look, we want to buy this piece of land and make this project with it, make a factory, or make a multimodal, or whatever. That's how they do it now. They got that land," he said, pointing to Punta Caucedo across the bay, "they got that land for nothing!"

The diverse interpretations of, and responses to, the Megaport underscore the multifarious composition of global capital and the peculiar, context-specific manner in which these global flows, material and discursive, congeal as they are realized in place and in a historical context. Aybar's portrayal of the FTZ system as a relic of cold war politics, as a tool to stem migration, and as a tributary arrangement designed to benefit U.S. corporations appealed to a historical reading of the asymmetrical relationship between the United States and the Dominican Republic—a view that found support in the protests against privatization that were erupting across the nation. Similarly, Zapata's comparison of the project to the seizure of the customshouse (which occurred before the 1916 U.S. occupation) historicized the Megaport, providing it with the face and agency of an aggressive nation-state rather than the shapeless aura of "free markets" and a global economy. Zapata, in fact, had been a student activist in the years after the 1965 U.S. intervention and had been forced into exile during the regime of President Balaguer.

In short, however diminished the capacity of nation-states to govern their economies, the state remains a key political field structuring the specific manner in which global flows of capital, people, and media are materialized in space, whether as multinational initiatives such as the Megaport or as discourses about the future of the international economy. From this perspective, "globalization" is less a description of the existing world system than a set of contested claims about how it *should* be structured in relation to nation-states and their peoples.

It was precisely these issues that were at the center of the dispute: what was the Megaport, who were its sponsors, and whose interests would be served by its construction? The answers to these questions were by no means given, top down, by transnational elites but rather took shape through struggles in situ. The Boca Chica TDA and the *hoteleros* framed the Megaport as a U.S.-sponsored project that would provide dubious economic benefits and also violate Dominican law by undermining the nation's natural and cultural patrimony. They sought to mobilize popular opposition to the project by presenting their eminently global interests as congruent with those of the nation and the local community and in opposition to U.S.-dominated capital.

The multinational sponsors of the Megaport challenged this narrative, emphasizing the economic prosperity that the project would generate and, by extension, the "popular" rather than elite interests that it would serve. Their case for the Megaport rested on the neoliberal claim that only free market openness to transnational capital, unfettered by the political space of the nation-state, would bring prosperity and modernization to the Dominican Republic. For their part, supporters of the Megaport constructed the tourism industry's interests as backward *(atrasado)*, partisan, and narrowly self-serving. Given the history of low-intensity conflict between the *hoteleros*, backed by state authorities, and the region's poor, this argument proved plausible.

TALKING NEOLIBERALISM: TRANSNATIONAL CAPITAL SPEAKS OUT

On March 2 the sponsors of the Megaport held their promised public meeting at the Coral Hamaca Beach Hotel and Casino to present their proposal to the community. The lobby outside the spacious meeting room was packed with people: clusters of local officials in business suits, merchants talking on cell phones, and families dressed in their Sunday best. Buses had been chartered (by labor union officials, a driver told me) to ferry residents from Andrés to Boca Chica to attend the meeting. At the entrance to the salon was a table displaying literature about the project: a small brochure providing an overview of the Zona Franca Multimodal Caucedo and a larger booklet in English describing Port Everglades, a port facility on the southeastern coast of Florida that was said to be similar to the one proposed for Punta Caucedo.

Inside the salon about eight hundred people were seated before the dais at the front of the room. The first couple of rows had been reserved for government officials and corporate executives representing CSX World Terminals and Mouchel Consulting, Ltd., a British firm that would be conducting the Environmental Impact Study (EIS). To the left of the dais, a wooden soundproof booth housed two simultaneous translators. To the right, an artist's rendering of the Megaport was projected onto a large screen. Smartly dressed hotel employees scurried about, checking microphone connections and tending stainless steel chafing dishes and trays that were being readied at the rear of the salon.

A Dominican woman and CSX employee approached the podium and welcomed the audience to the "informational" meeting before introducing the dozen or so CSX and Mouchel executives sitting in the first row. Mayra, as she introduced herself, then explained that headsets were available in the lobby for those who would need translation of the English-language presentations. A grumble rose from the audience. Only a few people left their seats to retrieve the headsets. "This is the Dominican Republic," the woman sitting next to me muttered, "why are they speaking to us in English?" Others grumbled their agreement. Mayra then introduced Manuel Enrique Tavares, one of the Dominican partners and the president of Itabo Industrial Park, a group of construction and real estate firms involved in FTZ development throughout the Dominican Republic.

Tavares, a tall, stately man with a deep voice, welcomed the audience and explained that the meeting was part of a long process of public review being followed in accordance with guidelines established by the General Law of Environment and Natural Resources. He then paused and looked up from his notes. "Having heard Mayra's introduction," he continued, "it occurred to me that one small issue was overlooked which requires mention. And that is the *local* partners. Because Mayra spoke only of CSX World Terminals, which is our partner. But it is also important to know who the Dominicans are who are moving this project." The CSX and Mouchel executives nodded their heads in agreement. Applause arose from the audience when Tavares introduced Samuel Conde, president of Samuel Conde & Associates, a Dominican construction firm, and

Jaak Rannik, president and CEO of Agencias Navieras B&R, a shipping firm.

The slight was telling, and the audience would remain alert to how issues of sponsorship and control of the Megaport were presented through both the content of the presentations and the meeting's format. Indeed, the charge that the project was a U.S.-dominated one, serving U.S. rather than Dominican interests, had been made by the *hoteleros* only the day before. Consequently, the issue of how "global," rather than Dominican, the interests controlling the Megaport were would remain a flashpoint that strongly influenced how residents interpreted and evaluated the competing claims about the project's economic impact.

Tavares described the Megaport as a logistics center for the regional transportation and distribution of goods and maintained that, since the port would handle containers rather than loose cargo, it would operate cleanly. Aided by bulleted discussion points projected onto the screen, he explained that the Megaport's proximity to the capital and its international airport would—with community support—create a "synergy" that could make the Dominican Republic into "the Taiwan of the Caribbean." Tavares also told the audience that the Megaport would contain docking facilities for cruise ships, which would contribute to Boca Chica's tourism economy, creating from 5,000 to 8,000 thousand jobs and contributing more than 30 million pesos per month to the local economy. He also stressed the fact that the project was financed by private sources rather than by the Dominican government and, for this reason, was required to comply with strict environmental rules and safeguards.

Next, Tavares explained the relationship between the Dominican interests and the multinational ones. "Our international partner, CSX World Terminals, contributes various things to this project. On the one hand, they contribute the technology, '*el* know-how,' and experience with developing this type of facility. We believe, with great conviction, that realistically we could not have put together a project of this magnitude if we did not have assistance from a company with the experience and prestige of CSX World Terminals." He added that only a company with CSX's "global reach" could have secured the international financing required for the project.

Tavares concluded his presentation by addressing the environmental issues that had been raised by the TDA and were being publicized in the media. He assured the audience that the port's construction would not interfere with ocean currents in the Bay of Andrés and that the Megaport's design features would prevent the polluting of coastal waters. Tavares then introduced Jim Rogers, an associate director at Mouchel.

Rogers spoke at length about the purpose and scope of the environmental impact study, discussing in mind-numbing detail the various components and stages of the study that would be done in Boca Chica. Many in the audience became restless and gathered in groups at the rear of the salon and in the lobby, ignoring the English-language talk. After an hour or so, Rogers completed his presentation, summarizing the process by which the EIS would be reviewed by the government. There was a flurry of applause, but few in the audience had been listening to the translation over the headsets. Mayra approached the podium to restore order and reassemble the audience. She then introduced Pedro García, the Dominican sociologist who would complete the social and economic component of the EIS.

As García approached the podium, a man in the audience called out, *"Hable en inglés, usted también!"* (Speak in English, you too!). The audience erupted in laughter. *"Aye mi madre!"* the woman next to me cried out in exasperation, as she removed her headset. Many of the headsets, it appeared, had not been working properly. Moreover, few in the audience had received them. Mayra approached the podium and apologized for the technical problems and, once again, encouraged the audience to obtain headsets for the remaining presentations in English. Hotel employees circulated through the audience distributing the headsets. Irritated, a man shouted out, "*After* he has already spoken?" referring to Rogers. The CSX executives looked on with growing concern.

García, speaking in Spanish, began by providing a brief history of Andrés and Boca Chica and a survey of the local economy, reciting statistics on, for example, the number of hotel rooms and the number of people working in Las Américas FTZ. Next, using data from a study of poverty that had been conducted by the National Planning Office, García presented demographic data on the area: the number of the "extreme" and "nonextreme" poor and the percentages of persons lacking basic services such as housing, potable water, and bathrooms, as well as jobs. García's hour-long presentation concluded with an account of the methods he would use to conduct the socioeconomic portion of the EIS.

When the last speaker was introduced, the meeting was entering its fourth hour. Allen Sosno, director of environmental affairs at Port Everglades, was to speak on the environmental lessons gained from the construction and operation of the Florida port. As he began his presentation in English, an uproar arose from the audience. Unable to resolve the problems with the headsets, the technicians had been instructed to feed the Spanish translation through the main sound system, which resulted in a choppy, drawn-out narrative, alternating between English and Spanish. There were shouts from the audience, "Turn it off!" referring to Sosno's microphone. The technicians complied, leaving the translator's voice alone audible. Muted, Sosno summarized the steps that had been taken at Port Everglades to protect the environment, culminating with an account of the port's successful campaign to protect the West Indian manatee.

After the presentations Tavares provided a summary in which he stressed once again the scientific rigor of the study that would be done and the economic benefits that the port would bring. He then opened the floor to discussion. Not surprisingly, the opening questions addressed the Megaport's impact on tourism and Boca Chica's coral reef.

Juana Sánchez, a *regidora* for the Partido de la Liberación Dominicana and member of the government commission reviewing the project, relayed the concerns of Boca Chica's *hoteleros* and merchants that the project's planners were not taking tourism into account. She argued that the EIS must address the area's need for "sustainable development," which would ensure the livelihoods of future generations. "We want you to give us assurances," Sánchez continued, "together with the *hoteleros,* who I think are defending the *zona [turística],* that you will not increase pollution and that you will also mitigate [existing pollution]. Because, for not only the residents of Andres–Boca Chica but also for those of the National District and nearby communities, Boca Chica is the only public beach used by the poor." The audience cheered at the mention of *los pobres.*

Tavares responded that the EIS would address the long-term environmental needs of the area and that the project's sponsors were committed to working with the government, the private sector, and the entire community to find solutions to all of the area's problems.

Next, José Antonio Pérez, representing the dockworkers of Andrés, rose to speak. He was surrounded by a group of about forty dockworkers and their families in the rear of the salon. Pérez asked what impact the construction of the Megaport would have on the existing port in Andrés. "And what," he continued, "will become of the dockworkers of Andrés? Will they be taken into account in this plan? Will they also benefit, the dockworkers who have worked in Andrés since the 1940s?"

Tavares placed both hands on the podium and solemnly replied, "I have to say, *caballero* (gentleman, a respectful term of address), that clearly . . . clearly the dockworkers of Andrés will be taken into account. Who *better* to work the ships than you who have worked here for so many years." Led by the dockworkers, the audience erupted in applause. Tavares added that, if anything, the Megaport would increase ship traffic to the existing port. What he did not repeat, however, was that the Megaport was to be a state-of-the-art containerport and that it was unlikely that the dockworkers of Andrés had the skills required for its automated operation.

One of the last to speak was González Troncoso, president of the Society for Ecological and Environmental Studies, a local community group. "What I see here," he began, surveying the audience, "is a conflict of interests between the hotel owners and this corporation. A conflict over which the residents of Andres and Boca Chica, to use the common expression, 'will lose no sleep.'" The audience laughed, applauded, and then quieted for him to continue. The CSX executives pressed their headsets to their ears for the translation.

> This project is excellent . . . on paper. What we are waiting for now is the *implementation* of the project. Because, just like Falconbridge [a Canadian-owned ferronickel mine] in Bonao—there they designed a marvelous project. And then we learned that the people of Bonao had taken to the streets, struggling and protesting against the environmental pollution. Because that project [i.e., its original plan] was not implemented. The same thing happened in Manzanillo and in Monte Cristi, everybody took to the streets because of the impact of the pollution. And we praise you for having developed a project so impressive. But you spoke to us of Hong Kong, and you spoke to us of Florida. In those places, there are strong institutions, where no one has the ability to violate the law . . . the mark of justice. But here, the multinationals come and do whatever they want. And if you violate this project that has been so well designed, Andrés, Boca Chica, and other communities will take to the streets, protesting and demanding the termination of this project.

Once again the audience erupted in applause as Troncoso's voice reached a crescendo. Tavares raised his hands and nodded his head in a gesture of understanding. "*Caballero . . . caballero,* and everyone," he began, his deep voice rising above the din.

> You are completely right. You are completely right. And fortunately, our country is making progress. Years ago, there was no—there was a dictatorship. And afterwards, we began a process of democratization that some say is still not complete. But fortunately, we have been making progress. Today, there is still much to do. But we have better justice today than ten years ago. And we will have still better. And if we violate our commitment and the law

> in constructing, and maintaining, and operating this port, in accordance with national and international norms, then the project will be removed and taken away.

There was a pause before polite applause as the audience wrestled, no doubt, with the image of the $250 million Zona Franca Multi-Modal Caucedo being "removed and taken away." But Tavares's assurances appeared to have tempered some concerns about the project. Five hours into the night, the meeting ended, and the audience regrouped around the tables at the rear of the salon where fruit punch and hors d'oeuvres were being served by hotel workers dressed in crisp white aprons and tall pleated chef's hats.

Tavares had succeeded, perhaps, in giving a Dominican voice and face to the project, skillfully parrying questions and comments, while the CSX personnel remained conspicuously silent. His manner was authoritative and respectful, suggested by his use of the word *caballero* to address male speakers. More significant, Tavares presented the transnational sponsorship and financing of the project as a guarantee that the EIS and, more generally, the port's operation would be conducted in accordance with strict guidelines rather than under the auspices of an implicitly corrupt and ineffectual state. To that end, Tavares had reframed the dumping of toxic waste in Bonao by Falconbridge as a consequence of the enduring legacy of Trujillo rather than as part of a pattern of abuses perpetrated by foreign corporations. As in modernization theory, it was the traditional backwardness of the Dominican Republic rather than its dependent relationship to U.S. and international lending agencies that hindered economic growth.

To be sure, many in the audience, Troncoso for one, remained skeptical about the project's "implementation," but the promises made by these most recent representatives of global capital had been received on a political and historical stage that, peculiar to this context, strongly influenced how the project and its sponsors would be appraised by the audience and the wider community. The development of tourism in Boca Chica had given rise to a dual economy in which the high-end, formal tourism sector was differentiated from the illicit and heavily policed informal economy. This order of things had fueled class antagonisms and resentment—a "routine contempt," as James Scott (1990: 14) put it—that undermined the appeal of the *hoteleros* to the nation's patrimony, let alone to the economic interests of the laboring poor; that is, class antagonisms, generated by this context-specific ordering of the division of labor, shaped how global flows of capital and information were structured within the political economy of the nation-state.

Not long after the Megaport's debut, a rumor began to spread in Andrés–Boca Chica that the project had been stopped by a court injunction initiated by the *hoteleros*. Although the rumor proved false, it was true that the special commission that had been appointed by the Chamber of Deputies to review the project was considering revising the contract that had been signed by its sponsors. At issue were preferential tariffs granted to the Megaport's sponsors, which dockworkers in Haina protested would undermine commerce to their port.

Nevertheless, many had come to the belief that the *hoteleros* had sabotaged the project, whether through the courts or through the political influence they exercised in the government, now ruled by the Partido Revolucionario Dominicano. For example, Manolo Sánchez, a laid-off sugar worker, assured me that the *hoteleros* had formed an alliance with the PRD to sabotage the project, which had been approved by the preceding PLD administration of Fernández. More generally, PLD supporters in Andrés and Boca Chica viewed opposition to the Megaport, in part, as a PRD attempt to roll back the previous administration's reputed accomplishments.

A WAR OF POSITION

On March 14 an editorial appeared in *El Nacional* criticizing the Megaport, based on the environmental arguments that had been made by the *hoteleros*. Later that day the editorial was discussed on *Rumbo al Progreso,* hosted by Hector Peña and Jose Beato, both of whom were PLD supporters of the Megaport. Beato accused the editorial's author of "yellow journalism" and argued that it was an attempt by "a certain interest group" in the community to sabotage the project by spreading false and misleading information about its environmental risks.

"Simply speaking," Peña followed, "there is hegemony *(hegemonía)* in this community, hegemony. We have to ask *them* for permission to do any kind of project. And we ask, 'Why should we request permission from them, from pirates, to secure the rights of all the people of Andrés, of Boca Chica, and of La Caleta?' For every project that comes into our community, we must ask the permission of *los señores hoteleros.*" Peña dragged out the polite term of address in biting sarcasm. Then, referring directly to Henry Pimentel, executive director of the Boca Chica TDA, he added, "Why doesn't he worry himself about the prostitution that is there [in the *zona turística*], where children are in the streets until two o'clock in the morning?" "Señores," Peña concluded, staring deadpan into the camera lens, "let *us* worry about the development of this community!"

Peña's comments lent support to beliefs and sentiments that were gaining ground in the community that cast the *hoteleros* as elitist "hypocrites," narrowly concerned about the *natural* environment but indifferent to the condition of the poor—the "human environment," as Peña would later put it. To counter the *hoteleros*' focus on threats to the coral reef, the Megaport's supporters pointed to poverty, crime, and prostitution, describing them as forms of "contamination" that were the effects, not only of unemployment, but of tourism as well. In this view, international tourism was a corrupting influence that was undermining public morality, Dominican cultural values, and the rights and obligations of citizenship. This argument, exercised often during the controversy, resonated with the resentment felt by many toward the tourism industry and in particular the system of all-inclusive resort hotels. And the icon of this multisource resentment came to be the figure of the sexually exploited female minor.

On the one hand, the all-inclusive resorts locked local vendors and merchants out of the lucrative high-end sector of the tourism industry. Consequently, considerable animosity was felt toward the *hoteleros*, not only by people working at the low end of the tourism economy, but also by Dominican visitors to the beach who were often treated as second-class guests.

On the other hand, the salience of male sex tourists among foreign visitors to Boca Chica fueled the widely held opinion that foreigners, both tourists and the expatriate owners of the sex tourism venues, were undermining the community's morality and, more to the point, the morality of its young women. For example, at the height of the debate over the Megaport, *El Nacional* published a three-issue exposé on prostitution in Boca Chica charging that "foreigners" were recruiting young women throughout the Dominican Republic to work as prostitutes in Boca Chica. The exposé provoked a quick response from government officials—notably, the chief of the National Police—and a flurry of local investigative reports and commentaries that were broadcast on Turivisión.

Soon afterward, an editorial published in *Listín Diario*, "Megaports Are Necessary," more forcefully made this link between foreign-induced moral corruption and opposition to the Megaport. "One preoccupation of the hotel owners," the editorial began, "is that the port will produce an 'environmental disaster' which will affect the beach at Boca Chica. We believe that this possibility is avoidable and that the authorities must remain vigilant so that this never occurs. But we also believe that this same level of concern must be shown to ensure that Boca Chica does not remain what it is today: a cavern in which unscrupulous foreigners promote all kinds of sexual aberrations, minors included, and without limits" (April 5, 2002, 2).

Mass support for the Megaport, bolstered by these appeals to moral and economic interests, increased rapidly as the terms of the debate crystallized and became common knowledge. A key venue for publicizing the debate was Turivisión, whose program hosts devoted considerable airtime to discussing the project. Public hearings on the Megaport were broadcast on Turivisión in their entirety. This publicity campaign provided an interesting case of cable television, the sine qua non of the global "mediascape," being put to eminently local use—in this case, by an interest group of local political elites to support one leg of transnational capital.

By mid-April the public buses in Andrés–Boca Chica carried bumper stickers with the entreaty, "*Apoye el Megapuerto!*" (Support the Megaport!), and graffiti began appearing in both towns bearing such slogans as "*Megapuerto Sí, Hoteleros No!*" (Megaport Yes, Hotel Owners No!) and "*Pimentel, fuera de Boca Chica*" (Pimentel, get out of Boca Chica).

On April 20 the government's special commission came to Andrés to gauge public opinion on the Megaport and to explain its own review process. The meeting was held at the office of the *ayuntamiento,* where an overflow crowd had assembled in the stifling midday heat. Members of the special commission sat at a long table placed under a huge Dominican flag painted on the wall. The audience was boisterous and agitated, some under the impression that the Megaport already had been "sabotaged" by the *hoteleros* and perhaps by the commission. A Turivisión camera crew hurriedly set up their equipment in the rear of the cinder-block room. An *ayuntamiento* official called the meeting to order, and then members of the commission spoke, each assuring the audience of the government's support for the project and stressing the need for economic development in the region.

For example, Victor Soto, a PLD deputy representing the eastern region of the National District, provided a macroeconomic argument for the Megaport, linking its construction to the future of free trade in the region. Moreover, speaking to local experience, Soto argued, quite paradoxically, that the closing of Ingenio Boca Chica had not been a result of its "capitalization" (i.e., its being leased to multinational corporations) but rather the reverse, a lack of capitalization.

> This community, as is the case in all of the country, in the capital of the Republic, is overpopulated. And there is a profusion of unemployment, of prostitution, of crime—the result of a lack of opportunities. We must create, in this part of the country, a free trade zone *(zona libre de comercio),* like that which will exist throughout Central America with CARICOM [Caribbean Community and Common Market], and which will eventually arrive in the Americas. And this country must modernize and create basic infrastructure that is fundamental to this [free trade zone]. And for this reason, we are in agreement with all megaprojects like this one. What destroyed the sugar mill [in Boca Chica] was not capitalization but a lack of capitalization to renovate the mill. Therefore, to capitalize Boca Chica, and to capitalize the Republic, we must have megaprojects like this one.

Soto's Malthusian argument located underdevelopment in the characteristics of the population rather than the organization of productive relations and their relation to the wider global order. Consistent with modernization theory, as well as IMF and World Bank ideology, progress could only occur by "clearing a space" within the landscape of traditional backwardness and moral corruption for the penetration of modernizing capital. And, as if to seal this logic in paradox, Soto advanced the peculiar, indeed, counterintuitive, explanation for the demise of Ingenio Boca Chica. Soto's remarks, nevertheless, were received with enthusiasm from an audience that had come expecting assurances of the project's approval against the interests and designs of the *hoteleros.*

Last to speak was PRD Deputy Tony Pérez, president of the commission. Pérez reaffirmed Soto's claims and then assured the audience that the revision of the contract for the Megaport had to do with *problemitas pequeñitos, very* minor problems, regarding tariffs. "The Megaport," he concluded, "is going to happen."

On July 27 CSX World Terminals and the Caucedo Development Corporation held their second public meeting at the Coral Hamaca Beach Hotel to present the results of the EIS. Since the March meeting, the project's name had grown; it was now called the Zona Franca Multi-Modal y Terminal Multi-Modal Puerto Caucedo. Residents of Andrés and Boca Chica circulated throughout the meeting room, examining the technical drawings and artist renderings of the facility that were displayed on easels. In one image of the Megaport, a luxury cruise ship—prominently out of scale—was docked in the port, bolstering its sponsor's assertion that the project would contribute to tourism.

32. Park benches donated by the sponsors of the Zona Franca Multi-Modal Caucedo in Boca Chica's town plaza. Photo by the author.

Manuel Tavares and the panelists repeated the claim that the Megaport would create 5,000 to 8,000 jobs and contribute 30 million pesos per month to the local economy. Tavares also informed the audience that a survey had indicated that 95 percent of the population of Andrés–Boca Chica were in favor of the project. Next, a marine biologist from Mouchel Consulting presented an incomprehensible mathematical model of tidal flows in the Bay of Andrés, concluding that there would be no damage to the coral reef or the beach. After three hours of EIS results, the audience had become restless, and many were gathered in the moonlit courtyard where refreshments were being served.

In the courtyard I ran into Fomerio Rodrigues, executive director of Turivisión and host of a popular talk show. He told me that initially he had been alarmed by the project, largely for environmental reasons. But now, he said, he believed that the project would bring economic benefits to the community. "The community, the country must progress," he added. Rodrigues introduced me (as "the protagonist" in the *telenovela*) to José Beato. I asked Beato what he thought of the EIS presentation and the Megaport generally. He replied that the EIS had been very thorough and scientific. "Many people," he said, "don't understand the process of changing from an industrial economy to a service economy. But it is necessary because we now live in a global economy *(economía mundial)*.

And *that* is what this project, the Megaport, is going to bring to the community."

I was surprised by their responses. Rodrigues, for one, had earlier expressed well-considered misgivings about the Megaport with respect to both its environmental hazards and the thornier question of its contribution in jobs and revenue to the region. Although there appeared to be a popular consensus in support of the project in Andrés–Boca Chica (a factor of no small significance for two public figures), both men had expressed their reasoning in the discourse of modernization theory, which views economic development, à la W. W. Rostow (1960), as a progressive ascent through Western-modeled stages of economic growth—from a "traditional" state of backwardness to modernity and prosperity. In contrast to dependency theory, advanced by left-leaning Latin American theorists, the modernization approach elided the historical processes through which "core" capitalist countries subordinated the economies of "peripheral" ones to their capital accumulation needs, rendering them dependent and, typically, exporters of cheap primary products and importers of value-added, manufactured goods.

Rodrigues's appeal to a notion of progress, externally imposed, gestured to this model of modernization, whereas Beato's narrative of an unavoidable progression from an industrial past to a service economy of the future recapitulated modernization theory's universalization of a Euro-American or, more accurately, an OECD-like path to economic development. Needless to say, the Dominican Republic never had an industrial economy, and the Megaport would, at best, provide subproletarian manufacturing jobs and further subordinate the nation's economy to the accumulation needs of U.S. and OECD capital. That modernization discourse, with its notion of an evolutionary progression from a tradition-bound past to economic growth, came to frame the ways in which many, though not all, residents interpreted and discussed the Megaport deserves some explanation.

With curious symmetry, the narrative of support for the Megaport writ large the drama of *La Negrita y el Turista* with its comparable, evolutionary narrative of an "up-from-the-countryside" progression. Not unlike Rostow's Weberian-inspired ascent from the shackles of tradition, la Negrita's development took her on an exodus from *el campo,* racialized and backward, through the civilizing mediation of urbanity, into the final embrace of Western [male] modernity. It is not by chance that the most compelling symbol of the corruptive selfishness of the tourism industry (and of the pro-Megaport position) was that of the underage, female prostitute, despoiled by "unscrupulous foreigners" who, as *Listín Diario* put it, promoted "all kinds of sexual aberrations."

If the story of la Negrita narrated a path to modernity that was mediated by male subjectivity and heteronormativity (progress as a pact among men), then the figure of the underage prostitute in debates over the Megaport embodied anxieties about the weakening of male power and Dominican sovereignty and the penetration of foreign capital. And if the *telenovela*'s gendered and racialized narrative of progress compromised, as Mabel put it, "the reality" of women's lives, then anxiety over the weakening of heteronormative male power derailed a more critical and historically attuned assessment of the Megaport, rendering modernization a more credible future than economic dependency. For just as modernization theory locates progress and development within the generative powers of the (white male) West, home to the tourist, so too did the consensus of public opinion fall in line behind "*el* know-how" of U.S. capital. In the end, I hazard to claim, the Megaport appeared to be more heteronormative and *más caballeroso* (more manly) than the tourism industry, which, putting women at risk, appeared as a corruption of the nation's body politic.

To be sure, if opposition to the tourism industry had centered more firmly on its asymmetrical division of labor and less on its "out of place" women, a more critical and experience-near deliberation and debate about both tourism and the Megaport might have taken shape. Instead, the paradoxical nature of the promise to transform the nation into the "Taiwan of the Caribbean" was muted and obscured by heteronormative anxieties. In short, economic progress required *above all* the shoring up of heteronormative male power. In a reversal of Marx's famous dictum, history had repeated itself, first as farcical *telenovela* and second (perhaps) as economic tragedy.

But this repetition did not go unmediated. Just as the narrative of la Negrita was disentangled from its heteronormative moorings through the interventions of Sonia and other women, so too did the Megaport remain subject to dispute and rumor grounded in the common sense of the laboring poor. In summer 2002 Minaya informed me of a rumor that he had heard about the Megaport: contrary to the promises that had been made by its sponsors, the Megaport would not have a dock and passenger terminal for cruise ships. Alarmed by this rumor, the Vendors' Union had met the week before to revisit the question of the Megaport, by then under construction. The sponsors' promise of cruise ship traffic to the Megaport had been critical to the support it received from workers in the tourism economy. Had a cruise ship terminal been included, Boca Chica would certainly have benefited, since, with the exception of Juan Dolio, other seaside areas were located too far from Punta Caucedo to benefit from cruise ship excursions.

One day, as I was perusing CSX World Terminal's web site back in New York, I happened to notice that in the artist's rendering of the Megaport that now appeared on the site, the oversized cruise ship had disappeared. The rumor was right. I then reexamined the EIS: the Megaport's potential impact on tourism would not require mitigation measures, its authors assured, because "[c]ruise ships *may* visit the terminal, increasing the tourism spend in the area *[sic]*" (Mouchel Consulting 2001: 15; emphasis added). At the end of the day, it seems, the Megaport had been sold on a ruse, one so self-assured that it did not require good grammar.

On February 21, 2002, President Hipólito Mejía, accompanied by officials of CSX World Terminals and the Caucedo Development Corporation, broke ground for the Megaport at Punta Caucedo. In a press release reporting the event, Arno Dimmling, vice president of CSX World Terminals, announced, "The new facility, and its associated systems and processes, will allow the Dominican Republic to become one of the most modern and efficient marine terminals in the world today, enhancing the country's ability to compete in the ever-increasing aggressive world market."

The struggle over the Zona Franca Multi-Modal Caucedo highlights the enduring role that the nation-state, as a contested political field, plays in configuring global flows of capital, technology, and labor, as well as in structuring discourses about the nature and future of the global economy. The tendency to discount this political significance by emphasizing the unfettered flows of transnational capital obscures the context-specific manner in which these processes are politically secured and materialized in space and time. Moreover, this strong deterritorialization argument obscures the fact that capitalism is, above all, a system for organizing labor—labor that must be disciplined, cajoled, and punished in specific spatiotemporal contexts. Time-space compression notwithstanding, capitalists must still act in time and space—and at times and in places not always of their own choosing.

The case of the Megaport also highlights the complex and sometimes antagonistic composition of transnational capital and the context-specific barriers and resistances as well as opportunities that it encounters in specific nation-states. In their struggle against the Megaport, the *hoteleros* were compelled, despite the legitimacy enjoyed by the tourism

33. The Megaport under construction at Punta Caucedo in 2002. Photo by the author.

industry, to appeal to the people and to the nation's cultural and natural patrimony. To that end, they argued that industrial development was incompatible with tourism and that the FTZs and their free trade ideology served the interests of U.S.-dominated, multinational corporations rather than those of the Dominican Republic.

To be sure, their appeal fell on deaf ears in an area that had received few benefits from tourism; one in which the vast majority of workers eked out a living on the margins of the tourism economy and, frequently, beyond the pale of legality and the safeguards of citizenship. Moreover, the tourism industry's eroticized race- and gender-stratified social division of labor rendered it particularly vulnerable to charges of sexual exploitation and moral corruption. In the end, class antagonisms, deformed by gendered anxieties and fueled by a symbolic economy that counterpoised "valued guests" against poor people to be avoided, exploited, and consumed, galvanized public support for the Megaport.

Against the *hoteleros*' construction of the nation's "patrimony," boosters of the Megaport advanced an alternative view that situated the nation's interests, albeit cynically, in the economic needs of the laboring poor and in opposition to the elitist landscape of the *zona turística*. CSX World Terminals and its Dominican partners constructed the Megaport as the solution to local problems, one that would integrate Andrés–Boca

Chica and the nation into the global economy. Nevertheless, this "global" argument was dressed in very local clothes, and the project's sponsors were hard pressed to present the project as one that would serve Dominican interests. On this score, the long-term, asymmetrical relationship between the Dominican Republic and the United States defined both the nature of the problem and the logic of its solution. Throughout the review process, Tavares and his Dominican partners were constructed as the agents behind the project while CSX World Terminals was backgrounded, portrayed as the experts who would contribute "*el* know-how" to the project. In addition, the Megaport's sponsors bent over backward to curry public support, lavishly catering events and responding to the linguistic preferences of their audience. These tactics bared, by means of transgression, the rigid class division underpinning the tourism economy. As a Turivisión cameraman remarked to me, as he surveyed the huge audience attending the EIS's presentation, "It's incredible. Few of these people have ever been inside of the Hamaca."

Nevertheless, many residents remained skeptical of the promises made by the Megaport's sponsors. Despite Tavares's attempts to disassociate the project from the abuses of other transnational corporations, few could fail to make the connection. Indeed, during the project's review process, communities throughout the nation were protesting the power blackouts, police repression, and a variety of abuses that had been committed by corporations such as Smith Enron and Falconbridge. Many residents of Andrés–Boca Chica remained bitter over the abandonment of Ingenio Boca Chica by its elusive, private sector managers. As Minaya told me after the release of the EIS, "They always promise a lot, *los empresarios* and the politicians. They promised to repair the *ingenio,* but it is still dead. They promise everything, but the poor are still hungry." Nevertheless, in this context and at this time, support for the Megaport against the "hegemony" of the *hoteleros* appeared the lesser of two evils.

It would be wrong, however, to view this community as having been simply duped, once again, by global capital and its promises of free market prosperity; or, for that matter, as lacking the political resources and expertise to oppose globalization globally. People resisted through mass protests that rendered sections of the nation ungovernable and provoked brutal repression. In fact, by 2002 unremitting protests against the punitive blackouts had provoked the Mejía administration to confront the private power distributors and threaten to revise, if not withdraw, their contracts. On June 18, 2002, the former director of the state power company, Radmamés Segura, called on the government to annul its contracts with the private power companies, describing them as a "foreign mafia" that should be expelled from the country (*Listín Diario*, June 19, 2002, 1). People power had produced some results.

The Megaport controversy incited public debate, not only about multinational corporations and the interests they serve, but also about "globalization" itself, forcing the project's sponsors to make explicit both their promises of prosperity and the economic assumptions underlying them. That transnational capital had to resort to a ruse (a cruise ship airbrushed onto an illustration of the Megaport) suggests the vulnerability and, indeed, paradoxical nature of the story that it is telling about itself. Whether, as in the case of the narrative of la Negrita, this story will be interrupted, disarticulated, and replaced with one that is closer to the needs and "reality" of the Dominican people and, indeed, the working people of the world remains to be seen.

Afterword

In June 2005 I returned to Boca Chica, a little less than four years after having completed fieldwork there. Much had changed since then. The Zona Franca Multi-Modal Caucedo had been completed, and from the beach I could see the huge unloading cranes perched over the docks, dwarfing the landscape around them. A group of children stood waist deep in the water, following the progress of a containership as it steadily navigated the narrow channel across the coral reef to the port and terminal.

Capital too had been on the move. Earlier in 2005, CSX World Terminals had sold its port facility at Punta Caucedo, along with its other overseas terminals, to Dubai Ports International (DPI), one of the world's largest owners and operators of ports, based in Dubai, United Arab Emirates. Commenting on the $1.45 billion acquisition, Sultan Ahmed Bin Sulayem, executive chairman of DPI, announced, "The acquisition of CSX complements DPI's existing network, giving us a truly global footprint that will benefit our customers and partners around the world" (CSX World Terminals 2005).[1]

However, the Megaport had not left much of a footprint in Andrés–Boca Chica. Although some people had found work as laborers during the construction phase of the project, those with whom I spoke in 2005

34. The Megaport's five gantry cranes dominating the horizon as viewed from Boca Chica in 2005. Photo by the author.

reckoned that relatively few permanent jobs had been created for local residents. The matter of local job creation had been a critical point of contention during the Megaport's public review process. In the Environmental Impact Statement, the project's sponsors claimed that between 3,000 and 5,000 direct jobs and 15,000 indirect jobs would be created through the operation of the port facility.[2] The EIS also avowed that 90 percent of those jobs would be made available to residents of Andrés–Boca Chica. To allay fears that local residents lacked the skills required, the project's sponsors had promised to provide basic skills training before the start of operations (Mouchel Consulting 2001). Although I have no hard evidence to ascertain whether this training was (or will be) provided, no one with whom I spoke in 2005 was aware of such a program. Moreover, there was little reason to assume that the Megaport's new owners would be bound by the promises made years earlier by CSX World Terminals.

Nor did the port facility contribute significantly to Boca Chica's struggling economy. Access to the multimodal terminal was achieved by widening and improving an existing dirt road that linked Punta Caucedo directly to the airport and highway to the north (see figure 33). As a result, traffic and commerce were channeled along this north-south corridor rather than east toward Andrés and Boca Chica. Although some hotels, restaurants, and other tourism-related concerns experienced a spike in business while the Megaport was under construction, this increase tapered off when the access road was completed. The owner of a restaurant put it to me this way: "Why should the workers and the engineers come here, to Boca Chica or Andrés, when they can go to the capital in twenty minutes." And the cruise ship pier and terminal, promised by the project's sponsors in 2001, never materialized.

In 2005 the tourism industry and the Dominican economy in general were still recovering from a financial crisis precipitated by the collapse of Banco Intercontinental (Baninter) in May 2003, after bank executives defrauded depositors and the Dominican government of U.S. $2.2 billion in account holdings—roughly 67 percent of the nation's annual budget. President Mejía's decision to bail out Baninter (and two other commercial banks) triggered a financial crisis that alarmed foreign investors and eroded the purchasing power of households. By the close of 2003 inflation had skyrocketed to 43 percent and the peso had lost half its value (Ribando 2005). Pressured by unrelenting protests over the daily power outages, the Mejía administration renationalized two of the power distribution companies (Edesur and Edenorte) that had been privatized in 2000, without notifying the IMF. In response, the IMF unilaterally suspended a $657 million standby agreement, resulting in the freezing of $500 million in loan payments to the nation's international creditors (*New York Times,* August 14, 2004, C1). In January 2004, in the midst of the skyrocketing cost of living, a two-day general strike organized by the Colectivo de Organizaciones Populares (a coalition of civic and labor groups) shut down the nation and achieved, according to its organizers, 97 percent participation.

In May 2004 former President Fernández was reelected to office in a resounding first-round victory over the incumbent, Hipólito Mejía. In September, under pressure from the IMF and other international lenders, the Dominican legislature passed a fiscal reform package, the provisions of which included an increase in sales taxes, a 20 percent cut in public expenditures, and the elimination of subsidies for electricity, propane, and food. The passage of this new austerity package cleared the way for a $670 million standby agreement with the IMF (Rabobank 2005; Ribando 2005). Though the economic reforms restored confidence among international creditors and investors, slowed inflation, and stimulated growth in the Gross Domestic Product (4.3 percent in the first quarter of 2005), the austerity measures—the elimination of subsidies in particular—threatened to further erode the lives and livelihoods of poor and moderate-income people. The consequences of the economic crisis and its aftermath were apparent in Andrés and Boca Chica in 2005.

Many of the people with whom I worked in 2000–2001 were unemployed or had otherwise suffered from worsening economic conditions and escalating social violence. Milquella, my research assistant, had been laid off from her job with a tour company in Juan Dolio and had been unemployed for six months. Minaya, my longtime friend, had been robbed at gunpoint in a March home invasion in the midst of a crime wave that was sweeping across the nation. Although he had offered no resistance, his assailants shot him in the hip. The debilitating injury had undermined his ability to earn a livelihood vending on the beach. Paredes, who worked as a welder next door to where I lived in 2000–2001, had made a second desperate attempt to emigrate to Puerto Rico in a small boat. His former coworkers told me that they were concerned that he had been among the fifty-five persons who perished at sea in a horrific migration attempt the year before. In 2004 alone more than five thousand Dominicans were intercepted by the U.S. Coast Guard en route to Puerto Rico (Ribando 2005). Finally, Jean Paul, a friend who had worked as a restaurant tout, had been deported to Haiti in a police crackdown on Haitian workers in 2004.

People working in the informal economy found their economic activities increasingly targeted by POLITUR, the specialized tourism police. Since 2001 the presence and policing intensity of POLITUR had increased dramatically; *cédula* and license checks had become routine and systematic. It was now commonplace for a team of POLITUR officers to surround groups of *motoconchos* and vendors to check identity cards, licenses, and other documents. Consequently, informal workers were debarred from the *zona turística*. On August 18, 2005, members of POLITUR destroyed more than three hundred food stalls and palm thatch umbrellas at the western end of Boca Chica's beach that had for two decades provided food, beverages, and picnic accommodations to Dominican visitors. The beach Vendors' Union charged that the police action, resulting in 300,000 pesos in losses, had been lobbied for by the Boca Chica Resort and the Boca Chica Tourism Development Association (*El Viajero Digital,* August 18, 2005).

This escalation in the policing of citizenship had also dramatically curtailed the presence of Haitians in the *zona turística*. In 2005 few persons of Haitian descent were working as vendors, touts, or salespersons in town or on the beach. This impression was confirmed by the merchants and vendors with whom I spoke. Those persons of Haitian descent whom I could identify were working as hair braiders and gallery painters—ethnic enclave occupations that, as I argued in chapter 5, were socially constructed as employing "natural" skills associated with Haitian (African) ancestry. Bruce, a Haitian painter, told me that many people had returned to Haiti voluntarily in an atmosphere of increasing hostility and persecution.

In fact, in summer 2005 an anti-Haitian pogrom occurred in the northwestern province of Monte Cristo, following the murder on May 9 of a Dominican woman, allegedly by three Haitians. On the same night, armed mobs attacked persons of Haitian descent in the town of Hatillo, burning down a number of homes. Elsewhere in the northwest, three Haitians were shot to death. The killing and ensuing mob violence incited a new round of deportations by Dominican authorities. By May 17 an estimated three thousand persons of Haitian descent, including Dominican citizens and persons in possession of valid work visas, had been deported. Still others, fearing the violence, fled to Haiti.

POLITUR's policing campaign had also suppressed the sex tourism industry and, in particular, the foreign-owned commercial venues that catered to it. Four bars, two discotheques, and the popular Zanzibar Bar and Café, all owned by foreign expatriates, had been shut down by the authorities for employing underage or otherwise undocumented women. Although the crackdown suppressed a long-standing source of embarrassment, frustration, and, some would say, crime for town residents, it also eradicated an important source of livelihood for perhaps hundreds of people who earned their living as vendors, hostesses, bartenders, and other occupations associated with Boca Chica's nightlife. POLITUR's reinvigorated policing campaign targeting social citizenship rights had succeeded, in effect, in privatizing the *zona turistíca*.

The situation that has evolved in Andrés–Boca Chica since I began preliminary fieldwork there in 1999 is that of an increasingly rigid dual economy: one tier centered on tourism and export manufacturing and, insulated from the surrounding society, highly integrated into transnational flows of capital, markets, and labor; and another tier consisting of an impoverished and increasingly immobile population of unemployed and underemployed persons who were improvising livelihoods in low-paying service jobs, declining sectors of the traditional economy, and the informal economy. In this key respect, Andrés–Boca Chica was a microcosm of the wider Dominican economy.[3]

The laboring poor have been increasingly prevented from moving through the social division of labor (i.e., into the enclaved "growth areas" of the economy controlled by transnational capital) and, indeed, through space itself. As a *motoconcho,* maddened by POLITUR's harassment, remarked to me in irony, "Look, I have a motorcycle, but I can't move." Movement here is not merely a metaphor for earning a living: it is precisely this movement—whether across the policed landscape of the *zona turística,* or the frontiers of the export manufacturing enclaves, or the international division of labor—that has been the target of neoliberal strategies of accumulation (Ong 1999; de Rivero 2001).

Moreover, in the wake of U.S. immigration reforms since the mid-1980s—in particular, the 1996 Illegal Immigration Reform and Responsibility Act—migration to the United States has ceased to be an option for the vast majority of Dominicans (Hernández 2002).[4] As capital has become increasingly mobile (illustrated by the sale of the Megaport to Dubai Ports International), labor has become ever more shackled to space—space that has been increasingly disciplined and privatized (Caldeira 2000).

Zygmunt Bauman, critical of the universalizing tendency in some globalization discourse, stressed the uneven and asymmetrical quality of space-time compression:

> What appears as globalization for some means localization for others; signaling a new freedom for some, upon many others it descends as an uninvited and cruel fate. Mobility climbs to the rank of the uppermost among the coveted values—and the freedom to move, perpetually a scarce and unequally distributed commodity, fast becomes the main stratifying factor of our late-modern or postmodern times. (1998: 2)

This process of "space-fixing," as Bauman (1998) called it, clarifies both the logic and the consequences of POLITUR's repression of the informal economy—a policing strategy that has fortified the barriers between the tourism economy and the populace, shoring up the near-monopoly of the all-inclusive resorts and their landscape of exclusion. Similarly, the Punta Caucedo Multimodal Terminal, like free trade zones elsewhere, promises to be an enclave of capital accumulation, shielded from revenue-generating tariffs and taxes and from the place-based needs and interests of the populace.[5]

It should come as no surprise, then, that the social function and meaning of space, far from losing its significance under conditions of globalization, is a key stake in the struggles of laboring people against the space-fixing practices of capital and the state. In Andrés and Boca Chica this spatial politics centered on the tourism industry and on its practices

35. Vendors surrounding tourists during the 2005 tourism slump. Photo by the author.

of social, economic, and symbolic exclusion, which fabricated the "atmosphere" of the *zona turística* over and against the economic needs and sociocultural hybridity of the surrounding community. The policing of citizenship, by means of document checks, as well as through race-, gender-, and class-influenced appraisals of identity, was a leading technology of power through which these social exclusions were secured in space.

Residents challenged these exclusions at various spatial scales. Workers in the informal economy defied state regulations governing participation in the tourist economy, transgressing the borders of the *zona turística* and, in some cases, contesting and reworking elite, power-laden definitions of the labor process and tourism experience. Against the static and bounded narrative of Dominican cultural identity, marketed by the tourism industry, these workers inhabited, performed, and sometimes commodified unruly and hybrid subjectivities that drew on Dominican cultural resources at home and abroad and within the wider African Diaspora. These workers infused a dynamic, creolized culture that celebrated black identities into a tourism industry that muted, devalued, and, at times, suppressed persons of African descent and their cultural practices. Transnational media, commerce, and migration (notably, the return migration and visits of Dominicans from the United States) provided cultural resources and capital to recalibrate the meaning of Dominican racial identities (Torres-Saillant and Hernández 1998).

Residential barrios such as Bella Vista, where I lived, also challenged the economic and symbolic hegemony of the tourism industry and, in particular, the priority and allowances that were given to the *zona turística* by the authorities over the needs of other areas. Junta La Unión's efforts to assert the identity and needs of Bella Vista were both a "defensive" measure against the evisceration of place-based meanings in the face of extraterritorial capital and a renegotiation of the meanings of community in a context of transnational migration and changing gender roles. La Gringa's opposition to the attempt of La Unión's male leadership to restrict the recognition of women's agency and work to their roles as "mothers" drew on the transnational experiences of Dominican women as laborers and independent heads of household. In this manner, the significance of community was renegotiated through its articulation to transnational processes—what Roland Robertson (1995) has called "glocalization," or the copresence and interaction of universalizing and particularizing tendencies.

This bilateral interaction of locality with transnational processes was also evidenced by the media-producing work of Fomerio Rodrigues and Turivisión. If, as Bauman (1998: 18) has argued, space-time compression has operated to denude the territories to which nonelites are confined of their "meaning and identity-endowing capacity," then Turivisíon's practices of representation worked to restore that capacity by recovering and asserting the temporality and spatiality of everyday life and struggle. Turivisión's broadcast of extended, unedited, and cinema verité narratives of everyday events in Andrés–Boca Chica thus served to "decompress" the time-space relation, fabricating a social geography that called into question the tourism industry's rhetoric of transnational movement and aspatial desire.

These resistances to the meaning- and space-fixing practices of global capital were uneven and were shaped and deflected by local arrangements of power, discourses of difference, and social histories. Like Junta La Unión's efforts to affirm the integrity of community, Turivisíon's aborted staging of the *telenovela La Negrita y el Turista* figured community and, by extension, national integrity and agency as male. In these gendered narratives of territory, women were interpolated as either mothers and managers of the household economy or as not fully formed adults whose sexuality was at risk when projected beyond the regulatory powers of men. Though these gendered constructions of agency and community were contested and, to varying degrees, reformulated by women, they nevertheless influenced how residents (notably, men) interpreted their problems and interests and devised strategies to address them.

In the political discourse of elites and nonelites alike, the socioeconomic problems confronting Andrés–Boca Chica were frequently indexed to, or expressed through, the issue of female prostitution and, more generally, male inability to govern the sexuality of women. Sex workers were viewed not only as women who were sexually out of place (in the street) and out of control (of male authority) but also as persons occupying particularly unstable and subversive positions within the division of labor, which rendered the social order vulnerable to threats and sources of disharmony, ranging from crime, drug abuse, and HIV/AIDS infection to the exploitation and abuses of foreign capital. This etiology of disorder drew on age-old, post-Enlightenment constructions of the female body as "intrinsically unpredictable, leaky and disruptive" and a source of danger and disorder, internal to the social body (Price and Shildrick 1999: 2).

This construction of the bodies and subjectivities of women proved of no small consequence in the debate over the Megaport. The charge, made by the project's supporters, that the tourism industry was deeply implicated in the moral corruption of women (minors, in particular) found fertile ground in Andrés–Boca Chica, undermining the tourism industry's appeal to the community's interests and condensing a variety of long-standing sources of resentment in the iconic figure of the fallen woman who had been corrupted by unscrupulous foreigners. In this and other political contexts, sex/gender and racial relations and ideologies shaped activists' discourse, if not the very perception of the nature and consequences of transnational capitalist investment.

The case of the Megaport also highlights the heterogeneous and, sometimes, mutually antagonistic composition of transnational capital even within the seemingly uniform narrative of neoliberal economic reform. Exploiting these differences, representatives of the tourism industry cast the Megaport and its free trade zone as a development strategy that was in decline in the post-NAFTA era and as an artifact of Reagan-era U.S. strategies to contain Cuba and promote political stability in the Caribbean basin. For their part, the Megaport's sponsors presented the multimodal terminal as essential to reaping the benefits of regional free trade and as the only hope for integrating the nation gainfully into the global economy. What is of interest here is that both emissaries of global capital were obliged to appeal to the interests of the nation-state and the community and improvise arguments that addressed their context-specific histories, arrangements of power, and cultural meanings. In short, place mattered not only in configuring the specific manner in which transnational flows of capital were materialized in space but also in shaping how that process was interpreted and contested by diverse and, often, conflicting interest groups within Dominican society.

This multifaceted, spatial politics has been overlooked in many recent discussions of globalization, largely because researchers have tended to emphasize the transnational mobility of capital while discounting, if not obscuring, the extent to which the organization and disciplining of labor under capitalism—the reproduction of the social division of labor—remains a critical function of nation-states and their governing regimes. That nation-states (though not all) are losing control over their economies and public policy making powers to transnational corporations and international institutions does not suggest that they are losing their political significance as battlegrounds where the future of the world system is being deliberated and contested.

This tendency to exaggerate the deterritorialized state of the contemporary world system has had important theoretical and political consequences. First, it has led to the view that globalization is a fait accompli, irresistible and a new historical horizon that has superseded not only the politics of nation-states but also enduring asymmetries in their relative powers—asymmetries that are firmly rooted in the continuing histories of imperialism (Petras and Veltmeyer 2001). In the case of the Dominican Republic, transnational capital, backed by the military might of the United States, exercised substantial control over the Dominican economy and state for much of the late nineteenth and twentieth century, underscored by the U.S. military interventions of 1916–1924 and 1965–1966. More generally, as James Petras and Henry Veltmeyer (2001) have pointed out, the origins of neoliberal economic reform in Latin America are rooted less in the inevitable unfolding of free market forces in the wake of failed, state-based development policies than in the U.S.-abetted overthrow of democratically elected governments in Chile, Argentina, Brazil, and Uruguay by violent dictatorships backed by national elites (see also Hicks 2000). To view the current regulatory and debt collection policies of the IMF, the World Bank, and WTO (fine tuned in the 1990 Washington Consensus) or the actions of transnational corporations as operating outside the framework of U.S. hemispheric power and intervention is naive at best and politically disabling at worst.

Equally important, the strong deterritorialization argument risks underestimating and obscuring the political agency and oppositional practices of those very actors who are experiencing, theorizing, and struggling against neoliberal economic policies. Although resistance to these policies in the Dominican Republic seldom caught the attention of the corporate media in the United States, it was unrelenting and multi-sited during the period of my fieldwork and, indeed, before. Throughout the 1980s adjustment policies met with widespread opposition from labor confederations and diverse, popular constituencies (Cassá 1995). This resistance, witnessed by the food riots of 1984 and by a succession of general strikes, contributed to the defeat of the IMF-receptive administration of Jorge Blanco (1982–1986) and to the critical position initially adopted by the administration of Joaquín Balaguer toward the IMF during his 1986–1990 term (Espinal 1995).

Strikes and popular protests against unemployment, price hikes, and the other consequences of neoliberal reforms continued through the 1990s and were typically greeted with violent repression from Dominican security authorities. Social unrest over the punitive power outages contributed to an atmosphere of crisis throughout the administration of Hipólito Mejía, culminating in the general strikes of 2003 and 2004. Although the return to power of Fernández in 2004 was welcomed by many as a departure from the failed economic policies of his predecessor, by summer 2005 the honeymoon appeared to be over.

This widespread opposition to neoliberal reforms, as well as the multilayered, everyday conflicts that are the focus of this book, suggest to me that the future of the Dominican and, indeed, global economy is far from settled. In Andrés and Boca Chica resistance to the space-fixing practices of neoliberal economic reforms permeated the everyday social practices and relations of the laboring poor. Locally, as well as nationally, the state assumed the task of enforcing this restructured division of labor and its constituent social exclusions and inequalities. Indeed, to the degree that states have relinquished control of their economies and public policies to transnational structures of political and economic power, they have been faced with crises of governance that are by no means new—that of repressing populations whose lives have become unsustainable (see Kotz 2002).

One may raise the question, can globalization be resisted? My response is that in the Dominican Republic and elsewhere, it *is* being resisted. Whether or not, and by what means, this resistance can give rise to a world order that is more just and more equitable is a political question—one that cannot be answered in advance. To paraphrase Stuart

Hall (1996) in a not unrelated context, we must think social transformation without guarantees.

There is a risk, I believe, of conflating what capital is saying about itself with the facts as they are on the ground. To overcome this risk, we must disentangle the disparate transnational processes that have become condensed in the notion of "globalization" and examine their effects in the situated lives of real people, communities, and nation-states. In short, it requires that we look behind and not into the mirror.

Notes

INTRODUCTION

1. *Boricua* (Puerto Rican) is derived from *Boríken* (or *Borinquen*), the name given by Puerto Rico's indigenous inhabitants, the Taíno, to the island.

2. In 2001 the exchange rate of the Dominican peso for the U.S. dollar averaged RD $16.43. I use this conversion rate throughout the text.

3. I adopt the term *globalization* with some misgivings since it has been used to refer to disparate transnational processes, the origins and effects of which are by no means congruent. As Bob Jessop (2001: 1) put it, "'Globalization' is a polyvalent, promiscuous, controversial word that often obscures more than it reveals about recent economic, political, social and cultural changes" (see also Bauman 1998). In this book I use *economic restructuring* to refer to broad changes in the Dominican political economy associated with neoliberal reforms and *transnational* as a modifier when referring to specific flows of capital, media, people, and so forth (see Ong 1999).

4. For example, see the reviews by Ray Kiely (2000) and Jeffrey Sommers (2003) of David Held et al., *Global Transformations;* see also Barrie Axford, *The Global System*. Anthropologists have been attuned to regional and national differences in their ethnographic studies of transnational processes. See, for example, Sherri Grasmuck and Patricia Pessar, *Between Two Islands;* Roger Rouse, "Mexican Migration and the Social Space of Postmodernity"; Linda Basch, Nina Glick Schiller, and Cristina B. Szanton, *Nation's Unbound;* Daniel Miller, *Capitalism;* Aiwa Ong, *Flexible Citizenship;* Carla Freeman, *High Tech and High Heels in the Global Economy;* Peggy Levitt, *Transnational Villagers;* Nina Glick Schiller and Georges Fouron, *George Woke Up Laughing;* and Paul Stoller, *Money Has No Smell.*

5. The G8 (Group of Seven plus One) consists of seven of the leading industrialized nations (the United States, Canada, Germany, France, Italy, the United Kingdom, and Japan) and, with limited participation after 1994, Russia. The Organization for Economic Co-operation and Development (OECD) is an inter-

national organization of thirty developed countries that accept the principles of democracy and free market economies.

6. For example, in their influential book *Global Transformations,* Held et al. discounted the significance of "earlier" imperial geographies: "North and South are increasingly becoming meaningless categories: under conditions of globalization distributional patterns of power and wealth no longer accord with a simple core and periphery division of the world, as in the early twentieth century, but reflect a new geography of power and privilege which transcends political borders and regions, reconfiguring established international and transnational hierarchies of social power and wealth" (1999: 429). As is often the case in the globalization literature, the past is presented through categories that are reductively simple (and thus untenable) as a means of emphasizing an unprecedented present. Clearly, a *simple* core and periphery division of the world has never adequately described the international system. Similarly, Justin Rosenberg (2000) has pointed out that the argument for the demise of nation-states often rests on a retrospective reading of the *ideal* of the Westphalian system as an actual historical past. For a contrasting view of the enduring significance of North-South differences, see Fernando Coronil, *The Magical State.*

7. For example, in *Globalization from Below* (2000), a book inspired by the now-legendary "Battle in Seattle" protests against the World Trade Organization, Brecher, Costello, and Smith wrestle with the challenges of coalition building between what they call "globalization from below" and other social movements marked by race, gender, and other distinctions. They observe: "Globalization from above has created common interests among an extraordinary range of people, but that doesn't mean they don't also have conflicting ones. The movement for globalization from below inherits a multitude of national, ethnic, religious, political, and economic conflicts from the *pre-globalization era*" (47; emphasis added).

More remarkable, perhaps, than the authors' proclamation of a new era is the notion of "inheritance." As in the colonial imaginary, in which an unmarked subject assumed the *mission civilatrice* (the Western subject's "burden" of enlightening the differentiated populations of the world), globalization from below inherits the project of global transformation, of interpreting and enfolding differences into a *universal* political subject—one that is cosmopolitan and no longer weighed down by race, gender, class, or other social distinctions.

Indeed, the authors suggest that it is "globalization from above" that calls into being globalization from below in a Manichaean, postglobalized universe. Though they make a strong case for building alliances with marked social movements, it is globalization from below, difference-free, indistinct, and transcendental, that is to function "as the tip of a spear, opening up issues and positions that represent broad but denied social interests" (106). It is only this unmarked subject, universal and absolute, that can fathom and act effectively against the totality that is conjured as "globalization from above." This claim of radical rupture with a preglobalized past, as in similar accounts, suggests a logic that is less political than theological.

The claim that the postglobalized world order is (or will soon be) divided into two warring camps, unmediated by sociospatial differences, rests at the foundation of Michael Hardt and Antonio Negri's (2000) prophetic account of Empire and its overthrow at the hands of "the multitude." In a bold and innovative effort to conceptualize a novel, immanent political subject, capable of undoing Empire, Hardt and Negri observe:

> Imperial power can no longer resolve the conflict of social forces through mediatory schemata that displace the terms of conflict. The social conflicts that constitute the political confront one another directly, without mediations of any sort. This is the essential novelty of the imperial situation. Empire creates a greater potential for revolution than did the modern regimes of power because it presents us, alongside the machine of command, with an alternative: the set of all the exploited and the subjugated, a multitude that is directly opposed to Empire, with no mediation between them. (393)

In contrast to the "mediated" subjects of history, embedded in anticolonial, sex and gender, or trade union politics, the radicalism of the multitude rests in its nomadism and incommensurability and, consequently, in its uncompromising negation of Empire's regime of biopolitical production. "Autonomous movement," Hardt and Negri observe, "is what defines the place proper to the multitude" (397). Although a logical and, indeed, imaginative possibility *given* Empire, there is little evidence to suggest that this politics of movement is either new or that nomadism has been, or will be, a real possibility for most of the world's population.

As Pramod K. Mishra (2001) has pointed out, the privileging of migration and "autonomous movement" as defining characteristics of the multitude risks leaving out those very peoples, particularly in the developing world, who have not moved and, importantly, the places that they inhabit. Mishra poses the axiomatic question, "Now, what kind of agency and biopower do Hardt and Negri impute to this vast majority of the Third World's population still toiling there under their own elites and traditional ideologies?" (97). The political risk here rests not only in privileging the demands (e.g., "global citizenship") and forms of agency that are most accessible to those who are on the move (not infrequently elites) but also in obscuring *precisely* the specific and novel modalities of political subjectivity and action that are taking shape in actually existing places in relation to the problem of movement

Hardt and Negri (2001: 399) then pose the challenging programmatic question, "How can the actions of the multitude become political?" The answer is unsurprising, if not tautological: the multitude becomes political when it directly confronts the repressive apparatus of Empire "with an adequate consciousness." Of interest here, as in *Globalization from Below,* is Hardt and Negri's evacuation of the politics of the present to a past that presumably has been already superseded. As in the millenarian movements that haunt premodern histories, the future can only be imagined by means of the utter obliteration of the past.

Hardt and Negri also address the equally daunting question of what is to be done—or, more exactly, what *should* the multitude do—politically? "This task for the multitude, however, although it is clear at the conceptual level, remains rather abstract. What specific and concrete practices will animate this political project? We cannot say at this point" (2000: 399–400). Having negated, a priori, all mediations between Empire and the multitude—and in the process evacuated history—there is, of course, little ground from which to answer this question. The multitude, disarticulated from the spatiotemporal and pulverized into "singularity," reveals itself to be nothing other than the text—an artifact of what Marx (1977: 157) called "contemplative materialism."

Indeed, Hardt and Negri's conception of social transformation, admittedly sketchy, is curiously Hegelian and, to paraphrase Marx's critique of Hegelian logic, converts subjects into the predicates of an ideal, universal political subject—in this case "the multitude." Louis Althusser (1977: 126) observed of this idealism, "Thus universality is not a predicate of the concrete individuals of this particular historical people, their basic element and daily bread; they themselves are, rather, the mere instruments of an ideal necessity that dupes and crushes them. They are not real people who are really free, but rather vassals of the freedom of the Idea, whose ways are unfathomable."

If, in the coalition building proposed by Brecher, Costello, and Smith, the marked multitudes are to be collated as predicates behind the spear of "globalization from below," for Hardt and Negri they exist only as an ideal possibility—as the *logical* antithesis of Empire. Just as civil society, the space of particular needs, was for Hegel incapable of embodying unmediated universality, being in and for itself (a role that he reserved for the Prussian state), actually existing "territorialized" social movements, for Hardt and Negri, can only realize their *positive* political power externally, in the Ideal of the multitude—"absolute spirit" for the new millennium. *Empire,* it appears, sets Hegel firmly back on his feet.

8. This recognition of the sociospatial contingency of the relations of production was present in Marx's formulation of the social division of labor. In Marx's writings the division of labor referred to the general organization of work in society and, under capitalism, to the allocation of social labor by capitalist enterprises. Marx used this category in two senses: first to refer to the organization of tasks and labor within and among capitalist enterprises, which he referred to as the "detail" division of labor. In this sense, Marx (1967: 348–349) stressed the specialization, or "parceling out," of productive operations among detail laborers that accompanied the rise of manufacturing. In the second, wider use of the category, Marx addressed the general order of social production, the social division of labor, which he noted "forms the foundation of all production of commodities" (351; see also Walker 1985).

9. For a critique of this state-economy dualism, see Timothy Mitchell, "Society, Economy, and the State Effect."

10. Meren-rap is a fusion of Dominican merengue music and rapping. The song that is credited with giving birth to the genre was "Soy Chiquito (No Inventes Papito, No Inventes)," recorded in 1990 by Santi y Sus Duendes and Lisa M. Reggaetón is a fusion of Jamaican dancehall and hip hop genres with bomba, plena, and other Latin music styles.

11. Two landmark ethnographic studies that address this problem are Daniel Miller's *Capitalism* and Coronil's *The Magical State.*

1. THE POLITICS OF LIVELIHOOD

1. Johnnycakes are deep-fried, pancake-shaped breads that are popular throughout the English-speaking Caribbean; they were introduced to the Dominican Republic by West Indian migrant workers.

2. This semirural area to the north of Carretera de Las Américas is referred to as "El Cruce de Boca Chica" (the Cross of Boca Chica). In-migration to the areas surrounding Andrés and Boca Chica led to the founding of unofficial communities or squatter settlements in El Cruce de Boca Chica and in the area to the east known as La Malena. As a result the boundaries of Andrés and Boca Chica proper have become increasingly blurred.

3. Elizabeth Garnsey (1981) attributed this neglect of the division of labor to the demise of classical political economy and the development of economics and sociology as distinct disciplines (see also Mitchell 1999). Noting that the analysis of the division of labor provides a means for understanding the interrelation of economic processes and social relationships, Garnsey (1981: 341) emphasized its significance for understanding the process of class formation: "It was not the identity of their sources of revenue that made of wage laborers, capitalists, and landlords three distinct social classes. Rather, it was the extent of control over the means of production, as embodied in property relations, sanctioned by the legal system and backed by the coercive powers of the state, which determined class formation."

4. As Richard A. Walker (1985: 175) has pointed out, the power differentials and relations that take shape through the formation of the social division of labor are relatively autonomous from, and irreducible to, class relations, "although they may easily become overlapped or even absorbed into the nexus of class power." The *social* division of labor is the result of a more extensive and multifaceted process of organizing and governing the productive and reproductive activities of populations, constituting, as Walker put it, "the material axis around which people develop capabilities, knowledge, associations—and power" (175). Thus, although the social division of labor expresses the allocation of labor within capitalist economies, the process of achieving that result implicates and harnesses power relations, strategies, discourses, and institutional resources that stretch well beyond "the economy."

5. This problem, elucidated in the exchange between Nancy Fraser and Judith Butler has often been posed as a distinction between "class first" positions and those stressing the relative autonomy of race, gender, sex, and other socially constructed differences from the relations of production or, more broadly, "the economic."

In an effort to clarify the distinction between class-based and other, ascriptive hierarchies, Fraser posited an analytic distinction between "injustices of distribution" and "injustices of misrecognition." She maintained that whereas the former are rooted in the unequal distribution of economic goods, the latter are rooted in "institutionalized patterns of interpretation and evaluation that constitute one as comparatively unworthy of respect or esteem" (1997: 280). Distinctions based on race, sexuality, and other ascriptive criteria, she suggested, have their origins in "social patterns of representation, interpretation and communication" rather than directly in the political economy and class structure of society (1995: 71).

Though injustices of recognition take concrete or "material" form and in existing social systems are deeply enmeshed in class-based injustices, Fraser held that they must be analytically differentiated, since they give rise to distinct justice claims and strategies of redress.

> Recognition claims often take the form of calling attention to, if not performatively creating, the putative specificity of some group, and then of affirming the value of that specificity. Thus they tend to promote group differentiation. Redistribution claims, in contrast, often call for abolishing economic arrangements that underpin group specificity. (An example would be feminist demands to abolish the gender division of labour.) Thus they tend to promote group de-differentiation. The upshot is that the politics of recognition and the politics of redistribution appear to have mutually contradictory aims. (1995: 74)

However, to sustain this analytic distinction in the face of existing social systems, where issues of recognition and redistribution are entangled, Fraser argued that the social organization of capitalist society "creates an order of specialized economic relations that are relatively uncoupled from relations of kinship and political authority" (1997: 284). It is for this reason that structures of economic distribution and social status can diverge.

However, Fraser's position requires a state-economy dualism that discounts, if not ignores, the state's "presence-action" in the organization of production (Poulantzas 1978). Moreover, this dualism serves to disembody and, in the process, depoliticize injustices of distribution by disassociating them from the ascriptive social hierarchies that enable economic exploitation and other distributive injustices. Indeed, it is the very structuring of this context-specific "coupling" between state and economy and ascriptive and class-based hierarchies that requires explanation. "Is it possible," Butler (1998: 6) asks, "to distinguish, even analytically, between a lack of cultural recognition and a material oppression when the very definition of legal personhood is rigorously circumscribed by cultural norms that are indissoluble from their material effects?" It is precisely this articulation of ascriptive differences to laboring bodies that is achieved through the sociospatial structuring of the division of labor—a process at once cultural, political, and economic. In short, class positioning is both experienced and secured through the articulation of differences to laboring bodies.

6. Whereas the notion of intersectionality stresses the importance of attending to the effects of multiple constructions of difference (e.g., race *and* gender) on the subject, my emphasis is on the process of their mutual constitution through the organization of production.

7. The Centro de Investigación Económica para el Caribe (CIECA 2001) concluded that this 2000 figure was an undercount and that the population of greater Boca Chica was closer to 100,000, if not higher.

8. Commercial sugar production was practiced during the sixteenth century in Hispañola, concentrated around Santo Domingo, but had virtually come to a halt by the early seventeenth century (Betances 1995).

9. Import-substitution industrial development was aggressively pursued by the Trujillo administration in the years after World War II. See Frank Moya Pons, "Import-Substitution Industrialization Policies in the Dominican Republic, 1925–61."

10. A report published by the Inter-American Development Bank also questioned this decline in unemployment and attributed it to a reduction in the rate of labor force participation rather than to an increase in employment (Inter-American Development Bank 2001).

11. In addition, Law No. 141–97 led to the privatization of mineral industries, an airline, a hotel chain, and other enterprises that had been under the management of the Corporación Dominicana de Empresas Estatales (CORDE), a state holding company.

12. I adopt José Itzigsohn's (2000) approach to conceptualizing informal economic activities in Latin America, which, following Alejandro Portes (1994a, 1994b), stresses the linkages between the formal and informal economies (as opposed to a discrete "sector" approach) and the role of state institutions in shaping urban labor markets and informality. For a survey of theoretical approaches to informal economies, see Tamar Diana Wilson, "Introduction."

13. Interestingly, vendors who sold food and beverages at the western end of the beach, which was frequented almost exclusively by Dominicans, were, with few exceptions, women. At issue here is the constructed boundary between the *zona turística* and "community." As Susan Vincent (1998: 133) has pointed out, social and physical boundaries determine the forms of women's work that are culturally acceptable according to gender and other norms. Within the *zona turística,* food vending (like the vending of other commodities) was viewed as a relatively lucrative and high status occupation; beyond the tourism sector, it was viewed as women's work and as an extension of domestic work. Beyond the tourism economy, women working informally were concentrated in clothing fabrication, selling and laundering, and food production and vending—a pattern of gender segregation that Rosario Espinal and Sherri Grasmuck (1997) also found among informal workers in the Dominican city of Santiago.

14. In their study of microproducers in Santiago, Espinal and Grasmuck (1997: 16) concluded that in contrast to accounts of informal economies in other areas of Latin America, the informal sector in the Dominican Republic "produces largely for the local market and sells primarily to individuals in the neighborhood. The absence of notable linkages between these producers and large-scale capital may relate to the Dominican context where production for export has primarily been organized in free trade zones. In these enterprise zones, cheap labor and lack of unionization make informal subcontracting of labor less essential to maintaining international competitiveness."

15. Article 11 of the Dominican Constitution extends citizenship to persons born in the nation "except for the legitimate children of foreigners resident in the country as diplomats or those in transit" (Gavigan 1995). It is this "in transit" exception that has been used to deny documents to children of Haitian descent (see also Human Rights Watch 2002).

16. *"Él/Ella sabe mucho"* is an idiomatic expression that conveys the sense of savoir faire and, in particular, the sense of being crafty, wily, and "slick."

2. THE SPATIAL ECONOMY OF DIFFERENCE

1. The historical reference is to the largely Kikuyu-led "Mau Mau Uprising" in Kenya (1952–1960) against the British colonial administration.

2. Sosúa is a seaside resort town on the northern coast of the Dominican Republic that is also reputed to be a destination for sex tourism. See Denise Brennan, *What's Love Got to Do with It?*

3. For an analysis of prostitution among minors in the Dominican Republic, see Julia O'Connell Davidson and Jacqueline Sánchez Tayor, *Child Prostitution and Sex Tourism.*

4. Nayan Shah (2001: 7) has noted the relationship between varying assessments of the capacity of subjects to reason and the recognition of citizenship: "Different forms of citizenship—from nationality status to suffrage to property rights to the access to social provision—have been abridged, circumscribed, and repudiated based on gender, race, nationality, and economic standing."

5. In 2002 Grupo BHD's Coral Hotels & Resorts entered into a strategic alliance with Hilton International to create the new brand Coral by Hilton.

6. Beachfront businesses relied on a system of service exchanges to maximize their customer base. For example, some bars established relationships with food vendors to provide meals for their customers. Typically, it was the *fisgones* who negotiated and conducted these transactions, for which they received a commission in the form of a markup in price.

7. The Coral Hamaca Beach Hotel had its own theater where it presented semiprofessional folkloric dance and theatrical performances. In 2005, for example, it presented a sanitized drama of Christopher Columbus's "discovery" of the island of Hispaniola that employed hotel staff as actors.

8. Remittances to the Dominican Republic grew at an annual rate of 12 percent between 1994 and 2003. In 2001 remittances amounted to US $1.8 billion dollars, or 8.34 percent of the GDP (Suki 2004).

9. I found it difficult, sometimes impossible, to manage perceptions of my identity. For example, among the tight-knit expatriate community from the United States, a rumor circulated that I was an Internal Revenue Service agent investigating tax evaders. Some Italian merchants thought that I was an agent with an undercover unit of the National Police, investigating drug and child trafficking. Late in my research I discovered that some members of the National Police believed that I was a drug trafficker because of my relationships with Elwin, Gérard, and others involved in the informal economy.

10. The bulk of Milquella's Avon commissions came from sales to tourists and foreign expatriates. Generally, most Avon products were a luxury beyond the reach of the working poor.

3. STRUCTURES OF THE IMAGINATION

1. For a discussion of Gagá (or Gagann) in Haiti, see Elizabeth McAlister, *Rara!* and Gage Averill, *A Day for the Hunter, a Day for the Prey.*

2. The Lenten Gagá festival provoked an equally nationalistic but costlier response elsewhere in 2001. In La Romana 137 Haitians and Dominicans of Haitian descent were deported by the Dominican government after they were falsely accused of having burned a Dominican flag. The flag in question had been displayed by the Gagá celebrants, as was customary (Human Rights Watch 2002). The incident in La Romana underscores what is politically at stake in these everyday negotiations of meaning, which can and often do attract the attention of the state.

3. Turivisión's programming can be viewed as constituting a "counterpublic"

that contrasted with the dominant narratives of tourism disseminated through the national electronic and print media. For a discussion of the concept of counterpublics, see Nancy Fraser, "Rethinking the Public Sphere."

4. The disclosure of this local or "indigenous" economy of pleasure was a frequent theme in Turivisión reporting. For example, Sucre produced a similar story about a group of teenage boys from the area who had taken up surfing in the waters off the coast of Punta Caucedo.

5. Rodrigues's philosophy of community television also resonated with other political and artistic currents concerned with the self-empowerment of the oppressed in Latin America during the 1960s and 1970s, exemplified by Paulo Freire's *Pedagogy of the Oppressed* (1970) and Augusto Boal's *Theater of the Oppressed* (1985). For discussions of the uses of grassroots media for local empowerment, see Deedee Halleck and Nathalie Mangan, "Access for Others"; Pat Aufderheide, "Latin American Grassroots Video"; and Tony Dowmunt, ed., *Channels of Resistance.*

6. In Boal's theater of the oppressed, the joker is a trickster figure who acts variously as master of ceremonies, narrator, and "wild card" actor who steps in and out of various roles, undermining rigid, potentially disempowering plots and characters.

4. SEX TOURISM AND THE POLITICAL ECONOMY OF MASCULINITY

1. The numbers of men of African, Asian, or Hispanic descent participating in Boca Chica's sex tourism industry were relatively insignificant in 2000–2001. During my stay in Boca Chica, totaling about fifteen months in three visits, I encountered only three dozen or so African American male tourists. Dominican men, other than those working in the tourism sector, do not frequent bars, discos, and restaurants in tourist areas. There is, however, a nontourism commercial sex industry that is discrete from the tourism sector (see Cabezas 1999; Brennan 2004).

2. The term *trabajadores sexuales* (sex workers) came into usage in the Dominican Republic in 1988 in the context of debates over the status of prostitution, prompted by the use of the term by sex workers themselves (Kempadoo 1998). In Boca Chica women who engaged in sex work used euphemistic phrases such as *salir con turistas* (to leave with tourists) or *trabajar con turistas* (to work with tourists) to describe their work. Jo Doezema (1998) has pointed out that the distinction between "voluntary" and "forced" prostitution made by many international rights organizations, while seeming to affirm sex workers' rights to self-determination, has led to a focus on campaigns to end forced prostitution rather than to efforts to strengthen the rights of all sex workers and challenge oppressive views of female sexuality. Instead, the forced versus voluntary dichotomy constructs the former as an innocent "victim" and the latter as a "whore" who "because of her transgression . . . deserves what she gets" (47).

3. For a discussion of ethnographic contributions to the study of the feminization of transnational labor regimes, see Aiwa Ong, "The Gender and Labor Politics of Postmodernity."

4. For a discussions of social scientists' lack of attention to heteronormativ-

ity in everyday experience, see Rosemary Pringle, "Absolute Sex? Unpacking the Sexuality/Gender Relationship"; and Steven Seidman, *Queer Theory/Sociology.*

5. See Donna Hughes, "Sex Tours via the Internet"; Beverly Mullings, "Globalization, Tourism, and the International Sex Trade"; and, in the Dominican Republic, Denise Brennan, *What's Love Got to Do with It.*

6. E. Antonio DeMoya, Rafael García, Rosario Fadul, and Edward Herold (1992), Amalia Cabezas (1998, 1999), and Denise Brennan (2004), working in Sosúa, on the north coast of the Dominican Republic, provide accounts of heterosexual and bisexual male escorts or "beach boys," referred to as Sanky-Pankies. Male sex workers were probably more active in Boca Chica than it appeared to me, a heterosexual male researcher. Male "guides" with whom I spoke denied that they exchanged sex for money through their interactions with tourists but nonetheless took pride in the "gifts" *(regalos)* that they received from both women and men. See Kempadoo (1999) for a discussion of how constructions of gender in the Caribbean differentially figure the identities available to men and women engaged in sex work and Herold, Garcia, and DeMoya (2001) on the importance of attending to the complex motivations shaping the relationships between tourists and hosts.

7. During my stay, I heard of three cases in which male tourists were evicted from their rooms in midsized hotels for admitting Dominican males. There was also an incident in which a German male tourist was robbed and severely beaten by two young Dominican men after he had allegedly propositioned them for sex. The alleged perpetrators were never caught. When I asked a policeman whom I knew about the case, he replied, "It's not worth it, [the tourist] asked for it."

8. See Cabezas (1999) for a discussion of the complex and highly ambiguous legal status of prostitution in the Dominican Republic.

9. In 2001 both the Zanzibar Bar and Café and the adjacent La Noria discotheque were owned by Italian expatriates who were part of a tight-knit Italian community invested in bars, restaurants, and real estate. Many working in tourism believed that these businesspeople had ties to the Italian mafia and that to run afoul of one *empresario* would lead to being blacklisted by all the Italian-owned establishments.

10. Midway through my stay in 2000–2001 this same sergeant had begun to ask me for *regalitos* (little gifts) in the form of a beer, a hamburger, or money to buy cigarettes. When I realized that he was setting me up for regular graft payments, I stopped making the gifts. The logic of graft is that only a person vulnerable before the law would make the gift to begin with and thus initiate the pattern of regular and, often, escalating payments. In short, the sergeant was testing my vulnerability and social connections.

11. Dominican men rarely patronized sex worker venues such as Pattaya that were associated with the tourism industry, in part because of their inflated prices. In 2001 Pattaya became, for a short time, a popular drinking spot for skilled foreign and Dominican workers (though not local men) who were involved in the construction of the AES power plant not far away.

12. The editors of *The Politics of Nature* (2003), the volume in which an earlier version of this chapter first appeared, alerted me to the potential for vignettes, such as this one, to incite a "voyeuristic complicity" between the

reader's gaze and the gaze of the sex tourist. This is a very real possibility for those on the "constitutive inside" of heteronormativity, where I must position myself. In the spirit of this chapter, I suggest that heteronormative males *are* complicit, willingly or unwillingly, and for that reason the voyeur's position is potentially more reflexive and disruptive of the heteronormative gaze than that of a more "detached [male] observer."

13. Clearly, this might not have been the case in other social settings or in relation to other interlocutors. Most sex workers in Boca Chica had not been raised there and commuted from other areas. Some women expressed the opinion that it was better to work elsewhere so as to not bring shame to one's family and, above all, to one's children.

5. RACE, IDENTITY, AND THE BODY POLITIC

1. Colonel William Regala was a member of the five-man National Governing Council that came to power after the departure into exile of Jean Claude Duvalier in February 1986. Promoted shortly afterward to major general in the Haitian army and assistant commander-in-chief, Regala was implicated in human rights abuses and drug trafficking.

2. I doubt that Gérard was ever involved in trafficking cocaine to the Dominican Republic. More than likely he was involved in transborder smuggling to and from Haiti during the OAS-sponsored embargo, which flourished before the return to power of President Aristide on October 15, 1994 (see Corten and Duarte 1995). Milquella told me that Gérard was once arrested by the police for attempting to sell two cars in Boca Chica that he had transported across the border from Haiti with a cousin.

3. The conviction expressed in this comment recalls the test that was given by Trujillo's soldiers during the 1937 massacre of Haitians in the Dominican border region. A person suspected of being Haitian was asked to pronounce the Spanish word *perejil* (parsley); if the *r* was not properly trilled, the person was killed (Wucker 1999).

4. In Rastafarian Creole (or "Dreadtalk") *livealect* (live + dialect) is used instead of "dialect" to avoid the sound and sense of "die."

5. To be sure, cultural mixing, or "creolization," has been a constitutive feature of all Caribbean societies from their beginnings, but in the Dominican Republic this process of mixing has been shaped and crosscut by the potent distinction between Haitians and Dominicans (see also Khan 2004).

6. Interestingly, Lauren Derby (1994) points out that one of the behaviors of Haitian women that troubled Dominican Nationalists in the border regions was the squatting of market women, which was viewed as being unwomanly and uncivilized.

7. Within Boca Chica's tourism sector bilingual Dominicans were very much in demand and paid high premiums, especially by the all-inclusive resorts. It was not uncommon for front desk personnel at the major hotels to be monolingual.

8. The exception, noted earlier, was in bartending, waitressing, and other jobs associated with sex tourism—jobs a "respectable" Dominican woman would not take.

9. For example, a survey of twenty Haitian sex workers in the Dominican Republic by the International Organization for Migration found that 40 percent of them believed that "those who live with HIV/AIDS are not good people, should not be allowed to work, and may be cursed by witches, and 74 percent believed that AIDS cannot be treated (IOM 2004: 35).

10. The *tonton makout* (or Volontaires de la Sécurité Nationale) were a dreaded paramilitary security force that operated in Haiti during the Duvalier dictatorships; FRAPH (Front for the Advancement and Progress of Haiti) was a paramilitary terrorist organization that sought to topple the Aristide administration.

6. THE POLITICS OF TRANSNATIONAL CAPITAL

1. The Punta Caucedo Multimodal Port is representative of a new generation of deepwater containerports and terminals designed to accommodate "post-Panamax" and "super post-Panamax" container vessels, that is, vessels too large to pass through the Panama Canal. These megaports require more dockside space than did earlier ports, as well as special gantry cranes capable of reaching across the wider beams (widths) of post-Panamax vessels.

AFTERWORD

1. In September 2005 Dubai Ports International merged with Dubai Ports Authority, which managed port operations in Dubai, to form Dubai Ports World (DP World). In February 2006 DP World won a takeover bid of Peninsular & Oriental Steam Navigation, a British company that operates port terminals in the United States. DP World's acquisition provoked controversy and opposition among members of the U.S. Congress and other public figures who maintained that the operation of U.S. ports by a UAE-owned company posed a threat to national security in the wake of the terrorist attacks of September 11, 2001. In the midst of mounting opposition, DP World announced on March 9, 2006, that it would transfer its newly acquired ports in the United States to an American-owned company. In this highly publicized case, national security interests trumped those of free trade (*New York Times,* March 10, 2006, A1, 18).

2. This assessment is based on anecdotal evidence. I informally questioned about forty people, who knew of five people who had been employed at the Zona Franca Multi-Modal Caucedo: three as construction workers, one as a security guards, and one as a truck mechanic.

3. The World Trade Organization's "Trade Policy Review, Dominican Republic" (2002), warned of this wider structural problem: "The Dominican Republic is approaching a juncture where the duality and enclave features of its economy may have to be addressed. Activities in FTZs and tourism are responsible for the lion's share of Dominican exports, and are important generators of employment and investment, but their backward linkages to the rest of the economy remain weak" (ix).

4. Ramona Hernández (2002: 178) reported that Dominican migration to the United States has been declining since 1996 as the number of deportations from

the United States has been increasing: "In 1998 only 20,387 Dominicans were admitted to the United States. This figure represents half the number of Dominicans admitted only seven years before. Unlawful Dominicans residing in the United States have fared no better. The number of those sent back to the Dominican Republic has systematically increased in recent years. In 1992, 1,082 Dominicans were deported from the United States. By 1996 this number had increased to 1,916, and by 1998, the latest figures available, the number of deported reached 2,498."

5. Writing about the meteoric growth of export-processing zones in the 1980s, Emilio Betances (1995: 129) observed, "The free-trade zones were not structurally linked to the Dominican economy: they offered no strategy for development and paid no taxes. Companies invested in the free-trade zones because the Dominican Republic offered low wages, political stability, and special access to the U.S. market. If any of these variables changed, the companies might simply decide to move elsewhere."

References

Abt Associates, Inc.
2002 *Diagnóstico ambiental y análisis económico/fiscal.* Santo Domingo: Secretaría de Estado de Medio Ambiente y Recursos Naturales.

Allison, Anne
1994 *Nightwork: Sexuality, Pleasure, and Corporate Masculinity in a Tokyo Hostess Club.* Chicago: University of Chicago Press.

Althusser, Louis
1997 *The Spectre of Hegel.* London: Verso.

Appadurai, Arjun
1996 *Modernity at Large.* Minneapolis: University of Minnesota Press.

Artaud, Antonin
1958 *The Theater and Its Double.* New York: Grove Press.

Aufderheide, Pat
1993 "Latin American Grassroots Video: Beyond Television." *Public Culture* 5(3): 579–592.

Averill, Gage
1997 *A Day for the Hunter, a Day for the Prey: Popular Music and Power in Haiti.* Chicago: University of Chicago Press.

Axford, Barrie
1995 *The Global System: Economics, Politics and Culture.* Cambridge: Polity Press.

Báez, Clara
1989 *La subordinación social de la mujer dominicana en Cifras.* Santo Domingo: Dirección General de Promoción de la Mujer/United Nations Research and Training Institute for the Advancement of Women/INSTRAW.

1991 *Mujer y desarrollo en la República Dominicana: 1981–1991.* Santo Domingo: Inter-American Development Bank.

2000 *Boca Chica: El impacto del turismo en la vida de la comunidad. Las mujeres y sus familias.* Santo Domingo: Caribbean Regional Gender Initiative.

Báez Evertsz, Franc
1978 *Azúcar y dependencia en la República Dominicana*. Santo Domingo: Universidad Autónoma de Santo Domingo.
Barry, Kathleen
1995 *The Prostitution of Sexuality*. New York: New York University Press.
Basch, Linda, Nina Glick Schiller, and Cristina B. Szanton
1994 *Nations Unbound*. Langhorne, Pa.: Gordon and Breach.
Baudrillard, Jean
1990 *Seduction*. New York: St. Martin's Press.
Bauman, Zygmunt
1998 *Globalization: The Human Consequences*. New York: Columbia University Press.
Betances, Emilio
1995 *State and Society in the Dominican Republic*. Boulder: Westview.
Betances, Emilio, and Hobart A. Spalding Jr.
1995 "Introduction. The Dominican Republic: Social Change and Political Stagnation." *Latin American Perspectives* 22(3): 3–19.
Boal, Augusto
1985 *Theater of the Oppressed*. New York: Theatre Communications Group.
Bolles, Lynn A.
1992 "Sand, Sea, and the Forbidden." *Transforming Anthropology* 3(1): 300–333.
Bourdieu, Pierre
1977 *Outline for a Theory of Practice*. Cambridge: Cambridge University Press.
Brecher, Jeremy, Tim Costello, and Brendan Smith
2000 *Globalization from Below*. Cambridge: South End Press.
Brennan, Denise
1998 "Everything Is for Sale Here: Sex Tourism in Sosúa, the Dominican Republic." Ph.D. dissertation, Yale University.
2004 *What's Love Got to Do with It*. Durham: Duke University Press.
Brotherton, David
2003 "Dominican Republic: The Deportees." *NACLA Report on the Americas* 37(2): 7–11.
Butler, Judith
1993 *Bodies That Matter: On the Discursive Limits of "Sex."* New York: Routledge.
1997 "Merely Cultural." *Social Text* 15(52–53): 265–277.
1998 "Left Conservatism, II." *Theory & Event* 2(2). http://muse.jhu.edu.
Cabezas, Amalia
1998 "Pleasure and Its Pain: Sex Tourism in Susua, the Dominican Republic." Ph.D. dissertation, University of California, Berkeley.
1999 "Women's Work Is Never Done: Sex Tourism in Susua, the Dominican Republic." In *Sun, Sex, and Gold: Tourism and Sex Work in the Caribbean*, edited by Kamala Kempadoo, 93–123. Lanham, Md.: Rowman & Littlefield.

Cabrera, Federico
2001 "La comunidad de Andrés: Una excursión al Lejano Oeste." *Listín Diario,* June 3, 4.
Caldeira, Teresa P. R.
2000 *City of Walls.* Berkeley: University of California Press.
Calhoun, Craig
1993 "Habitus, Field, and Capital: The Question of Historical Specificity." In *Bourdieu: Critical Perspectives,* edited by Craig Calhoun, Edward LiPuma, and Moishe Postone, 61–88. Chicago: University of Chicago Press.
Cassá, Roberto
1995 "Recent Popular Movements in the Dominican Republic." *Latin American Perspectives* 22(3): 80–93.
Chanan, Michael
1997 "The Changing Geography of Third Cinema." *Screen* 38(4): 372–388.
Chardon, Roland
1984 "Sugar Plantations in the Dominican Republic." *Geographical Review* 74(1): 441–454.
CIECA (Centro de Investigación Económica para el Caribe)
2001 *Diagnóstico: De la problemática de residuos sólidos en la ciudad de Boca Chica y Los Tanquecitos.* Santo Domingo: Centro de Investigación Económica para el Caribe.
Collier, Jane, and Michelle Rosaldo
1981 "Politics and Gender in 'Simple' Societies." In *Sexual Meanings,* edited by Sherry Ortner and Harriet Whitehead, 275–329. New York: Cambridge University Press.
Comaroff, Jean, and John L. Comaroff
2001 "Millennial Capitalism: First Thoughts on a Second Coming." In *Millennial Capitalism and the Culture of Neoliberalism,* edited by Jean Comaroff and John L. Comaroff, 1–56. Durham: Duke University Press.
Constable, Nicole
2003 *Romance on a Global Stage.* Berkeley: University of California Press.
Coronil, Fernando
1997 *The Magical State: Nature, Money, and Modernity in Venezuela.* Chicago: University of Chicago Press.
Corten, André, and Isis Duarte
1995 "Five Hundred Thousand Haitians in the Dominican Republic." *Latin American Perspectives* 86(22): 94–110.
Crichlow, Michaeline
1998 "Reconfiguring the 'Informal Economy' Divide: State, Capitalism, and Struggle in Trinidad and Tobago." *Latin American Perspectives* 25(2): 62–83.
Crick, Malcolm
1989 "Representations of International Tourism in the Social Sciences: Sun, Sex, Sights, Savings, and Servility." *Annual Review of Anthropology* 18: 307–344.
Cross, John
1998 *Informal Politics: Street Vendors and the State in Mexico City.* Stanford: Stanford University Press.

CSX World Terminals
2005 "Dubai Ports International Completes Acquisition of CSX World Terminals." Press release, February 22, 2005. http://csx.com.
Da Matta, Roberto
1987 "The Quest for Citizenship in a Relational Universe." In *State and Society in Brazil,* edited by John H. Wirth, Edson de Oliveira Nunes, and Thomas A. E. Bogenschild, 307–335. Boulder: Westview.
Davidson, Julia O'Connell, and Jacqueline Sánchez Taylor
1996 *Child Prostitution and Sex Tourism: Dominican Republic.* Bangkok: ECPAT International.
de Lauretis, Teresa
1990 "Eccentric Subjects: Feminist Theory and Historical Consciousness." *Feminist Studies* 16: 115–149.
DeMoya, E. Antonio, Rafael García, Rosario Fadul, and Edward Herold
1992 *Sosúa Sanky-Pankies and Female Sex Workers.* Santo Domingo: Instituto de Sexualidad Humana, Universidad Autónoma de Santo Domingo.
de Oliveira, Orlandina, and Bryan Roberts
1993 "La informalidad urbana en años de expansión, crisis y restructuración ecónomica." *Estudios Sociológicos* 11: 33–58.
Derby, Lauren
1994 "Haitians, Magic, and Money: Raza and Society in the Haitian-Dominican Borderlands, 1900 to 1937." *Comparative Studies in Society and History* 36(3): 488–526.
de Rivero, Oswaldo
2001 *The Myth of Development.* New York: Zed Books.
Diawara, Manthia
1998 *In Search of Africa.* Cambridge, Mass.: Harvard University Press.
Doezema, Jo
1998 "Forced to Choose: Beyond the Voluntary v. Forced Prostitution Dichotomy." In *Global Sex Workers: Rights, Resistance, and Redefinition,* edited by Kamala Kempadoo and Jo Doezema, 34–50. New York: Routledge.
Dowmunt, Tony, ed.
1993 *Channels of Resistance: Global Television and Local Empowerment.* London: British Film Institute.
Duany, Jorge
1998 "Reconstructing Racial Identity: Ethnicity, Color, and Class among Dominicans in the United States and Puerto Rico." *Latin American Perspectives* 25(3): 147–172.
Dworkin, Andrea
1981 *Pornography: Men Possessing Women.* London: Women's Press.
Ebron, Paula
1996 "Traffic in Men." In *Gendered Encounters,* edited by Maria Grosz-Ngate and Omari Kokole, 223–244. New York: Routledge.
Enloe, Cynthia
1989 *Bananas, Beaches, and Bases: Making Feminist Sense of International Politics.* Berkeley: University of California Press.

Espinal, Rosario

1995 "Economic Restructuring, Social Protest, and Democratization in the Dominican Republic." *Latin American Perspectives* 22(3): 63–79.

Espinal, Rosario, and Sherri Grasmuck

1997 "Gender, Households and Informal Entrepreneurship in the Dominican Republic." *Journal of Comparative Family Studies* 8(1): 103–128.

Family Health International

2005 *Final Report for the AIDSCAP Program in the Dominican Republic.* Arlington, Va.: Family Health International.

Fanon, Frantz

1965 *Wretched of the Earth.* New York: Grove Press.

1967 *Black Skins, White Masks.* New York: Grove Press.

Farmer, Paul

1992 *AIDS and Accusation: Haiti and the Geography of Blame.* Berkeley: University of California Press.

1997 "AIDS and Anthropologists: Ten Years Later." *Medical Anthropology Quarterly* 11(4): 516–525.

Foucault, Michel

1990 *The History of Sexuality: Volume I.* New York: Vintage Books.

1991 "Governmentality." In *The Foucault Effect: Studies in Governmentality,* edited by Graham Burchell, Colin Gordon, and Peter Miller, 87–104. Chicago: University of Chicago Press.

Fraser, Nancy

1993 "Rethinking the Public Sphere: A Contribution to the Critique of Actually Existing Democracy." In *The Phantom Public Sphere,* edited by Bruce Robbins, 1–32. Minneapolis: University of Minnesota Press.

1995 "From Redistribution to Recognition? Dilemmas of Justice in a 'Post Socialist' Age." *New Left Review* 212: 68–93.

1997 "Heterosexism, Misrecognition, and Capitalism." *Social Text* 15(3–4): 279–289.

Freeman, Carla

2000 *High Tech and High Heels in the Global Economy.* Durham: Duke University Press.

Freire, Paolo

1970 *Pedagogy of the Oppressed.* New York: Continuum.

Garnsey, Elizabeth

1981 "The Rediscovery of the Division of Labor." *Theory and Society* 10(3): 337–358.

Gavigan, Patrick

1995 *Beyond the Bateyes.* New York: National Coalition for Haitian Rights.

Gilroy, Paul

2000 *Against Race.* Cambridge, Mass.: Harvard University Press.

Ginsberg, Faye

1994 "Embedded Aesthetics: Creating a Discursive Space for Indigenous Media." *Cultural Anthropology* 9(3): 365–382.

Glick Schiller, Nina, and Georges Eugene Fouron

2001 *George Woke Up Laughing.* Durham: Duke University Press.

Grasmuck, Sherri, and Rosario Espinal
2000 "Market Success or Female Autonomy? Income, Ideology, and Empowerment among Microentrepreneurs in the Dominican Republic." *Gender & Society* 14(2): 231–255.
Grasmuck, Sherri, and Patricia Pessar
1991 *Between Two Islands*. Berkeley: University of California Press.
Grosz, Elizabeth
1994 *Volatile Bodies*. Bloomington: Indiana University Press.
Guarnizo, Luis Edwardo, and Michael Peter Smith
1998 "The Locations of Transnationalism." In *Transnationalism from Below*, edited by Michael Peter Smith and Luis Eduardo Guarnizo, 3–34. New Brunswick, N.J.: Transaction.
Hall, Stuart
1996 "The Problem of Ideology: Marxism without Guarantees." In *Stuart Hall: Critical Dialogues*, edited by David Morley and Kuan-Hsing Chen, 151–173. New York: Routledge.
Halleck, Deedee, and Nathalie Mangan
1993 "Access for Others: Alter(native) Media Practices." *Visual Anthropology Review* 9(1): 154–163.
Hardt, Michael, and Antonio Negri
2000 *Empire*. Cambridge, Mass.: Harvard University Press.
Held, David, Anthony McGrew, David Goldblatt, and Jonathan Perraton
1999 *Global Transformations*. Stanford: Stanford University Press.
Hernández, Ramona
2002 *The Mobility of Workers under Advanced Capitalism*. New York: Columbia University Press.
Herold, Edward, Rafael Garcia, and Tony DeMoya
2001 "Female Tourists and Beach Boys; Romance or Sex Tourism." *Annals of Tourism Research* 28(4): 978–997.
Hicks, Alexander
2000 Review of *Global Transformations: Politics, Economics and Culture. Social Forces* 78(4): 1571–1573.
Hirst, Paul, and Grahame Thompson
1999 *Globalization in Question*. Malden, Mass.: Polity Press.
Hughes, Donna
1996 "Sex Tours via the Internet." *Agenda: A Journal about Women and Gender* 28: 71–76.
Human Rights Watch
2002 "'Illegal People': Haitians and Dominico-Haitians in the Dominican Republic." *Human Rights Watch* 14(1[B]): 1–32.
Inoa, Orlando
1999 *Azúcar, árabes, cocolos y haitianos*. Santo Domingo: Editora Cole.
Inter-American Development Bank (IDB)
2001 *Dominican Republic Country Paper*. Washington, D.C.: Inter-American Development Bank.

International Monetary Fund (IMF). Staff

1999 *Dominican Republic: Selected Issues.* Country Report No. 99/117. Washington, D.C.: International Monetary Fund.

IOM (International Organization for Migration)

2004 *HIV/AIDS and Mobile Populations in the Caribbean: A Baseline Assessment.* Santo Domingo: International Organization for Migration.

Itzigsohn, José

2000 *Developing Poverty: The State, Labor Market Deregulation, and the Informal Economy in Costa Rica and the Dominican Republic.* University Park: Pennsylvania State University Press.

Jacobs, Jane

1996 *Edge of Empire.* New York: Routledge.

Jessop, Bob

1999 "Reflections on Globalization and Its (Il)logic(s)." Lancaster University, Department of Sociology. http://www.comp.lancs.ac.uk/sociology/soc013rj.html.

2001 "On the Spatio-Temporal Logics of Capital's Globalization and Their Manifold Implications for State Power." Lancaster University, Department of Sociology. http://www.comp.lancs.ac.uk/sociology/soc072rj.html.

Kempadoo, Kamala

1998 "COIN and MODEMU in the Dominican Republic." In *Global Sex Workers,* edited by Kamala Kempadoo and Jo Doezema, 260–266. New York: Routledge.

1999 "Continuities and Change: Five Centuries of Prostitution in the Caribbean." In *Sun, Sex, and Gold: Tourism and Sex Work in the Caribbean,* edited by Kamala Kempadoo, 5–33. Lanham, Md.: Rowman & Littlefield.

Khan, Aisha

2004 *Calloloo Nation.* Durham: Duke University Press.

Kiely, Ray

2000 "Book Review: Global Transformations: Politics, Economics and Culture." *Journal of Development Studies* 36(4): 182–183.

Kinnaird, Vivian, Uma Kothari, and Derek Hall

1994 "Tourism: Gender Perspectives." In *Tourism: A Gendered Analysis,* edited by Vivian Kinnaird and Derek Hall, 1–34. New York: John Wiley.

Knight, Melvin M.

1939 *Los americanos en Santo Domingo.* Santo Domingo: Universidad de Santo Domingo.

Kondo, Dorinne

1989 *Crafting Selves.* Chicago: University of Chicago Press.

Kotz, David M.

2002 "Globalization and Neoliberalism." *Rethinking Marxism* 14(2): 64–79.

Kutzinski, Vera

1993 *Sugar's Secrets: Race and the Erotics of Cuban Nationalism.* Charlottesville: University Press of Virginia.

La Forgia, Gerard, Ruth Levine, Arismendi Díaz, and Magdalena Rathe

2004 "Fend for Yourself: Systemic Failure in the Dominican Health System." *Health Policy* 67: 173–186.

Lefebvre, Henri
1991 *The Production of Space.* Cambridge: Blackwell.
Levitt, Peggy
2001 *Transnational Villagers.* Berkeley: University of California Press.
Ling, L. H. M.
1999 "Sex Machine: Global Hypermasculinity and Images of the Asian Woman in Modernity." *Positions: East Asian Cultures Critique* 7(2): 277–306.
Martínez, Samuel
1995 *Peripheral Migrants: Haitians and Dominican Republic Sugar Plantations.* Knoxville: University of Tennessee Press.
Marx, Karl
1964 *The Economic and Philosophic Manuscripts of 1844.* New York: International Publishers.
1967 *Capital. Volume 1.* New York: International Publishers.
1977 "Theses on Feuerbach. " In *Karl Marx: Selected Writings,* edited by David McLellan, 156–158. Oxford: Oxford University Press.
Massey, Doreen
1993 "Power-Geometry and a Progressive Sense of Place." In *Mapping the Future,* edited by Jon Bird, Barry Curtis, Tim Putnam, George Robertson, and Lisa Tucker, 59–69. New York: Routledge.
McAlister, Elizabeth
2002 *Rara! Vodou, Power, and Performance in Haiti and Its Diaspora.* Berkeley: University of California Press.
McClintock, Ann
1995 *Imperial Leather.* New York: Routledge.
MacKinnon, Catherine
1989 *Toward a Feminist Theory of the State.* Cambridge, Mass.: Harvard University Press.
Meyer-Arendt, Klaus J., Richard A. Sambrook, and Brian M. Kermath
1992 "Seaside Resorts in the Dominican Republic." *Journal of Geography* 21(5): 219–225.
Miller, Christopher
1985 *Blank Darkness.* Chicago: University of Chicago Press.
Miller, Daniel
1997 *Capitalism: An Ethnographic Approach.* Oxford: Berg.
Mishra, Pramod K.
2001 "The Fall of the Empire or the Rise of the Global South?" *Rethinking Marxism* 13(3–4): 95–99.
Mitchell, Michael J., and Charles H. Wood
1998 "Ironies of Citizenship: Skin Color, Police Brutality, and the Challenge to Democracy in Brazil." *Social Forces* 77(3): 1001–1020.
Mitchell, Timothy
1999 "Society, Economy, and the State Effect." In *State/Culture: State-Formation after the Cultural Turn,* edited by George Steinmetz, 76–97. Ithaca: Cornell University Press.

Moreno, Luis, and Deanna Kerrigan
2000 *HIV Prevention Strategies among Female Sex Workers in the Dominican Republic.* Research for Sex Work 3. Santo Domingo: Centro de Orientación e Investigación Integral.
Mosse, George
1985 *Nationalism and Sexuality.* New York: Howard Fertig.
Mouchel Consulting, Ltd.
2001 *Puerto Caucedo Multimodal Terminal: Environmental Impact Statement Summary.* Surrey, U.K.: Mouchel Consulting, Ltd.
Moya Pons, Frank
1990 "Import-Substitution Industrialization Policies in the Dominican Republic, 1925–61." *Hispanic American Historical Review* 70(4): 539–577.
1995 *The Dominican Republic: A National History.* Princeton: Markus Wiener.
2004 "Memoria de la diversidad perdida: Reflexiones iniciales." In *Desde la orilla: Hacia una nacionalidad sin desalojos,* edited by Silvio Torres-Saillant, Ramona Hernández, and Blas R. Jiménez, 48–54. Santo Domingo: Editora Manati.
Mullings, Beverly
1999 "Globalization, Tourism, and the International Sex Trade." In *Sun, Sex, and Gold: Tourism and Sex Work in the Caribbean,* edited by Kamala Kempadoo, 55–80. Lanham, Md.: Rowman & Littlefield.
Mutman, Mahmood
2001 "On Empire." *Rethinking Marxism* 13(3–4): 43–60.
Nandy, Ashis
1988 *The Intimate Enemy: Loss and Recovery of Self under Colonialism.* Delhi: Oxford University Press.
O'Connell Davidson, Julia, and Jacqueline Sánchez Taylor
1999 "Fantasy Islands: Exploring the Demand for Sex Tourism." In *Sun, Sex, and Gold: Tourism and Sex Work in the Caribbean,* edited by Kamala Kempadoo, 37–54. Lanham, Md.: Rowman & Littlefield.
ONAPLAN (Oficina Nacional de Planificación)
1997 *Focalización de la pobreza.* Santo Domingo: Secretariado Técnico de la Presidencia.
Ong, Aiwa
1991 "The Gender and Labor Politics of Postmodernity." *Annual Review of Anthropology* 20: 279–309.
1996 "Cultural Citizenship as Subject-Making." *Current Anthropology* 37(5): 737–762.
1999 *Flexible Citizenship.* Durham: Duke University Press.
Ortner, Sherry
1995 "Resistance and the Problem of Ethnographic Refusal." *Comparative Studies in Society and History* 37(1): 173–193.
1997 *Making Gender: The Politics and Erotics of Culture.* Boston: Beacon Press.

Overall, Christine

1992 "What's Wrong with Prostitution? Evaluating Sex Work." *Signs* 17(4): 705–724.

Pacini Hernandez, Deborah

1995 *Bachata.* Philadelphia: Temple University Press.

Pantaleón, Lourdes

2003 *Sexual Harassment in the Export Processing Zones of the Dominican Republic.* Santo Domingo: International Labor Rights Fund/Fundación Laboral Dominicana.

Pateman, Carol

1998 *The Sexual Contract.* Stanford: Stanford University Press.

Pattullo, Polly

1996 *Last Resorts: The Cost of Tourism in the Caribbean.* London: Cassell.

Pérez, Gina

2004 *The Near Northwest Side Story: Migration, Displacement, and Puerto Rican Families.* Berkeley: University of California Press.

Perraton, Jonathan

2001 "The Global Economy—Myths and Realities." *Cambridge Journal of Economics* 25: 669–684.

Petras, James, and Henry Veltmeyer

2001 *Globalization Unmasked. London: Imperialism in the 21st Century.* London: Zed Books.

Pettman, Jan Jindy

1997 "Body Politics: International Sex Tourism." *Third World Quarterly* 18(1): 93–108.

Portes, Alejandro

1994a "The Informal Economy and Its Paradoxes." In *The Handbook of Economic Sociology,* edited by N. J. Smelser and R. Swedberg, 426–452. Princeton and New York: Princeton University Press and Russell Sage Foundation.

1994b "When More Can Be Less: Labor Standards, Development, and the Informal Economy." In *Contrapunto,* edited by Cathy A. Rokowski, 113–130. Albany: State University Press of New York.

Poulantzas, Nicos

1978 *State, Power, Socialism.* London: Verso.

Price, Janet, and Margrit Shildrick

1998 "Opening the Body: A Critical Introduction." In *Feminist Theory and the Body,* edited by Janet Price and Margrit Shildrick, 1–14. New York: Routledge.

Price, Richard

1998 *The Convict and the Colonel.* Boston: Beacon Press.

Pringle, Rosemary

1992 "Absolute Sex? Unpacking the Sexuality/Gender Relationship." In *Rethinking Sex: Social Theory and Sexuality Research,* edited by R. W. Connell and G. W. Dowsett, 76–101. Philadelphia: Temple University Press.

Pruit, Deborah, and Suzanne Lafont

1995 "For Love of Money: Romance Tourism in Jamaica." *Annals of Tourism Research* 22(2): 422–440.

Rabobank

2005 *Update Dominican Republic.* Utrecht: Rabobank, Economic Research Department.

Raynolds, Laura

1998 "Harnessing Women's Work: Restructuring Agricultural and Industrial Labor Forces in the Dominican Republic." *Economic Geography* 74(2): 149–169.

Ribando, Clare M.

2005 *Dominican Republic: Political and Economic Conditions and Relations with the United States.* Washington, D.C.: Congressional Research Service.

Robertson, Roland

1995 "Glocalization: Time-Space and Homogeneity-Heterogeneity." In *Global Modernities,* edited by Mike Featherstone, Scott Lash, and Roland Robertson, 25–44. London: Sage.

Rosaldo, Michelle

1974 "Woman, Culture and Society: A Theoretical Overview." In *Woman, Culture and Society,* edited by Michelle Rosaldo and Louise Lamphere, 17–42. Stanford: Stanford University Press.

Rosenberg, Justin

2000 *The Follies of Globalisation Theory.* London: Verso.

Rostow, W. W.

1960 *The Stages of Economic Growth.* Cambridge: Cambridge University Press.

Rouse, Roger

1991 "Mexican Migration and the Social Space of Postmodernity." *Diaspora* 2(2): 8–23.

Rubin, Gayle

1975 "The Traffic in Women: Notes on the 'Political Economy' of Sex." In *Toward an Anthropology of Women,* edited by Rayna Reiter [Rapp], 157–210. New York: Monthly Review Press.

Rude, George

1995 *Ideology and Popular Protest.* Chapel Hill: University of North Carolina Press.

Rutherford, Jonathan

1997 *Forever England: Reflections on Masculinity and Empire.* London: Lawrence & Wishart.

Safa, Helen

1995 *The Myth of the Male Breadwinner.* Boulder: Westview.

1999 "Free Markets and the Marriage Market: Structural Adjustment, Gender Relations and Working Conditions among Women Workers." *Environment and Planning A* 31: 291–304.

Sagás, Ernesto

2002 *Race and Politics in the Dominican Republic.* Gainesville: University Press of Florida.

Sagawe, Thorsten

1996 "Industrial Free Zones in the Dominican Republic: National vs. Local Impact." *Journal of Geography* 95(5): 203–210.

Said, Edward
1978 *Orientalism*. New York: Vintage.
Sambrook, Richard Alan, Brian M. Dermath, and Robert N. Thomas
1992 "Seaside Resort Development in the Dominican Republic." *Journal of Cultural Geography* 12(2): 65–75.
Scheper-Hughes, Nancy, and Margaret M. Lock
1987 "The Mindful Body: A Prolegomenon to Future Work in Medical Anthropology." *Medical Anthropology Quarterly*, n.s., 1(1): 6–41.
Scott, James
1990 *Domination and the Arts of Resistance*. New Haven: Yale University Press.
Sedgwick, Eve Kosofsky
1985 *Between Men: English Literature and Homosocial Desire*. New York: Columbia University Press.
Seidman, Steven
1996 *Queer Theory/Sociology*. Cambridge, Mass.: Blackwell.
Singer, Linda
1993 *Erotic Welfare: Sexual Theory and Politics in the Age of Epidemic*. Edited by Judith Butler and Maureen MacGrogan. New York: Routledge.
Soja, Edward
1980 "The Socio-Spatial Dialectic." *Annals of the Association of American Geographers* 70(2): 207–225.
Sommers, Jeffrey
2003 Review of *Global Transformations*. *Journal of World History* 14(1): 111–116.
Sontag, Susan
1978 *Illness as Metaphor*. New York: Farrar, Straus and Giroux.
Stoller, Paul
2002 *Money Has No Smell*. Chicago: University of Chicago Press.
Suki, Lenora
2004 *Financial Institutions and the Remittances Market in the Dominican Republic*. New York: Earth Institute at Columbia University.
Taylor, Diana
1994 "Performing Gender: Las Madres de la Plaza de Mayo." In *Negotiating Performance: Gender, Sexuality, and Theatricality in Latin America*, edited by Diana Taylor and Juan Villgas, 275–305. Chapel Hill: Duke University Press.
Tilly, Charles
1995 "Citizenship, Identity and Social History." *International Review of Social History* 40(3): 1–17.
Torres-Saillant, Silvio
1998 "The Tribulations of Blackness: Stages in Dominican Racial Identity." *Latin American Perspectives* 100(25): 126–146.
1999 "Nothing to Celebrate." *Culturefront* 8: 41–44.
Torres-Saillant, Silvio, and Ramano Hernández
1998 *The Dominican Americans*. Westport, Conn.: Greenwood Press.

Tripp, Aili Mari
1997 *Changing the Rules: The Politics of Liberalization and the Urban Informal Economy of Tanzania.* Berkeley: University of California Press.
Trouillot, Michel-Rolph
1994 "Culture, Color and Politics in Haiti." In *Race,* edited by Steven Gregory and Roger Sanjek, 146–174. New Brunswick, N.J.: Rutgers University Press.
Truong, Thanh-Dam
1990 *Sex, Money and Morality.* London: Zed Books.
Tsing, Anna
2000 "Inside the Economy of Appearances." *Public Culture* 12(1): 115–144.
Turner, Bryan S.
2000 "Review Essay: Citizenship and Political Globalization." *Citizenship Studies* 4(1): 81–86.
van der Veen, Marjolein
2001 "Rethinking Commodification and Prostitution: An Effort at Peacemaking in the Battles over Prostitution." *Rethinking Marxism* 13(2): 30–51.
Veeser, Cyrus
2002 *A World Safe for Capitalism.* New York: Columbia University Press.
Vincent, Susan
1998 "Gender Ideologies and the Informal Economy: Reproduction and the 'Grapes of Wrath Effect' in Mata Chico, Peru." *Latin American Perspectives* 25(2): 120–139.
Walker, Richard A.
1985 "Class, Division of Labour and Employment in Space." In *Social Relations and Spatial Structures,* edited by Derek Gregory and John Urry, 164–189. New York: St. Martin's Press.
Weston, Kath
2002 *Gender in Real Time.* New York: Routledge.
Wilk, Richard
2002 "Television, Time, and the National Imaginary in Belize." In *Media Worlds,* edited by Faye Ginsburg, Lila Abu-Lughod, and Brian Larkin, 171–186. Berkeley: University of California Press.
Wilson, Tamar Diana
1998a "Approaches to Understanding the Position of Women Workers in the Informal Sector." *Latin American Perspectives* 25(2): 105–119.
1998b "Introduction." *Latin American Perspectives* 25(2): 3–17.
World Trade Organization
2002 "Trade Policy Review, Dominican Republic." Report to the Secretariat.
Wucker, Michelle
1999 *Why the Cocks Fight: Dominicans, Haitians, and the Struggle for Hispaniola.* New York: Hill and Wang.

Index

Note: Page numbers in *italics* indicate photographs.

Text: 10/13 Sabon
Display: Akzidenz
Compositor: BookMatters, Berkeley
Indexer: Thérèse Shere
Cartographer Bill Nelson Cartography
Printer and binder: Thomson-Shore, Inc.